Succeed in
IELTS

9

Practice Tests

GlobalELT

English Language Teaching Books

Introduction

IELTS is the International English Language Testing System. It tests all four language skills: listening, reading, writing and speaking. It is intended for people who want to study or work in an English-speaking country.

There are **two** versions of the test, the **Academic** module and the **General Training** module. The Academic module is for those who want to study or train in an English-speaking university. University admission to undergraduate and postgraduate courses is based on the results of the Academic test.

The General Training module is mainly for those who are going to English-speaking countries to do secondary education or get a job and focuses on basic survival skills in social and workplace environments.

All candidates have to take the Listening & Speaking Modules. There are different versions for the Reading and the Writing Modules, depending on whether candidates are taking the Academic or the General Training module of the test.

The 9 complete IELTS Practice Tests included in this book are for the Academic version of the test.

Published by **GLOBAL ELT LTD**
www.globalelt.co.uk
Copyright © **GLOBAL ELT LTD, 2011**

Contributors:
Sean Haughton, Christina Oliver and Linda Collins

Every effort has been made to trace the copyright holders and we apologize in advance for any unintentional omission.
We will be happy to insert the appropriate acknowledgements in any subsequent editions.

British Library Cataloguing-in-Publication Data
A catalogue record of this book is available from the British Library.
- Succeed in IELTS - 9 Practice Tests - Student's Book - ISBN: 978-1-904663-33-1
- Succeed in IELTS - 9 Practice Tests - Teacher's Book - ISBN: 978-1-904663-34-8

The authors and publishers wish to acknowledge the following use of material:
The photos in the reading section of the Test 1 - 9, 10 © Ingram Publishing Image Library

Contents

IELTS FORMAT

Academic	General Training
For entry to undergraduate or postgraduate studies or for professional reasons.	For entry to vocational or training programmes not at degree level, for admission to secondary school and for immigration purposes.

The test Modules are taken in the following order:

MODULE	QUESTIONS	TIME	QUESTION TYPES
Listening	4 sections, 40 items	*approximately 30 minutes*	multiple choice, short-answer questions, sentence completion, notes, form, table, summary, flow-chart completion, labelling a diagram/map/plan, classification, matching
Academic Reading	3 Sections, 40 items	*60 minutes*	multiple choice, short-answer questions, sentence completion, notes, form, table, summary, flow-chart completion, labelling a diagram/map/plan, classification, matching, choosing suitable paragraph headings, identification of author's views, -yes, no, not given, -true, false, not given questions
General Training Reading	3 sections, 40 items	*60 minutes*	
Academic Writing	2 tasks	*60 minutes*	**Task 1** (150 Words - 20 minutes) Candidates have to look at a diagram, chart, or graph and present the information in their own words. **Task 2** (250 Words - 40 minutes) Candidates have to present a solution to a problem or present and justify an opinion.
General Training Writing	2 tasks	*60 minutes*	**Task 1** (150 Words - 20 minutes) Candidates have to respond to a problem with a letter asking for information. **Task 2** (250 Words - 40 minutes) Candidates have to present a solution to a problem or present and justify an opinion.
Speaking		*11 to 14 minutes*	It consists of three parts; **Part 1** - Introduction and interview, **Part 2** - Long turn, **Part 3** - Discussion.
		Total Test Time *2 hours 44 minutes*	

IELTS

LISTENING SECTION

EXAM GUIDE

This section contains a detailed analysis of the Listening section of the exam with Exam Tips and Guidance for all the different Listening tasks that students will encounter taking the IELTS exam, with reference to the tasks included in the Practice Tests.

Listening Section Format

Section	No. of Questions	Text Type	Context	Task Types
1	10 (usually 1 / 2 tasks)	a conversation / interview between two speakers	giving or exchanging information on an everyday topic	note completion form completion table completion sentence completion flow-chart completion map labelling diagram labelling matching multiple choice
2	10 (usually 2 tasks)	a monologue (occasionally introduced by a second speaker)	giving information on an everyday topic e.g. on a talk show	
3	10 (up to 3 tasks)	a conversation between 2/3/4 speakers	an educational or training context	
4	10 (up to 3 tasks)	a monologue	an academic setting e.g. a lecture / presentation / talk / speech	

Time: **40 minutes** (including 10 minutes to transfer your answers onto the answer sheet)

Marking: 1 mark for each correct answer

SECTION 1

is...
- a face-to-face or telephone conversation
- about a topic of general interest
- usually comprised of one or two tasks (there is a pause between tasks)
- ten questions long WITH an example at the beginning

tests...
- your understanding of specific information (i.e. dates, everyday objects, places etc.)
- spelling (all words must be spelt correctly)

spelling:
- if you are asked to write the name of a street, person, company etc., it will be spelt for you
- you should be very familiar with the names of the letters of the alphabet to aid you in spelling what you hear

numbers:
- you may have to write down a year, phone number, part of an address etc.
- remember that '0' can be pronounced 'oh' or 'zero' when saying a phone number
- when talking about money, we typically say amounts in the same way as in the examples below:
  £4.50 = four pound(s) fifty / four fifty
  $31.85 = thirty-one dollar(s) and eighty-five cents / thirty-one eighty-five
- most years are pronounced in the same way as in the examples below:
  1985 = nineteen eighty-five
  2015 = twenty fifteen
  (we put the first two numbers together and then the second two)
  except for the years 2000 - 2009, example:
  2000 = two thousand
  2009 = two thousand and nine or two thousand nine
  (we say the year as we would a number)
- you can write dates in different ways and still get full marks:
  3rd March, March 3rd, March 3 and 3 March are all considered the same two-word answer
- for measurements, you can write either the whole thing or an abbreviation, for example:
  25m = 25 metres = 25 meters

SECTION 2

is...
- a talk / speech / announcement / recorded message / radio excerpt with one speaker talking (possibly introduced by another speaker)
- about a topic of general interest
- usually comprised of two tasks (there is a pause between tasks)
- 10 questions long - there is NO example

tests...
- your understanding of factual information
- your ability to select relevant information from what you hear

SECTION 3

is...
- a discussion between two to four speakers (e.g. between two students and a university lecturer)
- concerned with some aspect of academic life
- up to three tasks (there is a pause between tasks)
- 10 questions long - there is NO example

tests...
- your ability to identify key facts and ideas and how they relate to each other
- your ability to identify speakers' attitudes and opinions

SECTION 4

is...
- a lecture / talk / presentation / speech, often in front of an audience
- concerned with a topic of academic interest, like a scientific subject for example
- up to three tasks (there is no pause between tasks)
- 10 questions long - there is NO example

tests...
- your ability to follow the speaker's opinion
- your ability to spell accurately
- your ability to understand and distinguish between different ideas (e.g. causes, reasons, effects, consequences)
- your ability to follow the way the ideas are organised (e.g. main ideas, specific information and attitude)

TASK TYPES: (1) NOTE COMPLETION

Remember...

1. Always check the word limit in the instructions.
2. Use the time before the recording starts to look at the heading and read through the notes.
3. Look at each gap individually and think about what kind of word(s) would fill it i.e. numbers, a date, an address, a noun, a verb etc.
4. Follow the introduction carefully when the recording starts; the narrator will tell you what the section is about.
5. Focus on each question in turn as you listen to the recording. Keep up with the recording as it moves from one question to the next and do not dwell on gaps you have missed; there isn't time and this will possibly cost you the answer to the next gap as well.

> If you don't know an answer, guess it at the end when you are filling in your answer sheet; you have nothing to lose!

EXAMPLE:
TEST 1 - SECTION 1

> There will always be an example in Section 1. While this is being played you have an opportunity to establish a context for what you would expect to hear in the rest of the recording. Also use the point in the recording where the example finishes as a cue to listen carefully for your first answer.

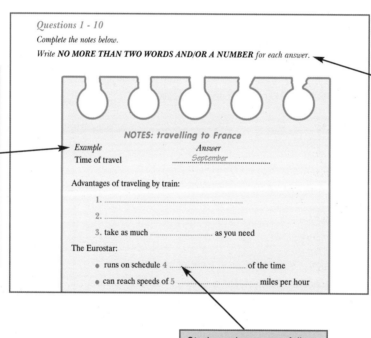

Questions 1 - 10
Complete the notes below.
Write **NO MORE THAN TWO WORDS AND/OR A NUMBER** *for each answer.*

NOTES: travelling to France

Example	*Answer*
Time of travel	*September*

Advantages of traveling by train:

1. ....
2. ....
3. take as much .... as you need

The Eurostar:

- runs on schedule 4 .... of the time
- can reach speeds of 5 .... miles per hour

> Always stick to the word limit; you can write one, two or three words for each answer in this case.

> Study each gap carefully to predict what kinds of words you should look for. In 4, for example, we might need to listen out for a percentage (a number).

Succeed in IELTS

9 Practice Tests

- Audioscripts & Key
- Writing Supplement including model compositions and example candidate answers at varying levels, followed by detailed justifications of the marks awarded.
- JUSTIFICATION of the Answers for the Listening (the answers are underlined in the audioscript) and the Reading sections of each practice test

SELF-STUDY GUIDE

GlobalELT
ENGLISH LANGUAGE TEACHING BOOKS

ISBN 978-1-904663-36-2

9 781904 663362 >

WRITING SUPPLEMENT

This **Writing Supplement** includes model answers for all the writing tasks from the Practice Tests. Example candidate answers at varying levels are also provided followed by detailed justifications of the marks awarded.

Test 1

Task 1 - Model Answer

This is an example of a very good answer. There are many different approaches that could be taken, however, and this is just one of them.

> This graph illustrates the volume of passengers that travel on the metro in Toronto at different times of day on a typical weekday in July.
>
> The volume of passengers during the week using the Toronto Metro system varies significantly according to the time of day. The system opens at 6 a.m. and passenger volume averages around 100,000 people using the system at that time. By 8 a.m., the system is at its maximum daily volume, averaging around 400,000 people. At around 6:30 p.m., the volume is again near this peak number, but does not quite reach the 400,000 point. Between these two times volume is at its lowest level at around 4 p.m. and the second-lowest level at around 10 a.m.. Between the hours of 12 p.m. and 3 p.m. passenger volume seems to even out at around 300,000 people. After 6:00 p.m., the volume of passengers drops steadily until slightly before 8 p.m., when volume picks up again. This trend continues until a little after 9, and then the volume drops by the 10 o'clock closing time to around 140,000 people.
>
> This graph can be best explained by people's work schedules. Most people begin work between 8 and 9 a.m. and finish between 5 and 7 p.m.. This would mean commuting would be at its heaviest before 9 a.m. and 7p.m., as reflected in the graph. The midday plateau could be explained by activity during lunch breaks.

Task 1 - Example Answer

This is an example of an answer that satisfies the requirements for **band 5**. The answer successfully summarises the main points of the graph, though there are some details left out which could have been included. There are frequent errors in grammar and some lexical inaccuracies, but although they are distracting, they do not generally obscure the intended meaning. Sentences tend to be short and use simple structures. A strong point in this composition is the organisation of ideas into logical paragraphs.

> Here is a graph of the passengers travel on the Toronto Metro system in July. It shows very busy in the morning and very busy in the evening and other times not so much busy. The most busy time is 7 the morning and again 6 the evening. These times have 400 thousands of passengers. This is when the people are going to work.
>
> Before the two times of very busy, it is the most quiet. At 6 the morning and 4 in afternoon, are only 100 thousands of passengers traveling. Here, people are at home or they are at work and they are not going anywhere.
>
> Another time that is busy, but not so much busy as other times is from half 11 to half 2 in the day. In these time it is different because there is not so much change. There are always around 300 thousands passengers. It is very stable in that. Here perhaps the people are going for lunch or for shopping or to do small jobs on the lunch break. And perhaps the people who do not work are going for shopping.

Task 2 - Model Answer

This is an example of a very good answer. There are many different approaches that could be taken, however, and this is just one of them.

In my country, how much schools focus on traditional subjects varies widely. In recent years there has been a push to include more courses that would prepare students for the working world. Programmes that emphasise real-life skills such as construction studies or information technology are important to those students who will not go on to higher education. However, in my opinion, when schools put too much emphasis on less traditional skills, they are robbing students of a knowledge base that will no-doubt help them throughout their lives.

The purpose of primary and secondary education is to build well-rounded students and well-rounded citizens. Even though English literature classes may seem trivial to a 16-year old planning a career in construction, the basic thinking skills he or she may gain could be priceless in the future. Education should go further than simply preparing students for the workforce or even for higher education. Children should not be forced to think about their careers at such a young age; instead they should focus on learning basic skills.

A basic traditional curriculum should be present in all schools, but the choice should be there for students to branch out more into less traditional and more modern subjects. By offering a wide variety of subjects and incorporating information from our ever-changing world into traditional ways of teaching, students can graduate from school with a well-balanced knowledge base that will help them to succeed in countless ways in the future.

As in all facets of life, balance is the key to this issue. A balance needs to be sought between the traditional subjects on offer and those subjects that aim to prepare students for careers in a more practical manner.

Task 2 - Example Answer

This is an example of an answer that satisfies the requirements for **band 8**. The task is achieved and an opinion is clearly expressed and supported. The paragraphs are logical, and the text flows due to effective use of linking phrases. A wide variety of vocabulary is used effectively, as are a variety of sentence forms although there is occasional awkwardness of grammatical structure, which is the weakest point of the essay.

Many subjects in my education turned out not to be useful to me. Since school I have used very little the algebra, and not at all the knowledge of ancient wars of my country. So, yes, I agree with the statement that schools too much concentrate on traditional subjects and do not prepare students adequately for the demands of the modern working world.

Every student will have a different life and will need a different preparation. Therefore, the traditional curriculum that is taught to everyone is not a very good solution. Schools should be more flexible and curricula should be tailored more closely to the student's individual needs. A student that wil become an artist has little need for mathematics or science, for example, and likewise, a student who will be an engineer would have little need for art or biology. When students focus on their own applicable subjects, they will have more time to go into these subjects in depth, and will therefore excel. This is of critical importance because the modern world is very competitive.

Also, important learnings are missing from a traditional curriculum. The most important of things in our modern world is computer, internet, and other electronic resources. If a student does not leave school with an excellent knowledge of these he or she is at a disadvantage. Likewise, to succeed in the working world, we must be very skilled in our personal interactions and cooperation with others, and most leave school with no skills in this area and must work them out quickly in their first job. Also, basic financial teachings could benefit students.

In conclusion, for schools to produce students that are ready to meet the demands of the working world today, some changes are clearly necessary. I believe if schools modernised and made more practical their curricula, students would benefit greatly.

Test 2

Task 1 - Model Answer

This is an example of a very good answer. There are many different approaches that could be taken, however, and this is just one of them.

> This graph shows the average number of hours worked each day by men and women in eight countries in the developing world, spanning a period of six years from 1998 to 2003. The different countries vary a great deal in terms of the hours worked, but across all countries women consistently work more hours than men.
>
> On average, in the 8 developing countries, women work one hour and eight minutes more each day than men. The country with the biggest discrepancy between working times of men and women is Benin, where women work an average of 2 hours and 25 minutes more than men each day. There is a marked discrepancy in Mexico as well, where women work an average of one hour and 45 minutes more than men each day. In contrast, the country with the least difference is Mauritius, where women still work an extra 24 minutes each day. In the other five countries, the extra time that women work each day is fairly uniform, more or less an hour.
>
> What is strikingly different, however, is the variation in the hours that people, both men and women, work in the different countries. For example, although women work on average more than men, the men in Mongolia work more than women in any other country, while women in South Africa work less than men in any other country. Indeed, the difference in time worked by people in these two countries is nearly four hours, which is much more dramatic than the difference between hours that men and women work in any one country.

Task 1 - Example Answer

This is an example of an answer that satisfies the requirements for **band 7.5**. The answer successfully summarises some of the main points of the graph, though only working hours of men and women are compared, not hours between countries, so not all features have been discussed, and this has affected the score. Cohesion and coherence are good; the paragraphs are logical and the sentences flow, even though use of linking words is not extensive. The vocabulary is varied and appropriate to the task, and there is a good range and accuracy of grammatical forms.

> This graph shows the daily working hours for women and men between the years 1998 and 2003 in different countries in the developing world. It indicates that during this period, women tended to work more hours than men. On average, in the eight developing countries, a typical woman worked 1 hour and 9 minutes more than a typical man each day.
>
> The smallest difference in hours worked by men and women was in Mauritius where a woman worked only 24 minutes more than a man. This was followed by Mongolia where a woman worked 44 minutes more than a man. The biggest difference in working in the two genders was in Benin where a woman worked an average of an additional 2 hours and 25 minutes. In Mexico a woman worked 1 hour more than a man, which was the second biggest difference between the working hours of men and women.
>
> In all 8 developing countries analysed, women worked more hours per day than men, establishing that this trend was most likely the norm for developing countries of this time period.

Task 2 - Model Answer

This is an example of a very good answer. There are many different approaches that could be taken, however, and this is just one of them.

While almost everyone must work to earn a living, people have different value systems when deciding what sort of job to do. Some have the predominant aim of earning as much money as possible. Others make their choice based on what they love to do. While there is more than one way for people to build a happy life, I think, ideally, the decision should be based on a balance of both financial and personal rewards.

There are people who live very rewarding lives working lucrative jobs that do not offer any non-monetary rewards. People who earn a lot of money have many opportunities to do things in their free time that can be very personally rewarding; they might travel the world, play a musical instrument, write, do charity work, whatever makes them feel happy. Even if they have little free time while they are working, they could save their money and retire early to pursue some activity they are passionate about. Or perhaps there are some people who derive their sense of reward from having material possessions - a luxurious house, a new car, expensive clothes. Basically, money gives people many opportunities that they would not otherwise have.

On the other hand, a person who is passionate about his or her work does not need a lot of extra money to have a personally rewarding life. His reward comes from doing a job to the best of his ability or producing something important. This kind of work is often creative, artistic, or involves helping others or advancing society, but it can also be more mundane work, if a person has the right attitude. A person who is passionate about his work takes pride in whatever he does, and enjoys where he is each day.

An ideal job, of course, would be both personally and financially rewarding. Sometimes this happens, because people who love what they are doing are usually the people who do exceptional work, and sometimes they get recognition for this. More often this ideal situation does not materialise, however, and what we all hope for is a job that has an acceptable balance of financial and personal rewards - a job we like well enough, that allows us to meet our necessary expenses.

Task 2 - Example Answer

This is an example of an answer that satisfies the requirements for **band 6.5**. The script addresses the question in the task, and opinions are expressed, but in a rather confusing way. Paragraphs are not always logical, and contain a variety of different ideas, and this is the weak point of the script. However the text flows and there is a good use of linking and connecting phrases. The range of vocabulary and complexity of grammatical structures is very good, often natural, and omissions and errors are infrequent. The formal register is not consistently maintained, and contractions are present, which has negatively affected the score.

Before choosing a career, one must decide which is more important: money or the enjoyable job. Of course, for some, they can have an enjoyable job that's also good financially. However, for many, a choice, at least for some extent, have to be made. With citizens of developed countries relying more and more on money and material goods, jobs that pay well are becoming more important to many than jobs that are enjoyable. This leads to problems, both personally and with professions, but it is an issue that goes deeper than only choice and more connected to what lifestyle communities and societies embrace.

I think that job satisfaction is more important than financial gain as the main consideration when deciding what job to take. However, there's always a line that needs to be drawn between the two. I require a certain standard of living and even if the job is very rewarding in some way, if it does not meet the requirements financially, I wouldn't do that job. I think that if possible, everyone should choose happiness over wealth. As the saying goes, money doesn't buy happiness, so doing a job that doesn't make you happy won't help you to purchase the contentment.

However, it is also to be emphasised that some people do not have the choice. Many citizens in countries around the world do not have a choice in what work they do and how long they do it for. People are working in sweat shops and other terrible conditions for very little money and other people can't find any work at all.

For most people, money must be taken into consideration when choosing a job, but, if possible, other rewards of a job or career should be taken into consideration by anyone who is lucky enough to have that choice.

Test 3

Task 1 - Model Answer

This is an example of a very good answer. There are many different approaches that could be taken, however, and this is just one of them.

This graph shows the percentages of boys and girls attending both primary and secondary school in the years between 2000 and 2004 in industrialised countries, developing countries and the least developed countries. It reveals that children in the least developed countries are far more likely to miss out on education, particularly at a secondary level.

In industrialised countries, education levels are quite uniform. The percentages of boys and girls in both primary and secondary education differ by only one percentage point, and the percentages of children in primary and secondary education, both in the case of boys and girls, differ by only four percentages points.

In developing countries the case is rather different. A fairly high percentage of both boys and girls receive a primary education; 88 percent and 83 percent respectively, but notably, the gap between girls and boys is greater than it is in industrialised countries. For secondary school, however, the numbers are much lower, with only 50 percent of boys and 49 percent of girls enrolling.

In the least developed countries, education rates are lower still. Only 71 percent of boys, and 65 percent of girls attend primary school, while a mere 30 percent of boys and 26 percent of girls attend secondary school. It is clear that children in the least developed countries have little opportunity to get a secondary education.

Task 1 - Example Answer

This is an example of an answer that satisfies the requirements for **band 7**. The summarization of the graph is successfully achieved, although presentation of more complex details is not done in a way that helps the reader to understand clearly, for example over use of "these" and unspecified subjects. There is evidence of successful use of linking words, however an extensive lexical resource is not demonstrated. The grammar is accurate, but the range is not extensive.

There are large differences in attendance by children in primary and secondary schools between industrialised and developing countries. Children in the least developed countries were significantly less likely to attend these schools than those in more developed and industrialised countries. The biggest differences came between secondary school enrollments for girls. Only 26% in the least-developed countries were enrolled in secondary school, while 92% in industrialised countries were. Coming in somewhere between these two extremes, in other developing countries, 49% of girls were enrolled in secondary schools.

The smallest difference in attendance was in primary school enrollments by boys. 71% of boys in the least developed countries, 88% of boys in other developing countries and 95% of boys in industrialised countries attended primary school.

Enrollment by girls in primary schools was similar to these figures and enrollment by boys in secondary schools was similar to the figures for girls in secondary schools. Generally, those children living in the poorest countries seem to be least likely to attend primary and secondary school.

Task 2 - Model Answer

This is an example of a very good answer. There are many different approaches that could be taken, however, and this is just one of them.

The question of what to do about people who break the law is not an easy one. Prisons are over-crowded, expensive, and often don't seem to work because people who are released keep ending up re-offending and being locked up again. Rehabilitating law breakers sounds like a better solution, but it is not easy to demonstrate that it works. I think the best thing to do about law breakers depends on the crime they have committed.

Some people would definitely not be suitable for rehabilitation. Serial killers, for example, would pose too large a risk to others if they were released. Also, someone who could commit such crimes is clearly psychopathic and could probably not be taught more correct behaviour. Those who are a danger to others or who have committed serious crimes in a calculated way simply need to be punished.

On the other hand, many offenders could probably benefit greatly from some kind of rehabilitation programme. These people would include those who have been arrested for drug-related offenses, or petty theft, and who have probably been led into crime because of difficult life circumstances. If their addictions could be treated, and they could be taught some skills that would increase their options, then they would likely be able to escape from the cycle of reoffending. Another group who would benefit are the mentally ill. These individuals need medical treatment and not incarceration; prison is entirely inappropriate for them.

In situations where there is a possibility of rehabilitation, I believe it is very important to try, because the re-habilitation of any individual is of huge benefit, not only to the rehabilitated person, but to all of society. Except for cases when an individual is clearly not suitable for rehabilitation, I believe it is a far better option than being locked in prison.

Task 2 - Example Answer

This is an example of an answer that satisfies the requirements for **band 5.5**. The task is achieved and complex ideas are expressed, although they are sometimes expressed in a disorganised manner. The formalities of essay structure are not consistently followed. The paragraphs are logical, but the argument does not progress from paragraph to paragraph in an organised manner. A wide variety of vocabulary is used, as are a variety of sentence forms although there is awkwardness of grammatical structure, and frequent grammatical mistakes, which occasionally causes misunderstanding.

In my country, prisons are too much crowded and many people that go from prison end up back in prison soon after they are released. This is proof that prisons do not succeed in rehabilitating offenders, which must to be the focus of the system. Of course, each one the individual prison is different and each one person inside them is different, but broad averages show that the prison is inherently flawed. This could be true and for the prison systems of countries across the world.

The best way to solve the problems of the prison would be to make again the system with a focus on rehabilitation instead of punishment. Many people who have committed the crimes have not because they are bad, but because they have bad situation that leave them hopeless so that they turn to crime.

Many people grow up only knowing life of crime. A child born to poverty and with drugs around or other illegal things may automatically do drug-dealing or other crimes simply because he or she doesn't know anything other. Instead of throw them in prison and release back into the same life and then back into prison etcetera, this same person goes through drug-rehabilitation and then through a job-training, when he is released he will be more likely and able to be a functioning member of society.

Obviously, rehabilitation is not possible in all situation. The criminal who have committed very serious crimes should be dealt differently than those who have not committed so serious or harmful crimes. However, at least to try the rehabilitation, especially in certain types of crimes, could benefit taxpayers, and workers in the country's legal system, the prisoners themselves.

Test 4

Task 1 - Model Answer

This is an example of a very good answer. There are many different approaches that could be taken, however, and this is just one of them.

> This graph shows the amount of water used in homes each day in the U.S. both with and without water conservation methods. The water conservation methods offer a considerable reduction in water consumption in most activities.
>
> Each day, every American consumes many gallons of water for a variety of reasons. The most water is used when flushing toilets, followed respectively by washing clothes (in a washing machine), taking showers, using faucets, leaks, other uses and washing dishes (in a dishwasher.) In total, per day, every American uses nearly twenty gallons of water just flushing the toilet. On the other end of the spectrum, washing dishes uses only about one gallon of water a day. In total, Americans use, on average, about seventy gallons of water a day.
>
> However, if water conservation methods were put in place, these numbers would be reduced significantly. The savings would be most considerable in the case of toilet-flushing; water used would fall from around 20 gallons a day to only slightly more than ten gallons with water conservation methods. Around four or five gallons of water would be saved for most 'other uses'. The exceptions are using faucets, and the other uses category, where water conservation methods would have no effect. Still, over all, implementation of conservation methods would mean that total water consumption would drop from a daily average of nearly seventy gallons per person to around fifty gallons per person.

Task 1 - Example Answer

This is an example of an answer that satisfies the requirements for **band 4.0**. There is partial command of the language, and the main points of the graph are addressed, although not always to the extent that they could be. There is limited use of connectives and the information does not flow. Vocabulary is mostly accurate but limited. Most sentences are short with simple grammatical structures. They are generally clear, in spite of some grammatical inaccuracies, though a few times grammatical mistakes cause misunderstanding. There is considerable borrowing from the prompt.

> The graph shows the daily water consumption for Americans in their homes. The most of the water is used for flushing a toilet. The littlest is for washing dishes (in a dish washer) Americans to not use much water with this way. Much water is used and for washing clothes (in a washing machine)and taking a shower. Then there is using faucets, leaks and other uses.
>
> The gallons of water an American uses at home daily with water conservation methods is not so much. It is less than without about 55 gallons and not 70 gallons. Particularly for flushing a toilet it is less. It is 10 gallons less for flushing a toilet. Using faucets, washing dishes and other uses, however, does not help the water conservation methods.
>
> It shows that the water conservation methods are very good and they must to be used.

Task 2 - Model Answer

This is an example of a very good answer. There are many different approaches that could be taken, however, and this is just one of them.

Racism and xenophobia are serious problems which most people have experienced personally. Maybe someone you know has felt afraid of others who are different from them, without being able to explain exactly why. Perhaps you have a friend of a different race who has been denied career opportunities. Or perhaps you have heard someone say something racist to you or to someone else. But what did you do in these situations? Did you let it go, or did you say something? Only if we all speak up and bring attention to cases of racism and xenophobia will the problem start to disappear.

If indeed people are taught and not born with attitudes that are racist or xenophobic, it is critically important to challenge any examples of these forms of discrimination that we are exposed to. First of all, this is true because children learn by example and by imitation, and they are very preceptive - picking up on things the adults around them may not even be aware of. If children do not hear racist 'talk', they will not repeat it. Furthermore, if adults are made to answer for any racist statements they make, perhaps they will think twice about expressing them, and if they stop expressing them, this could break the cycle and prevent children from learning that it is acceptable behaviour.

Even in the increasingly frequent, but unfortunate cases where people from relatively homogenous societies are just naturally afraid of those persons of different ethnic or cultural descent that they inevitably come in contact with in the new 'global village', it would be benefical to challenge any expressions of racism and xenophobia. The truth is, that whatever people feel, if they learn that certain opinions are socially unacceptable, they will not air them publicly. This is an important first small step. It will reduce tension in societies and allow for more positive interactions between individuals of different races and cultures, which will in turn bring familiarity and lessen the fear of the unknown.

I believe that people can modify their nature, although it may be difficult. So, whether racism and xenophobia are taught or are an inherent part of our nature, I believe that as long as awareness is increased and a social atmosphere that does not condone them is maintained, gradually these destructive attitudes will be diminished.

Task 2 - Example Answer

This is an example of an answer that satisfies the requirements for **band 7**. An adequate response is made to the topic with evidence of detailed reasoning; however, the formalities of essay structure are not followed, for example a clear introduction and conclusion are lacking, and information is poorly organised in support of the argument. Contractions are used which are inappropriate in a formal essay. There is evidence of an extensive range of vocabulary, and natural expression, but there is also occasional inaccuracy and a notable level of repetition. Grammatical range is extensive, accurate, and often natural.

Racism and xenophobia are huge problems at both national and global levels. Every country deals with these problems and every person, every global citizen, has responsibility to combat them. The only way that either of these problems can be combated is through a grassroots social movement aimed to eliminating these feelings. Children need to be taught from young age that different doesn't mean bad. They should be informed about other cultures and other races and should be taught to be understanding rather than hostile. For this to happen, adults need to take the initiative to realise that their own racism and xenophobia is unfounded.

With increased globalization and increased ease of travel, the need to combat racism and xenophobia is becoming more and more important. As modernisation takes hold of the world, different people from different cultures are living their lives in nearer theoretical proximity of each other. This creates situations without much room for racism and xenophobia.

Because parents and grandparents often pass on their racism and xenophobia towards other groups to their children and grandchildren, racism and xenophobia as well as other hatreds can be difficult to stop. Every person needs to sit down and really consider whether or not their prejudices are valid. The more someone experiences cultures other than their own, the more he or she understands that people everywhere aren't very different from each other. Little cultural or social differences don't make such a big difference in the long run. People are simply people and everyone should be trying their best to be understanding of everyone else's differences in the hope that others will do the same.

Task 1 - Model Answer

This is an example of a very good answer. There are many different approaches that could be taken, however, and this is just one of them.

> This chart compares the different things that Canadian households spent their money on in the years 1972 and in 2002. It shows that the spending habits of Canadians have changed a great deal in thirty years.
>
> In 1972, most of the annual expenditure, 39 percent, went towards food. A large percentage, 22 percent, was also spent on cars, and smaller, roughly equal percentages were spent on petrol, furniture, restaurants and books. Only three percent of the annual expenditure went towards computers.
>
> In contrast, in 2002, 40 percent of the annual expenditure went towards cars. Only 14 percent was spent on food, and an equal amount was spent on restaurants, so people seem to be cooking less. The amount spent on petrol and furniture only changed slightly, and the amount spent on books decreased. Expenditure on computers, however, increased to 11 percent, which is even more than what was spent on petrol.
>
> In conclusion, it seems that people in 2002 spent a higher proportion of their money on luxuries, such as nice cars or eating out, in contrast to 1972 when more seemed to be spent on necessities such as food and furniture.

Task 1 - Example Answer

This is an example of an answer that satisfies the requirements for **band 6.5**. Description of the main points of the chart was achieved, although it would have been improved if more time was spent on comparison and less was spent on speculation. Information is included that is not contained in the chart, and is not necessarily accurate, and this is a weak point. The lexical resource is appropriate to the task, but not extensive. There is evidence of complex grammatical structures used with accuracy, although at other times the grammar is simple, and there is simple listing of facts from the chart, for example.

> In Canada, annual spending for households changed dramatically from 1972 to 2002. In 1972 Food was 39% of household spending. In 2002 this number was less than half, only 14%. This doesn't mean that Canadian households are spending less money on food; it means that they are spending more money on other things. After food, the next biggest thing Canadians in 1972 spent money on was cars (22%), then furniture (11%), petrol (10%), restaurants (8%), books (7%) and computers (3%). In 2002 this order changed completely. Cars came first, comprising 40% of spending. Next came food (14%), restaurants (14%), computers (11%), furniture (9%), petrol (9%) and books (3%).
>
> This information shows that the values, as far as spending, of Canadian households have changed in recent years. It also implies that spending has increased, as it is unlikely that Canadians have stopped buying food in exchange for cars. Instead, their spending has most likely increased. This doesn't necessarily mean income has increased, but could imply that with the increased emphasis on material things such as cars and computers that debt has increased.

Task 2 - Model Answer

This is an example of a very good answer. There are many different approaches that could be taken, however, and this is just one of them.

Few people can deny that the environment has become a global issue. The effects of global warming have begun to become more apparent, and climate instability is beginning to take its toll in the form of droughts, floods and dangerous storms. Governments seem unable to agree to take any action. The outlook may seem grim, but there are plenty of things that each of us, as individuals, can do to minimise damage to the environment.

The most obvious thing we can cut back on is our use of electricity. The creation of electricity is very damaging to the environment, whether it is created by burning coal, damming rivers, or nuclear means; none are good methods. By replacing standard light bulbs with energy efficient bulbs considerable energy - as well as money because the bulbs last so long - can be saved. Also, it is important to turn off computers and TVs when they are not in use, and to try to wear jumpers or pullovers if it is cold in the winter and turn the thermostat down a few degrees. Finally, if a house is insulated properly, it takes much less energy to heat or cool it to comfortable levels.

In addition, we can consume less in general. Everything we buy, be it clothes, toys, furniture, gadgets - whatever it is - it used up energy and caused pollution in its making. If we buy less, and do not buy things that we do not need, then we can cut back on both pollution and energy consumption. For this reason it is very important not to purchase things we do not need, and when we need something, to try to choose items that will last a long time and not be thrown out and replaced promptly.

Finally, we can also try to be mindful of how we travel since cars and planes create a large amount of pollution. Planes are one of the worst culprits when it comes to using up fossil fuels, so it makes sense not to travel by plane if there is any alternative. Cars, too, pollute a lot, although less than planes. If you drive them every day, however, it adds up rapidly. We should all try to commute to work using public transport if it is available, or better yet, go on foot or on a bicycle.

So, even though things might seem hopeless when we see how governments can not agree to take action, we must remember that there are ample things we can each do at a personal level in order to help prevent more environmental damage from occurring.

Task 2 - Example Answer

This is an example of an answer that satisfies the requirements for **band 6**. A response is made with some degree of complexity. There is a clear conclusion, however the support that leads to this conclusion is not presented in a logically ordered way, and there is some content that is irrelevant to the conclusion. There is a natural flow of language, an extensive lexical resource is made use of and a wide range of grammatical forms are used with some degree of control. However, in some places misuse of complex grammatical structures leads to a lack of clarity of meaning.

The words "global warming" have become an intimate part of almost every global citizen's lexicon. Pollution has become a big problem all over the world. The destruction of forests and habitats are growing issues. The environment is the one issue that it affect every person, plant or animal on the planet. Economics, wars and social problems wouldn't even be able to exist without a safe, good environment. Countries around the world are taking measures to help combat what damage we a global community, have done the environment. This, of course, makes a difference, but the really differences must be made on a smaller level.

Each person in the world must understand how their actions make a difference and their choices could be choices that help saving the world. In America, most the people seem to own inefficient large cars, they drive more than is necessary and they don't focus on the conserving energy in their own homes. They also use too much water, produce too much litter and generally contribute to polluting our earth. These lifestyle choices make America, per person, the worst contributor to global climate change and one of the main polluting county. However, it isn't Americans just that need to make changes.

Simple changes such as using environmentally friendly products, like, for example, energy efficient appliances, not littering, recycling, reusing things and generally not focusing on consumerism could make all the difference in whether or not our world will stand for generation to come.

In conclusion, every person has power to make a difference and every person has responsibility to do.

Task 1 - Model Answer

This is an example of a very good answer. There are many different approaches that could be taken, however, and this is just one of them.

The chart illustrates how the use of different payment methods by consumers in the United States has changed from 2002 to 2005. In 2002, more consumers used cash than any other payment method. This accounted for nearly 35% of their purchases. The use of cheques and credit cards came in closely behind cash, with cheques accounting for about 27% of purchases and credit cards being used only slightly less. The use of debit cards was significantly lower, accounting for only around 13% of purchases.

By the beginning of 2003, the hierarchy of use of these methods of payment had changed. The use of cheques rose by around 5%, while the use of cash dropped by around 4%. The use of credit cards rose parallel to cheque use. Debit cards, in this period of time, stayed relatively even.

From early 2003 until mid-2004 the use of cash dropped by about 4%. At the end of 2004 into 2005 cash-use began a gradual rise but did not reach 2002 levels. The use of cheques rose nearly 9% until mid-2004 and then began to drop slightly in 2005. The use of credit cards rose until the middle of 2003 and then began to gradually drop by about 2% in 2005. Debit-card-use dropped very gradually by about 3% in 2005.

As a whole, cheques and credit cards were the only payment methods that were used more often as the four-year time period progressed.

Task 1 - Example Answer

This is an example of an answer that satisfies the requirements for **band 7.5**. Description of the chart is fully achieved. Information is effectively organised and the writing flows naturally even though more use could have been made of linking devices. The lexis is appropriate to the task. There are a few minor inaccuracies in the grammar, which do not negatively affect communication. Grammatical range tends to be conservative - with a preference for simpler rather than more complex structures, and this is the main reason the answer does not achieve a higher band.

This chart follows the use of four payment methods - cash, check, credit card and debit card - over a period of four years from 2002 to 2005. Over that time, there were some significant changes.

The first thing that is noticed about the chart is there are two groups in the methods. The debit card is alone and much lower of percentage than the cash, check, and credit card. It falls slowly throughout the years. The other three methods are a lot closer together and form second group. They change position compared to one another by the end.

Cash use begins highest at almost 35 percent of the time and falls until the middle of 2004. After, it rises slowly but not as high as it was a first, only to perhaps 29 percent. Cheque and credit card begin together at around 27 percent use each, then rise slowly for about a year and a half. Then credit card use levels out and falls slowly for the rest of the time. Cheque continues to rise until the middle of 2004 then falls very little to end just below 35 percent of use. Cheque and cash end in very close positions, around 28 percent of usage.

If we consider the graph only shows the area of 40 percent, we can see that all the changes were, relatively, quite small. All methods changed only between about 2 to about 8 percent in the four years.

Task 2 - Model Answer 1

This is an example of a very good answer. There are many different approaches that could be taken, however, and this is just one of them.

Advertisements are everywhere nowadays. We are exposed to them on the radio, on TV, in the trailers for movies, on buses, billboards, and even via the clothes and possessions of celebrities. It is impossible to avoid them. Because of this, I think it is inevitable that they will influence our choices as consumers and impact our lifestyles.

Decision making processes are seldom simple, and this is why they are vulnerable to the influence of advertisements. If someone is feeling insecure about her appearance, and she sees a beautiful model wearing certain clothes in an advertisement, she may feel that if she had those clothes she would be more beautiful. Or if advertisements show enough happy families eating in a fast food chain, parents might automatically think of taking their children to such food outlets during difficult times to cheer everyone up. Finally, if an advertisement shows successful young professionals going for holidays on a tropical island, young professionals might not feel they are successful unless they also get away for a tropical holiday. No demographic is immune. Of course, everyone would like to think they are making their own autonomous decisions but, in reality, people often cannot say just what their decisions are based on, and in these cases, it is, most likely, the influence of advertisements is at work.

The influence that advertisements have can impact our lives in various ways. The most obviously worrying influence is that people who feel the need for a constant stream of new possessions will of course be under considerable extra financial strain. They may have to work longer hours and spend less time with loved ones, or perhaps they might even get into debt. Additionally, people may be more inclined to feel discontented with their lives if they witness a barrage of advertisements showing them all the things they 'need' in order to lead a worthwhile life.

In conclusion, due to the pervasiveness of advertisements, it seems very unlikely that anyone can escape their influence in today's world.

Task 2 - Example Answer

This is an example of an answer that only satisfies the requirements for **band 3.5**. There is a partial response to the task. Lack of coherence sometimes puts a strain on the reader, but generally meaning can be understood in spite of frequent mistakes in anything other than simple grammatical forms. There is a variety of lexis, but it is not always used appropriately.

Advertising, in the modern world, influence our choice as consumers and it effect on our lifestyles. It is impossible, in most of places, to go for any time without seeing some of advertising. People are constantly at the television, radio, print, internet and billboard advertising. Even like a logo on a clothing or the name of a politician written at a bus. Advertising is so much everywhere most people don't even understand how much they see, hear each day.

Consumers we always making choices. We are always deciding what we buy and what not buy and what we choose or not choose. People maybe not know to seeing a billboard advertises the certain product every day or on their way to work or school, they might later to purchase or choose that product in the future.

When consumers, make decisions by advertisements, we are not necessarily making informative decision. Why should someone choose one or another because a catchy phrase or a colourful advertisement? But, on the other hand, what other ways to make decisions about purchasing product or service? If anyone living at a developed country, regardless in a village, counting times of day they see or hear advertising, they have very surprised at just how much constantly exposed to advertising.

Task 1 - Model Answer

This is an example of a very good answer. There are many different approaches that could be taken, however, and this is just one of them.

> This chart follows the value of four international money markets over four years. All four of the market indices rose steadily in value from 2005 to 2007 inclusive, registering a sharp drop in value at the end of 2008. The four markets seem to mirror each other's performance, suggesting that there is a strong correlation in market trends; a rise or fall in one index is reflected in the other indices.
>
> The American index was the strongest in each of the four years, peaking in value at around 13,000 points in 2007, before dropping off to its lowest level at around 9,000 points in 2008. The British market index was the second-most valuable throughout the four years, peaking in 2007 at about 6,500 points before registering a 2,000 point drop in value by the end of 2008. The French and British markets are closely aligned in terms of value and performance, suggesting their economies may be of similar size, while the Korean market was the lowest-valued in each of the four years, though it exhibited a similar performance trend.
>
> From 2005 until 2007, the graph suggests that the global economy may have been performing strongly since all four markets registered steady increases in value. It is also clear that, in 2008, the economy contracted, both locally and globally, as is reflected in the significant fall in market value registered across all four indices.

Task 1 - Example Answer

This is an example of an answer that satisfies the requirements for **band 6**. The answer successfully summarises the main points of the graph, is coherent, with logical paragraphing. Better use could be made of linking devices, however. The lexis is not extensive, but is accurately used and appropriate for the task. There is some awkwardness in expression and some minor grammatical mistakes but they do not obscure the intended meaning.

> This is a chart that shows the end of year value for four international money market indices, over four years. The four markets show many things common and some different.
>
> The Dow Jones is the strongest value in all the years but also it goes down the most. It has the biggest changes rising as high as 13500 and falling as low as around 9000. This drop is more than all the value of the KOSPI which is the weakest market. The KOSPI goes up and down again the least. It has stability. The two European markets, the British FTSE 100 and the French CAC 40 are very close to each other with value.
>
> Some things are true for all the markets. All rise steadily from 2005 to 2007. Each are highest in 2007 and fall lowest in 2008. The relationships between the markets stay the same in each year. The markets change in value, but never change in their relationships to each and the other.

Task 2 - Model Answer

This is an example of a very good answer. There are many different approaches that could be taken, however, and this is just one of them.

Sometimes it seems that all of society cares only for material goods and image. We see reality shows involving people living luxurious lifestyles, and we see well dressed people in advertisements enjoying life with their expensive gadgets. Even our local shop windows display flashy cars, designer labels, and new electronics. It might seem like no one cares about the important things any more and our whole value system is disintegrating; however, I don't believe this is the case.

To some extent, I believe what we see is a highly visible minority. It is mostly the very wealthy who are living such flashy lifestyles, and this is nothing new. What is new is how visible they are because of current increased media activity. We see celebrities on their reality shows, and we watch how they live. We are inundated with gossip about their holidays, their parties, and their fashion, in magazines, on TV and on internet gossip blogs. They are everywhere, and everyone seems interested in watching them. However, this does not necessarily mean everyone is going to try to emulate them. Most people will stare at car crashes, too, and I think some of the obsession with the flashy celebrity lifestyle is fuelled by that same motivation.

In addition, we are entering an economically challenging time, and I think this will bring about big changes in society's value systems. Fewer and fewer people will be able to afford material things, even if they might covet them. It will become more obvious that the flashy lifestyles portrayed by the media are largely a fairy tale. When people find that they must worry about keeping the rent paid or food on the table, this acts as a very powerful distraction from worrying about the brand of their neighbours' clothing. When the well-being of their families is threatened, most people will quickly remember just how important that is.

Finally, there are many people out there who are working to remind everyone about the important things in life. Even though they are less visible, we must not forget about the volunteers who teach sports or art or music to poor children. We must not forget about the doctors who travel to third world countries to share their skills, or the environmental workers trying to secure a better world for the next generation. If we turn off the TV and get out into our communities we will see that there are still strong family ties and strong friendships.

In conclusion, although it may seem that all of society is obsessed with material goods and has forgotten about the important things in life, I believe we are only seeing a highly visible minority, mostly involved with the media, with such materialistic values. Many people still believe the family, community, and environment are important, and are working to keep their values alive.

Finally, I believe the difficult economic times ahead will help their cause and remind everyone that having friends and family around and having physical safety and enough to eat is really far more important than having the newest model of car or the latest accessory.

Task 2 - Example Answer

This is an example of an answer that satisfies the requirements for **band 7.5**. The task is achieved and an opinion is clearly expressed and supported. The paragraphs are logical, and the text flows due to good use of linking expressions. A wide variety of vocabulary is used effectively, as are a variety of sentence forms, although there is occasional awkwardness of grammatical structure, which is the weakest point of the essay.

Nowadays, people everywhere seem to spend more time concerned with looking good and keeping up appearances than ever before; more and more emphasis is put on owning big cars, living in upmarket homes and wearing designer labels. And perhaps our attention to detail in such superficial aspects of life is leading us to neglect the more important things like building strong family bonds and good relationships, and looking after the ones we love. Our values seem to have been turned upside down as we now prioritise the superficial over the meaningful.

This could indeed be reflected in the worrying social trends we are seeing, such as higher divorce rates, increasing relationship problems and juvenile delinquency. After all, if parents are wrapped up in their own little superficial worlds, focus on keeping up with the Joneses, the children and the relationships will suffer a consequence.

Society today seems to be obsessed with celebrity, and material wealth. Perhaps, it is the very thing that we are seeking to attain – celebrity – that is causing to change our behaviour to the detriment of our personal and family lives. Celebrities lead very unreal lifestyles, and scandal, divorce and unethical behaviour follow them wherever they go, it seems. They are poor role models to seek to immitate.

It is clear that we need to start reassessing our priorities and return to the old value system of which family and friends came first. It is a sad reflection on the country today that suicide rates are so high, and perhaps if more focus are put on attaining happiness rather than material goods and celebrity, we might start to see a return to the traditional values of the past, which emphasised the simpler aspects of life such as family and friendship.

Task 1 - Model Answer

This is an example of a very good answer. There are many different approaches that could be taken, however, and this is just one of them.

> These two graphs present information about sales in pounds sterling of three different kinds of music. Taken together, the graphs cover five decades, from the 1960s to 2003. The graphs show that the popularity of pop music, classical music and rock has changed dramatically over the years.
>
> In the 1960s, classical music was by far the most popular type of music. Yet throughout the following decades, its popularity steadily declined. The top graph indicates that, as an exception, classical music sales increased by almost a billion pounds in 2002 before falling again to the previous low in the following year.
>
> In contrast, the popularity of pop music has had a constant and dramatic upward trajectory from the 1960s to the 1990s. This trajectory is interrupted, however, in 2000, 2002, and 2003, and sales from pop music end 2003 earning a billion pounds less than they earned in the 1990s. Still, it has been the most popular type of music since approximately 1988.
>
> Finally, the popularity of rock music has gone through many rises and falls. It rose rapidly in the 60s and 70s, and was the most popular type of music then, before falling sharply in the 80s.

Task 1 - Example Answer

This is an example of an answer that satisfies the requirements for **band 5.5**. The main points of the graphs are summarised in a basic way. It is coherent, however there is no paragraphing used which interferes with the reader's ability to follow the information, as does an absence of linking and referencing phrases. Vocabulary is generally appropriate for the task, however there are some inaccuracies. Some complex grammatical structures are attempted, but some basic errors are also occasionally present.

> In the 1960s, classical was the most popular music with up to four billion pounds in sales generated, but this has been decreasing in popularity ever since. By the 1990s, it has become the least popular of the three music with sales of just 2 billion pounds. Rock, on the other hand, went from being one of two of least popular themes in the 60s to become the most popular during the seventies and early eighties with the sales of above four billion in a year. In the 1990s, rock became slightly less popular again, and has remained the second-most popular music ever since. Pop Music has risen steadily in popularity throughout decades from 1960 to 1990. By the middle 90s it has easily become the most popular theme with doubling its sales to around five million in a year. Pop remained the most popular theme in the early 2000s, though by 2003 sales had dropped back somewhat around 4 billion. Rock, remained the second-most popular music but saw many changes in sales in the 2000s, at one point in 2001 reaching a two-decade high of four billion. Classical continued to see its sales declining remaining at or below two billion pounds.

Task 2 - Model Answer

This is an example of a very good answer. There are many different approaches that could be taken, however, and this is just one of them.

These days going into debt is a normal thing. It is almost impossible to buy a house without the help of a mortgage, and people hardly give this a second thought. Credit card use is ubiquitous. Even cars and stereos are sometimes bought on credit. Although borrowing money can give people some opportunities they would not have otherwise, I believe that, generally, going into debt is very risky.

On some occasions, borrowing money can help people improve their circumstances. If a person does his or her maths carefully, he or she can pay less, monthly, for a mortgage than they would for rent, and enjoy the added advantage of owning property. It is undoubtedly a good feeling to live in your own home, and in the right circumstances it can also be a great investment. Another situation when borrowing can be beneficial is in the case of starting a new business. Sometimes a bit of financial help can allow someone to earn the money back many times over, but this requires business skills and a bit of luck as well.

In spite of these benefits, going into debt can also pose quite a lot of dangers. If someone gets a mortgage on a house at a bad time, he or she can end up stuck paying much more than the property is actually worth. People with mortgages also lose flexibility, because for the first few years they pay off only interest, and if they need to sell the house and move, they simply lose this money. Even more risky is borrowing money on a credit card. Generally this does not involve investment, but rather the acquisition of material goods and when these goods are bought on credit, they end up costing far more than they would otherwise because of high interest rates. It is very easy for people to not realise how much they owe a credit card company and get themselves into an amount of debt that is very hard for them to ever pay off. This can literally destroy lives.

In conclusion, although borrowing money can be a good idea in some circumstances, without a great deal of caution and forethought it can pose serious dangers. In general, I believe taking on debt is a bad idea.

Task 2 - Example Answer

This is an example of an answer that satisfies the requirements for **band 4.** The answer partially addresses the task, expressing a supported opinion on one part of the more complex topic. There is evidence of structure and logical paragraphing, and even some basic linking words. However vocabulary is limited and not always appropriate for what is being expressed, and only very simple sentence structures are attempted, with frequent mistakes. There is borrowing from the prompt in the first paragraph.

Most the people it is common to borrow money. Most people have a credit card, a mortgage, and of then they will buy a car on time as well. It is to risky. It is very risky to use a credit card.

Using the credit card is not the good idea. It is because the credit card is not real money it is not money that the person he has in his hand. So when he buy the thing with the credit card they take the money and he takes the new thing but the money is not paid. So the money is bigger and bigger because it grows up. This makes a very big problem for the people.

In the end the people who they use the credit card they have a big debt and they must to find a way to pay for it. This is very hard and it takes them many years.

I believe that it is not so often that people use the credit card. The most of the people know about it is so risky. So they are careful with it themselves. Also the people all can not get the credit card easily. They must to do an application so they can not take the risky and they are safe.

In conclusion it is very bad and very risky to use the credit card. You should not do that.

Task 1 - Model Answer

This is an example of a very good answer. There are many different approaches that could be taken, however, and this is just one of them.

This chart shows that the percentage of people in the Irish republic, and in each province, who speak the Irish language has increased between the years of 1981 and 2002.

This trend of increasing numbers of speakers each year is generally consistent. There is a similar pattern in each province, with slow increases until 1991, and then a large increase in 1996, and a smaller increase again in 2002. The only exception to this trend occurs in Leinster, Connacht, and Ulster in the year 1986 when the percentage of language speakers actually drops slightly. However, for the whole state, in 1986, there appears to be a very small increase.

Although the trend is the same, the percentages differed widely between provinces. Connacht has the highest number of Irish speakers, rising to between 47 and 48 percent. It is closely followed by Munster, with around 46 percent. Ulster has about 42 percent, with Leinster showing the lowest values with less than 40 percent. This relationship between numbers of speakers and province is also consistent between years; in other words, Connacht always has the highest percentage, and Leinster the lowest.

Perhaps the most striking point that is illustrated by this chart is the large rise in the number of Irish language speakers in the year 1996. In every province, it is close to a 10 percent increase. I would guess that some action must have been taken to encourage people to learn the language in the years between 1991 and 1996.

Task 1 - Example Answer

This is an example of an answer that satisfies the requirements for **band 6.5**. The answer successfully summarises the main points of the chart in logical paragraphs which flow due to good use of linking words. Lexis is appropriate to the task, and there is use of idiom. Grammar is generally accurate, although the level of complexity varies; sometimes sentences show control of complex structures, and other times simple structure is used.

This chart shows percentages of people who speak Irish language in four provinces and then the whole Irish state combined. It show this for five years and covers a bit more than 2 decades; twenty one years to be precise. The chart reveals some patterns.

First of all there are patterns in language use in the different years. In every one of the province, and of course the whole state, language use is each year rising. It is rising a little for the first decade, with as an exception Leinster and Ulster where it fell only a little in the year 1986. A very important feature in this graph is that in 1996 everywhere the language use rose a great deal.

Secondly there are patterns between provences. In every year, Connacht has the most speaker, and Munster has the second most speakers. Ulster and Leinster have considerably less. These two are close in value but Leinster is the least of all.

Finally, the take home message from this chart could be said to be that outlook for the Irish language seems to be improving, and also that whatever happened between 1991 and 1996 was very successful at increase in the number of Irish speakers.

Task 2 - Model Answer 1

This is an example of a very good answer. There are many different approaches that could be taken, however, and this is just one of them.

Few would argue that we do not face an energy crisis. However there are many different ideas about how to solve it. Among the suggestions is nuclear power, which some feel is the only solution; however, I strongly disagree that nuclear power is a necessary evil.

First of all, there are far too many risks to make nuclear power an acceptable solution. If there is an accident with the nuclear reactor, the consequences are huge – many people would die, and the environment would be damaged for many years to come. Governments always say that the reactors are safe - there is no way there could be an accident - yet the past has shown us, time and time again, that human error will occur and there will be accidents. Also, even when the reactors are working properly, they produce dangerous radioactive waste. This waste will last for a very long time - longer than any material we can create to safely contain it. We are already seeing the consequences of waste, from some early reactors, that was irresponsibly dumped - in the discovery of seriously polluted land and negative health consequences for local residents. If you want to find out more about this, you can Google the Hanford site in Washington state in the USA.

Luckily there are different options for generating and using power, so we need not be dependent on nuclear energy. There is solar energy, wind energy, wave and tide energy, and energy can even be created by burning our rubbish. Although it may be true that our technology is inadequate today to use these forms of energy to completely replace non-renewable sources, we should be focusing on advancing these technologies so that they can meet the demand. Also, energy usage today is incredibly wasteful, so many more advances could be made by giving some attention to creating appliances that use less energy, and changing our lifestyles to make them less energy hungry.

So, in conclusion, although certain results of nuclear energy could be called evil, it is hardly necessary to subject ourselves to them. We would be much better off supporting researchers who are developing new energy forms, and new ways of managing our lifestyles to consume less.

Task 2 - Example Answer

This is an example of an answer that satisfies the requirements for **band 5**. A relevant response is made and an opinion is expressed, although it does not cover the full complexity included in the prompt. It is mostly coherent and cohesive and the ideas move logically from paragraph to paragraph. The paragraphs are also organised in a clear and logical way. Lexis is accurate but limited for the subject, and there are many grammatical errors. Simple sentences are expressed accurately, but more complicated structures are not used effectively.

Nuclear power has dangers and drawback like the radioactive fallout and if it breaks there is disaster. But also it is an alternative when we are running out of oil and coal. There are advantages too.

The dangers of nuclear are many. There is pollution to the environment with radioactive chemical. These last for a very very long time and can make people sick like cancer and to lose the hairs. Also they are dangerous if they break. They do an explosion like what happened at Chernobyl or what happened in Japan.

What was on the news recently is really bad in Japan. Japan has so much danger from the nuclear reactor after the earthquake. The people are scared and all over the word too. Radioactive fallout went into the sea and into the air but certainly the people near the reactor are the most dangerous. They had to leave their homes and it is very sad.

On the other hand there are and advantages. It is easy because it makes a lot of energy as much as we want and it never runs out. Maybe it is cheap, I don't know but I think this. Also it makes no smoke like coal and it is not black or smelly. Also the countries that they do not have oil can build the nuclear and have it and they do not need to pay money or fight wars with other countries that have oil. This is a very big advantage for the politics in the world.

In conclusion there are good and bad things of nuclear power. It has some things very good for us but also the bad.

Succeed in IELTS
AUDIOSCRIPTS

TEST 1

You will hear a number of different recordings and you will have to answer questions on what you hear. There will be time for you to read the instructions and questions and you will have a chance to check your work. All the recordings will be played once only. The test is in four sections. At the end of the test you will be given ten minutes to transfer your answers to an answer sheet.
Now turn to section one.

SECTION 1

You will hear a conversation about different options for travelling to France. First you have some time to look at questions 1 to 5.
(Pause the recording for 30 seconds)
You will see that there is an example that has been done for you. On this occasion only, the conversation relating to this will be played first.

F= Travel agent   M= Student
F: *Good morning!*
M: *Hi.*
F: *How can I help you?*
M: *I'm looking for information about travelling to France. I'm studying in Nice next year and need <u>to go there in September</u>. I'm thinking of driving, so I guess it's either through the Channel, or by ferry. Um.... I think the ferry's a lot slower, isn't it?*
F: *Indeed it is; it takes around nine hours from London to Paris, including the overland bits, and usually it's more expensive too, unless you book well ahead of time; then sometimes the ferry's more affordable.*

The answer is "September" so the time of travel has been filled in for you. Now we shall begin. You should answer the questions as you listen because you will not hear the recording a second time. Listen carefully and answer questions 1 to 5.

[REPEAT]
M: How much does it cost?
F: Well, when you take the train and the ferry now, you must buy your tickets separately ...
M: Actually I'd prefer to take the Chunnel. How much does that cost?
F: That depends on your travel date and availability of tickets, but you can expect to pay about 50 pounds each way for the car, in addition to your passenger fares.
M: It's not cheap.
F: No; will you be using your car a lot while you're in France?
M: Uh, not really, but I'll have a lot of luggage, so it seems like the easiest way. Besides, I hate flying.
F: Driving is never the easiest way to get from the UK to France, I'm afraid! And of course, your steering wheel will be on the wrong side when you get there! If you're not going to need your car when you arrive, may I suggest leaving it at home and travelling by train? **(1)** <u>It's much faster,</u> **(2)** <u>more affordable</u> **(3)** <u>and you can take as much luggage as you need</u>, there aren't limits.
M: Oh, I didn't know that about the luggage - that's good. It would certainly be more relaxing, I suppose. Ok, tell me about the train.
F: It's definitely the most popular option these days. Eurostar has

now captured over 70% of the London to Paris market from the airlines, and maybe this has something to do with the fact that **(4)** <u>92.4% of Eurostar trains run on time</u>, against just 65% of flights on the same routes. From central London to central Paris, Eurostar is faster than flying as well.
M: And the Eurostar is ... what exactly? A train company?
F: Oh, sorry! The Eurostar is the high-speed passenger train that runs from London to Paris via the Channel Tunnel. **(5)** <u>Eurostar can reach 186 miles per hour</u>, and the journey takes just 2 hours 15 minutes.

Before you hear the rest of the conversation, you have some time to look at questions 6 to 10.
(Pause the recording for 30 seconds)
Now listen and answer questions 6 to 10.

M: All right, so it's easy to get to Paris, but what about Nice? It's a fair bit farther.
F: Yes, but it couldn't be easier. There are two main options; you can leave London at seven twenty-seven in the morning, then transfer in Paris to **(6)** <u>catch the TGV train at eleven forty-six</u>, which takes about five and a half hours, and be in Nice in time for an evening meal. Or, you can take any Eurostar to Paris in time **(7)** <u>to catch the twenty-two twenty-five from Paris</u>, which arrives in Nice at eight fifty-four. **(8)** <u>It's a longer journey, but many people prefer the convenience of travelling overnight</u>.
M: Yes, that appeals to me. About how much does the overnight journey cost?
F: The example I've pulled up on the computer now costs a hundred and thirty-five pounds return, but sometimes it's lower; as low as 97 pounds. I'll write down a couple of website addresses for you, and you can search for various times and fares on your own.
M: Thanks, that's great ... oh ... one more thing. I'll need a single fare, because I won't be returning for a while. Is that going to be more expensive?
F: No, don't worry. **(9)** <u>Singles are approximately half of the return fare</u>, though this wasn't true several years ago, when it wasn't uncommon for a return to be cheaper than a single.
M: Ok, this sounds good, but what about flying? Is that an option?
F: If you aren't going to opt for taking the train, flying is another good option. While the train's the fastest way to travel from London to Paris, you can actually save time by opting to fly from London to the South of France.
M: I guess there's an airport in Nice, isn't there?
F: Yes; the Nice Cote d'Azur Airport. It's about 7km from the centre of Nice. Since it's the third most important airport in France after Charles de Gaulle and Orly in Paris, there's no shortage of flights.
M: Do you know exactly how long it takes?
F: **(10)** <u>Two hours</u>.
M: That's quick!
F: Yes, but you need to consider that you'll lose time checking in and waiting to collect luggage and such. And of course, there's a baggage allowance.
M: True. All right, thanks very much for your help. I've got a lot to think about now.
F: No problem at all! Feel free to come back if you have more questions.

That is the end of section one. You now have half a minute to check your answers.
(Pause the recording for 30 seconds)
Now turn to section two.

SECTION 2

You will now hear a guide talking about an architectural development in the city of Birmingham.
First you have some time to look at questions 11 to 15.
(Pause the recording for 30 seconds)
Now listen carefully and answer questions 11 to 15.

Good morning ladies and gentlemen! Thanks for joining me on our monthly excursion to visit new architectural and city planning developments in our city of Birmingham. Today, as you can see, we're here at the development site of "the Cube", and its construction is well underway. Indeed, the year ahead will be an exciting year for Birmingham Development Company and its construction arm, Buildability, as the construction of "the Cube", the most spectacular building in Birmingham, continues at speed. This new building, valued at over £100 million, has been designed by the internationally renowned architects, MAKE. Their design team, led by Ken Shuttleworth, has created a 17-storey cube aimed at providing a spectacular contrast to the increasing number of towers appearing on the Birmingham cityscape.

(11) The complex 142-week building programme that will transform the Birmingham skyline upon its completion, is currently over halfway through its development. The building will continue to rise, over the coming year, **(12)** with each floor taking 2-3 weeks to complete. As you can see, to your right, the first shipment of the special gold anodised cladding that will adorn the cube has now arrived on-site, **(13)** and from February, the glistening golden exterior will begin to be installed, bringing the unique building to life. **(14)** Late summer will see the 'topping out' of the concrete frame of the cube structure, with the intricate metallic **(15)** fretwork screen beginning to take shape in the early autumn.

Before you hear the rest of the talk, you have some time to look at questions 16 to 20.
(Pause the recording for 30 seconds)
Now listen and answer questions 16 to 20.

What has been accomplished to date in the city's regeneration has been nothing short of amazing, yet we hope to set a new benchmark for developments in Birmingham. The Cube will bring forward a new standard of architecture and a building, which will not only be Birmingham's most striking waterside location, but also one which is identifiable around the world. The Cube breaks all the boundaries of what has been achieved in Birmingham so far.

The finished Cube will be a mixed-use building. It will house the city's first **(16)** rooftop restaurant with panoramic views whilst **(17)** a boutique hotel and residential apartments below will feature internal views over the twisting atrium. **(18)** Further down, high specification Grade A office space is planned with more **(19)** exclusive retail **(20)** and waterside restaurants at the base. The Mailbox has already raised the bar in the quality and calibre of our architecture and the retail offerings, worldwide brand names and stylish restaurants have given Birmingham a contemporary profile rivalling the capitals of Europe.

From the outset, the Cube's design team sought to create a new landmark building for Birmingham which fits into its context and which draws people in. Lined with coloured glass and with an exterior clad in shimmering metal fretwork, the Cube has visible links to Birmingham's heritage in engineering and jewellery manufacture. It was essential that the building created a strong visual presence, immediately identifiable as a gateway to the canal and city centre area to the north.

Our city is a city of the future and as a futuristic building with phenomenal foresight in style and design, the Cube is indicative of our plans in how we see Birmingham developing. The Cube will help to elevate us onto a global stage. Now, let's go and have a look at the progress of the entrance gateway.

That is the end of section two. You now have half a minute to check your answers.
(Pause the recording for 30 seconds)
Now turn to section three.

SECTION 3

You will hear a conversation between four students: Lynn, Thomas, Sophie and David. They are talking about one of their tutors, Marlena.
First you have some time to look at questions 21 to 25.
(Pause the recording for 30 seconds)
Now listen carefully and answer questions 21 to 25.

L= Lynn T= Thomas S= Sophie D= David
L: Thomas, let's not go to the lab. Let's just stay here in the student lounge and drink tea and review the chapter.
T: You know we can't do that. We've a responsibility to turn up and make sure our tutor has understood the week's lectures. If we don't go, no one will ever even realize she's got the theories all muddled up!
S: Oh really?
L: Sophie, it's awful! Marlena just opens her mouth and I'm confused. Really, she...
T: Marlena's our tutor.
S: Yeah, I gathered that...
L: You lot have got no manners; I was in the middle of saying something! ..... **(21)** She'll say things that make no sense whatsoever, and I'm thinking I've misunderstood something, and I'm looking around the room and everyone has these looks on their faces of...
T: **(22)** Disbelief and merriment!
L: Maybe **you** do, Thomas, but we're not all geniuses. Really, I'll be so worried that I've got it all wrong, then people start asking questions, and by and by we figure out that she's mixed something up.
S: (23) That's too bad. It's not a good situation at all.
D: (24) But surely you're exaggerating a bit, Lynn...
L: No, it's awful! I don't know how she got through her undergraduate studies, much less got accepted as a postgrad here. **(25)** You'd think our professor would have some idea about her abilities.

Before you hear the rest of the conversation, you have some time to look at questions 26 to 30.
(Pause the recording for 30 seconds)
Now listen and answer questions 26-30.

D: Marlena's an unusual name. Is she English?
L: She's Spanish, David. She's got a really strong accent...
T: Really that's a lot of the problem, I think. I don't think she's thick; she just doesn't communicate very well. I'm not sure she understands us completely, **(26)** especially when someone's joking around. And we do tease her a bit, I must admit.
S: What a nightmare! I'd hate to have you in my class if I was a tutor, Tom!
T: As long as you're clever Sophie, you'd have nothing to worry about. . .
S: But you've just said she's not thick!
D: I think I've met her, actually; I think we had a class together, maybe last year. She was really shy and quiet. Hardly spoke the whole term. But she was always smiley and friendly. She seemed nice, actually, and I think she got one of the highest marks in the class. **(27)** Maybe you've all picked on her so much that she's so nervous that she can't think clearly. Ever think of that?
L: But we don't need to baby-sit; we need help! It's a difficult subject!
S: Has anyone ever gone up and asked her for help individually?
T: Yes, actually, I have. I couldn't understand one of the formulas in the first chapter - the theory about why it worked just made no

sense to me, so I went and asked her about it and she cleared it right up. She was very helpful. She's not thick; I already said that.

S: She's just so much fun to torment, right?

T: Yep, that's it!

S: **(28)** <u>Lynn, if you are having trouble with something why don't you make an appointment to meet with her individually</u> and see if she can help you that way? **(29)** <u>Maybe you'd see a different side of her.</u> I reckon she just hates getting up in front of the class and I can hardly blame her.

L: Yes, I could try that I suppose.

D: Guys, the tutors aren't old academics who've been teaching for thirty years; they're just like us, two years down the road, if we're clever enough to continue with our education. I know I'd be mortified to get up in front of you lot, and I don't think I'll feel that differently in a couple of years' time. **(30)** <u>You know, we're far more experienced as students than they are as teachers.</u>

T: You're right, David. Really, it's more like one of our mates is trying to help us out, but you know, our mates aren't so frightened of us!

S: Yeah, but you aren't so horrible to your mates, are you?

That is the end of section three. You now have half a minute to check your answers.
(Pause the recording for 30 seconds)
Now turn to section four.

SECTION 4

You will hear a lecture on the illness, tuberculosis.
First you have some time to look at questions 31 to 40.
(Pause the recording for 1 minute)
Now listen carefully and answer questions 31 to 40.

Hello there; can I have your attention please? We've got a lot to cover today and we need to get started. If you recall, last week we discussed the AIDS epidemic, and its effect on health care systems in the countries with the highest incidence. Well, today I'm going to speak about **(31)** <u>another significant disease that is rather closely associated with the AIDS epidemic - Tuberculosis.</u>

In the UK, active Tuberculosis, otherwise known as TB, was common in the nineteenth century - the old 'consumption' of romantic novels. Since then, **(32)** <u>better living conditions, better nutrition, immunisation and effective treatments</u> in the twentieth century have all combined to make TB uncommon in the UK today. **(33)** <u>However, TB is still common in developing countries and parts of</u> **(34)** <u>Eastern Europe.</u> It causes more deaths worldwide than any other infectious disease - **(35)** <u>about three million per year.</u> This is a tragic statistic since TB is now generally a curable disease. **(36)** <u>Overall, one third of the world's population is currently infected</u> with the bacteria that cause TB. However, people infected with TB bacilli will not necessarily become sick with the disease. The immune system "walls off" the TB bacilli which, protected by a thick waxy coat, can lie dormant for years. It's estimated that 5 to 10 percent of people who are infected with TB bacilli, but who are not infected with HIV, become sick or infectious at some time during their life. Left untreated, each person with active TB disease will infect on average between 10 and 15 people every year.

....

Pause (4 seconds)

There are certain risk factors that make certain people more likely to become ill with TB. When people's immune systems are weakened, their chances of becoming sick are greater, **(37)** <u>for example, due to HIV infection, immune-suppressing treatment, or alcohol or drug addiction.</u> Age is also a factor, with babies, young children and the elderly being most susceptible. In addition, poor nutrition and lack of vitamin D are linked to TB. Finally, **(38)** <u>TB is more common in certain environments such as among homeless people, among prisoners,</u> in large cities and in more impoverished areas.

(39) <u>Until 50 years ago, there were no medicines to cure TB.</u> Finding medicines to cure TB was a tremendous breakthrough. But now, strains that are resistant to a single drug have been documented in every country surveyed; what's more, strains of TB resistant to all major anti-TB drugs have emerged. Drug-resistant TB is caused by inconsistent or partial treatment, when patients do not take all their medicines regularly for the required period because they start to feel better, because doctors and health workers prescribe the wrong treatment regimens, or because the drug supply is unreliable.

A particularly dangerous form of drug-resistant TB is multidrug-resistant TB, abbreviated as MDR-TB, which is defined as the disease caused by TB bacilli resistant to at least the two most powerful anti-TB drugs. Rates of MDR-TB are high in some countries, especially in the former Soviet Union, and threaten TB control efforts. While drug-resistant TB is generally treatable, it requires extensive chemotherapy - up to two years of treatment - with second-line anti-TB drugs. These second-line drugs are more costly than first-line drugs, and produce adverse drug reactions that are more severe, though still manageable.

(40) <u>The recent emergence of extensively drug-resistant TB,</u> called XDR-TB, particularly in settings where many TB patients are also infected with HIV, <u>poses a serious threat to TB control</u> and confirms the urgent need to strengthen basic TB control and to apply the new WHO guidelines for the management of drug-resistant TB.

That is the end of section four. You now have half a minute to check your answers. *(Pause the recording for 30 seconds)*
That is the end of the listening test. In the IELTS test you would now have ten minutes to transfer your answers to the listening answer sheet.

TEST 2

You will hear a number of different recordings and you will have to answer questions on what you hear. There will be time for you to read the instructions and questions and you will have a chance to check your work. All the recordings will be played once only. The test is in four sections. At the end of the test you will be given ten minutes to transfer your answers to an answer sheet.
Now turn to section one.

SECTION 1

You will hear a telephone conversation between Jason and Laurel. They are arranging to meet later to go to an art gallery. First you have some time to look at questions 1 to 7.
(Pause the recording for 30 seconds)
You will see that there is an example that has been done for you. On this occasion only, the conversation relating to this will be played first.

J = Jason   L = Laurel

J: *Hi Laurel, it's Jason. How are you?*

L: *Jason, so glad you called. I'm fine. You must have got my message on your answerphone. I wanted to know if you were <u>free tomorrow</u> to go to the opening of a Gaudi exhibition.*

J: *Yes, I heard about it and thought of you straight away.*

The answer is "tomorrow" so the time of the visit has been filled in for you. Now we shall begin. You should answer the questions as you listen because you will not hear the recording a second time. Listen carefully and answer questions 1 to 7.

[REPEAT]

L: So, you're free tomorrow?

J: Yes. What time did you want to go?

L: **(1)** Well, I have a class at college in the morning until 11.15. Wait, no, 11.30, so any time after then.

J: **(2)** I have a lecture until about 12.15. Well, that works perfectly. Do you want me to come and pick you up?

L: No, you're much closer to the gallery than I am.

J: Which gallery is it?

L: The Tate, which is really good because I can get there pretty easily by tube.

J: Oh, right. Okay, where do you want to meet and at what time?

L: If I leave when I finish my class, I can probably make the 11.55 tube. That should get me into central London in about 25 minutes.

J: **(3)** I can come to the tube to meet you by 12.30.

L: It's probably easier to meet at the Tate. The tube is pretty quiet at that time. Not the usual rush of people, so I should be ok, and they've installed a new device in the lift for wheelchairs, so I can get to the street without having to wait for long. Do you remember the old lift?

J: Yes, it was horrible. It made that loud clanking noise and the smell would make anyone pass out.

L: The new lift is quicker and the wheels of the chair lock into a safety system that allows you, and whoever else is in there with you, more room. It's a lot quicker.

J: That's a relief. Okay, so where are we meeting?

L: **(4)** How about at the ticket office at the Tate?

J: If I get there first do you want me to buy you a ticket?

L: No, I get a concession and need to show my card.

J: Lucky you. How much do you pay?

L: **(6)** About 10 pounds for major exhibitions on Tuesdays.

J: **(5)** That's pretty good. The normal price is another 5. Hang on, did you say Tuesdays?

L: Yes. Tomorrow's Tuesday.

J: Yes, yes. You're right. Why did I think it was Wednesday? Oh, because our lecture times have all changed this week and it's put me off. Okay, hang on. I have no class so I can come and pick you up.

L: Can your car take my wheelchair?

J: **(7)** Yes, I've got the van, so there's plenty of room in the back.

Before you hear the rest of the conversation, you have some time to look at questions 8 to 10.
(Pause the recording for 30 seconds)
Now listen and answer questions 8 to 10.

J: What's your address?

L: It's **(8)** flat 6, 83 Alexandra Avenue, West Hampstead.

J: Let me write this down. Flat 6?

L: Yes. **(9)** That's 83 Alexandra Avenue.

J: **(10)** Alexandra Avenue?

L: Yes, West Hampstead.

J: Got it. Okay, I'll be there at 12.30. Will you be home by then?

L: Sure will. Thanks, Jason. See you tomorrow.

J: Okay. Bye.

That is the end of section one. You now have half a minute to check your answers.
(Pause the recording for 30 seconds)
Now turn to section two.

SECTION 2

You will hear a tour guide talking about the Newgrange passage tomb in Ireland. First you have some time to look at questions 11-16.
(Pause the recording for 30 seconds)
Now listen carefully and answer questions 11 to 16.

Good morning, and welcome to the Brú na Bóinne Visitor Centre. Newgrange is one of the finest examples, not only in Ireland, but in Western Europe, of the type of structure known as a passage tomb. It was probably built about 3000 BC — that makes it around 500 years older than the pyramid at Giza, in Egypt, and 1000 years older than Stonehenge in England!

Before we start our tour, let me tell you a little bit about what you'll be seeing. Newgrange consists of **(11)** a long narrow passage and chamber, which, if we imagine looking down on it from above, would have the shape of a cross. In the **(12)** two rooms of the chamber forming the arms of the cross, you will see **(13)** large stone basins, which are a feature of many Palaeolithic Irish tombs, though researchers can only guess about what their purpose would have been.

(14) Outside of the tomb, **(15)** in front of the entrance to the **(14)** passage, sits the large carved entrance stone, which I'm sure you've all seen pictures of in magazines or textbooks. After all, this stone is about the most famous example in the entire repertory of Palaeolithic rock art. The spirals and zigzag lines covering it are strikingly beautiful. Some of the large kerbstones lining the inside of the passage are also decorated, although they're not as famous. An eleven-metre-high circular mound made of stones covers the tomb, making it appear even larger and more imposing than it is, especially from a distance. The final thing I want to mention before we set off is **(16)** the light box, which is an opening that you will see in the roof of the passage, above the entrance, which allows the light of the sun to enter and illuminate the tomb at sunrise on the day of the winter solstice.

Before you hear the rest of the talk, you have some time to look at questions 17-20.
(Pause the recording for 30 seconds)
Now listen and answer questions 17-20.

Actually, I want to tell you a bit more about the winter solstice at Newgrange. The alignment of the tomb to the winter solstice sunrise is without a doubt one of the most amazing features of Newgrange, and has led researchers to speculate that the site may not have been only a place of burial but may have had broader cultural importance as a place of spiritual or scientific significance. Indeed, to witness the winter solstice sunrise illuminate the tomb is breathtaking and still has a deep resonance with people today.

The general public are welcome to gather at Newgrange for the sunrise on the morning around the Solstice, **(17)** but access to the chamber itself is limited on the Solstice mornings, and is **(18)** decided in advance by lottery. It's proved to be extremely popular; last year there were 25,349 entries for the Solstice lottery's 50 places. But don't despair — in recent years the event has been transmitted live by the Office of Public Works to hundreds of thousands of people around the world via internet and television stations.

This year's draw will take place on September 30th, **(19)** and the winning applicants will be notified by mid October. To ensure that everything is fair and square, children from three local schools will choose the winning applicants. Fifty names will be drawn, **(20)** and each of the lucky winners can bring a guest. But of course, one hundred people won't fit in the tomb; we have room for ten lottery winners and their guests in the chamber on each of the five mornings around the Winter Solstice. If you're interested in signing up, you can do so at the information desk on your way out.

That is the end of section two. You now have half a minute to check your answers.
(Pause the recording for 30 seconds)
Now turn to section three.

SECTION 3

You will hear a dialogue between a doctor and a patient.
First you have some time to look at questions 21 to 24.
(Pause the recording for 30 seconds)
Now listen carefully and answer questions 21 to 24.

P = patient   D = doctor

P: **(21)** Hello Dr Smith, can I come in?
D: Yes, please sit down. I won't be a minute.
P: Thank you.
D: You would be Mr Garrison?
P: Yes, Peter Garrison.
D: Okay, what seems to be the problem, Mr Garrison?
P: **(22)** I've been having some pains in my stomach and it's been bothering me for nearly two weeks. Actually, ten days to be exact.
D: What happened at the time the pain started?
P: I was having dinner with my family and I thought I must have eaten something that didn't sit well in my stomach.
D: Then what did you do?
P: I drank a glass of alker seltzer to ease the pain, but it didn't work.
D: Do you remember what it was that you ate at the time the pain started?
P: Yes, I was eating pumpkin soup with bread, and then we had roast chicken, potatoes, some vegetables, and afterwards dessert. I think it was chocolate pudding with cream.
D: That's quite a lot of food.
P: Yes, well, I do like to eat.
D: Do you do any form of exercise?
P: No, not really. I mean, sometimes I might go for a walk.
D: How often?
P: **(23)** Maybe once a month.
D: And for how many hours?
P: Oh, no, not a long walk. I might walk to the local shops instead of taking my car.
D: How far away is the shop?
P: About 5 minutes.
D: By car?
P: No, on foot.
D: Well, I think the problem here is that you're quite overweight from the looks of things. You don't exercise and you eat far too much, so I'd say the issue you're having with your stomach is something that was inevitable. I'm going to suggest a few things, but you have to comply, otherwise there's no point in me going on.
P: So it's serious.
D: **(24)** It will be if you don't take steps to change your lifestyle.

Before you hear the rest of the conversation, you have some time to look at questions 25 to 30.
(Pause the recording for 30 seconds)
Now listen and answer questions 25-30

P: What should I do?
D: First of all, I'm going to give you a list of what you can and can't eat for the next month. I want you to follow this quite strictly. Do you understand?
P: Em, yes.
D: For breakfast I want you to have a cup of hot water and lemon juice.
P: Is that all?
D: No, let me finish.
P: Sorry.
D: **(25)** After 20 minutes I want you to have a freshly-squeezed juice of either fruit or vegetables. Then eat either cereal without sugar, and with low-fat milk, or if you don't like cereal, then have some toast. You can use honey or jam that is organic only. **(26)** But I don't want you to use any butter and no sugar or salt.
P: For a whole month?
D: Yes. Then for a mid-morning snack you can have two pieces of fruit.

Lunch will be two pieces of brown, organic bread with either avocado or hummus instead of butter, and salad. Then in the afternoon you can have a handful of nuts, but not too many. Okay so far?
P: Well, it all sounds a bit hard. You know. It doesn't seem like much.
D: **(27)** For dinner you are allowed a small quantity of about 100 grammes of either brown rice or pasta with steamed or baked fish, and vegetables. If you must have dessert, you can either have another piece of **(28)** fruit or some low fat organic yogurt.
P: Where do I buy all this organic food?
D: There's a shop in the high street and I want you to walk there. **(29)** It's just opposite the town hall.
P: Okay.
D: I want you to be 100% dedicated to this diet.
P: Is that it?
D: Yes, and I'll see you in a month's time to reassess you.
P: Okay, Doctor. Well, I'll see you in a month.
D: **(30)** Oh, and absolutely no alcohol, coffee or cigarettes.
P: Oh, dear.

That is the end of section three. You now have half a minute to check your answers.
(Pause the recording for 30 seconds)
Now turn to section four.

SECTION 4

You will hear part of a lecture on photography. First you have some time to look at questions 31-40.
(Pause the recording for 1 minute)
Now listen carefully and answer questions 31 to 40.

Last week, we focused on the creative side of photography - composition etc. - but this week it's time to get a bit more technical. Today, our focus is going to be on exposure. The term exposure simply refers to the amount of light your film is exposed to. Or, put another way, **(31)** the amount of light you allow to strike your film.
A good photographer has got to know two things; (i) how much light is required to capture a particular image and (ii) how to control the light reaching the film. **(32)** The former is usually determined by the camera's inbuilt light metre, **(33)** and the latter is taken care of by means of the aperture and shutter settings. Essentially, exposure time is controlled by opening the aperture and allowing light to pass through it for a fixed duration. Aperture sounds like a fancy word, but, in simple terms, **(34)** it is basically a hole whose size can be varied to allow more or less light to pass through it. **(35)** Aperture size is described in f-numbers, with each f-number being half as bright as the previous one. The difference in value between one full f-number and the next is known as a 'stop'. The smaller the f-number, the larger the aperture and the greater the amount of light being let pass through it.

....

Pause (4 seconds)

(36) Shutter controls also play a crucial role in determining the exposure for a shot. The shutter prevents light from reaching the film **(37)** until the instant of exposure when a picture is being taken. Then, it opens for a predetermined amount of time, allowing light to pass through the aperture and onto the film. **(38)** Shutter speed is expressed in seconds or fractions of a second. A one-unit change to the shutter speed is also known as a 'stop', and a change of one stop to the shutter speed has a similar outcome to a one-stop aperture size adjustment.
Overexposure, as the name suggests, **(39)** occurs when you give your film more exposure to light than is necessary to capture a clear image. Telltale signs of overexposure include pictures domi-

nated by pale or light shades and poor washed-out colours. Underexposure, then, occurs when there is not enough light and produces the opposite result; a dark image **(40)** <u>with poor detail and shadows.</u>

Before we go on to look at how to ascertain the correct exposure settings for a particular shot, let's take a short break..

That is the end of section four. You now have half a minute to check your answers.

(Pause the recording for 30 seconds)

That is the end of the listening test. In the IELTS test you would now have ten minutes to transfer your answers to the listening answer sheet.

TEST 3

You will hear a number of different recordings and you will have to answer questions on what you hear. There will be time for you to read the instructions and questions and you will have a chance to check your work. All the recordings will be played once only. The test is in four sections. At the end of the test you will be given ten minutes to transfer your answers to an answer sheet. Now turn to section one.

SECTION 1

You will hear a conversation between a computer technician and a woman whose computer has crashed.
First you have some time to look at questions 1 to 4.

(Pause the recording for 30 seconds)

You will see that there is an example that has been done for you. On this occasion only, the conversation relating to this will be played first.

M = computer technician
F = woman whose computer has crashed.
M: *Hello. Tom's computer maintenance; how may I help you?*
F: *Hello. I...um... seem to have* <u>a problem with my computer.</u>
It's really inconvenient too, because I've a deadline tomorrow I'm rushing to meet.

The answer is "computer problem" so the reason for the phone call has been filled in for you. Now we shall begin. You should answer the questions as you listen because you will not hear the recording a second time. Listen carefully and answer questions 1 to 4.

[REPEAT]
F: Suddenly **(1)** <u>the screen went blank.</u> Blue. A blank, blue screen. I don't know if you can do something about it?
M: Ah, the dreaded blue screen. I think I can do something about it - it's my job after all. There are a few different scenarios, though, that could be going on with your computer. You've tried re-starting it, right?
F: Oh, yes. Nothing.
M: And **(2)** <u>it's plugged in, not running on battery?</u>
F: Yes.
M: Are you sure? Can you check again?
F: Ok. *(pause)* **(2)** ... <u>Yes, it's plugged in.</u>
M: Ok. Can you give me a bit more information about what happened?
F: The screen went blank.
M: No, I mean, what activity were you doing when the problem occurred? Your computer was on, I presume; you were working, right? What did you do immediately before the blank screen appeared? **(3)** <u>Were you using the internet?</u>

F: **(3)** <u>Yes, I was.</u> Is it a virus?
M: That seems likely. What anti-virus software are you using?
F: Uh... **(4)** <u>I'm not sure.</u> How embarrassing!
M: Never mind. I'll have to come and have a look at your computer.
F: Ok, that's great.

Before you hear the rest of the conversation, you have some time to look at questions 5 to 10.
(Pause the recording for 30 seconds)
Now listen and answer questions 5 to 10.

M: Alright, let's see. What about tomorrow morning about 10?
F: Oh, no. That won't do I'm afraid. I've got a very important project on the computer that absolutely must be finished and handed in by 9 a.m. tomorrow. By ten it's too late, I'm afraid. Can't you come now?
M: Well, I'm at a job at the moment, and my wife and kids are expecting me home by 8 for dinner.
F: Can you at least suggest someone else who can work? I know it's Sunday evening, but surely there's somebody, I mean, people have emergencies! *(beginning to sound stressed)* I've been calling numbers in the phone book, and you're the only one out of about twelve that even answered!
M: Just a moment, don't panic. Where are you located?
F: **(5)** <u>I'm in the Morningside area.</u>
M: Well, you're in luck. I have to pass your area on my way home anyway. Now I should be finished here by half past seven, **(6)** <u>so what about around seven forty five?</u> Is that ok?
F: That's great, thank you.
M: What's your address?
F: 14 Branston Crescent 2F3
M: That's b - r - a - n - i - s - t
F: **(7)** <u>No, sorry, b r a n s t o n crescent</u>
M: Oh, alright; and your name?
F: **(8)** <u>Sandra Sarrencen. That's [s a double r e n c e n].</u>
M: And the name on the buzzer?
F: The same.
M: Alright, I'll be there shortly.
F: Thanks. Ah, can I ask you how much it's going to cost?
M: Certainly. **(9)** <u>My call-out fee is 60 pounds,</u> and that covers the first hour's work, and after that the fee is 40 pounds an hour.
F: Oh, gosh. That's rather expensive. How long do you think it will take?
M: If we're lucky it will be fairly quick. Honestly, though, if it takes **(10)** <u>much more than half an hour I'll have to finish it tomorrow morning. But I doubt that will happen.</u>
F: I hope not! Will you take a cheque, or do you prefer cash?
M: A cheque is fine.
F: OK, so, I'll be waiting...
M: OK, bye.

That is the end of section one. You now have half a minute to check your answers.
(Pause the recording for 30 seconds)
Now turn to section two.

SECTION 2

You will now listen to a talk by the Water Project Manager of a charity called 'Charity-Water'.
First you have some time to look at questions 11 to 17.
(Pause the recording for 30 seconds)
Now listen carefully and answer questions 11 to 17.

As Charity-Water's Water Project Manager, **(11)** <u>I travel to some of the most desperate places on earth in search of clean water.</u> And while the landscape changes, there's always one thing that remains the same: the women are always walking. Whether I'm in the mountains of Haiti, in rural Liberia, or the jungles of the Central African Republic, the women are always carrying water. **(12)** To give you an idea of the work that Charity-Water does, I'll tell you the story of one of these women.

Driving down a bumpy road in the middle of Northern Uganda, our truck suddenly swerves off the road and up over an embankment. **(13)** We usually prefer to surprise communities by our arrival because it makes it easier to monitor how our water points are functioning without hundreds of people watching. But once you visit a few communities in the neighbourhood, rumours of your presence spread like wildfire. **(14)** We jump out of the truck and walk into a party.

This is when I met Helen Apis. She told me about the new freshwater well in her village. **(15)** "I am happy now," Helen beamed. "I have time to eat, my children can go to school. And I can even work in my garden, take a shower and then come back for more water if I want! I am bathing so well."

A few of the men chuckled to hear a woman talk about bathing. **(16)** But all I noticed was Helen's glowing face, the fresh flowers in her hair, and the lovely green dress she wore for special occasions. Touching her forearm, I replied, "Well, you look great." "Yes," she paused. Placing both hands on my shoulders and smiling, she said, "Now, I am beautiful." That really hit me. My job is to focus on sustainable development, health, hygiene and sanitation; to make sure Charity-Water's projects are working in 20 years. **(17)** But nowhere on any of my surveys or evaluations was a place to write, "Today we made someone feel beautiful."

Before you hear the rest of the talk, you will have some time to look at questions 18 to 20.
(Pause the recording for 30 seconds)
Now listen carefully and answer questions 18 to 20.

Before she had clean water, Helen would wake up before dawn, take her only two 5-gallon Jerry Cans, and walk almost a mile and a half to the nearest water point, which happens to be at a school. Because there simply wasn't enough water for the area's population, she'd wait in line with hundreds of other women who also valued clean water. Helen's only other option was to skip the wait and collect contaminated water from a pond.

Helen spent most of her day walking and waiting. She told me each day she'd say to herself, "How should I use this water today? Should I water my garden so we can grow food? Should I wash my children's uniforms? Should I use it to cook a meal? Should we drink this water?" With two children, one husband and 10 gallons, Helen had to make choices. I saw the shame in her eyes when she described how she would return from her long trek to find her two young children waiting for her. They were often sent home from school because their uniforms were dirty.

With the new well in her village, her life was transformed. **(18,19)** She now had choices; free time; options. **(20)** Also, Helen had been chosen to be the Water Committee Treasurer, collecting nominal fees from 51 households to use for the maintenance of their well. Water Committees are often the first time women ever get elected to leadership positions in villages. Last month, Helen was standing in line waiting for water. This month, she's standing up for her community. And now, she is beautiful.

That is the end of section two. You now have half a minute to check your answers.
(Pause the recording for 30 seconds)
Now turn to section three.

SECTION 3

You will hear a conversation between a student, Jessica, and Dr. Kitching, a university advisor.
First you have some time to look at questions 21 to 25.
(Pause the recording for 30 seconds)
Now listen carefully and answer questions 21 to 25.

J = Jessica   K = Dr. Kitching

J: Hello Dr. Kitching, my name's Jessica. I work for the student newspaper. **(21)** I called you last week to ask if I could interview you for an article about how to ask for references.
K: Oh, yes; I remember! Come in. Have a seat.
J: Thank you. Do you have a few minutes now to do the interview?
K: Yes, that's fine.
J: Great! I got the idea to do this article because, well, **(22)** everyone I know is rather puzzled about how to get references from professors when they need them for applications for jobs or postgraduate studies. And I thought, since you're a professor, and you've been working as a student advisor for many years also, what better person to ask.
K: Yes, I have got some advice I can share on this topic. Where shall we begin?
J: **(23)** First of all, do you mind if I record our conversation?
K: No, I don't mind.
J: Thanks. Do you write many references yourself?
K: Oh yes, I certainly do! Let's see, it's variable of course, **(24)** but I'd say I average at least 50 per year.
J: My goodness! That's nearly five per month! It's more than one per week!
K: Yes, it's a lot. And of course, **(25)** most of the requests are made in the spring or early summer, when students are starting to think seriously about where they will be heading after they graduate in June.
J: Do most professors do so many?
K: Yes, it's part of the job. Of course, because I'm an advisor, students probably feel like I know them rather better than some professors, so I probably get a few more than I would otherwise.

Before you hear the rest of the conversation, you have some time to look at questions 26 to 30.
(Pause the recording for 30 seconds)
Now listen and answer questions 26-30.

J: Alright, so what do we students need to know in terms of asking for references or letters of recommendation? It's incredibly daunting, actually, particularly since we have such large classes. I'm not sure if my professors even know who I am!
K: Yes, that's probably the biggest issue students face in getting references. You will invariably have to contact former Professors even if you have never spoken to them outside of class. Following on this, if I were giving a first year student advice, I would say to make sure you've had contact with several Professors outside of class so you won't be a stranger. All it takes is visiting during office hours, even if it's just to say "Hello, I'm enjoying your lectures".
J: But what if we didn't do that?
K: Then you'll just have to contact your professor anyway.
(26) Make a telephone call; tell him or her who you are, and what classes you attended, this sort of thing. Remember, for your professor, recalling an average student out of hundreds and hundreds isn't easy. **(27)** So tell him or her what course you took, and what semester and year it was. Include what grade you got and anything memorable. Perhaps you spilled your coffee. Though at the time it wasn't funny it might be enough for Professor Brown to remember you and it won't shed any negative light on you; it was an accident. Or perhaps, although you never spoke outside of class, you went up and asked a question that was a great one. **(28)** Any information you can give to identify yourself is going to help you out.
J: Should I visit Professor Brown in person?
K: Yes, that would be ideal. I would suggest giving the information first over the phone, **(29)** then follow up by e-mailing it to your professor. During the phone conversation, **(30)** ask if you could meet briefly. This will be both a physical reminder of who you are and also another chance to make a good impression.
J: Isn't it very difficult to write references for all these students you've never spoken to or really even met?

K: Yes; for example, I was recently called by a student from 20 years ago! He lived in another country. I really didn't recall him. He told me a little about himself and I looked back at his records. I told him that all I could do was verify that he was in my class, that he showed up for all the classes and that he received a 3.4 in my class. Sometimes I'm very surprised that students who did very poorly in my class ask me for a reference.

J: What do you do in that case? Give a poor reference?

K: I, like most Professors I know, never say anything negative about the student; however it is what is unsaid that can say it all. So you really want to make sure you're remembered in a positive way and have left a good impression.

J: Ok, thanks very much for all this information. The story should come out in our next printing, so if you're interested I'll drop one copy over to you.

K: I'll be looking forward to seeing it.

That is the end of section three. You now have half a minute to check your answers.
(Pause the recording for 30 seconds)
Now turn to section four.

SECTION 4

You will hear a lecture about the behaviour of primates - the group of animals that includes monkeys and humans. First you have some time to look at questions 31 to 40.
(Pause the recording for 1 minute)
Now listen carefully and answer questions 31 to 40.

Good morning; today's lecture will be about primate behaviour. Up until now I've talked mostly about physical features: how they apply to living primates; how we use them for classification; **(31)** how they apply to the fossil record. **(32)** But human evolution isn't simply about how we've changed physically over the last 70 million years; it's also about how our behaviour has changed.

Now, if I asked you to define what is meant by the term "human", you could probably, hopefully, give me a list of characteristics that physically define us. But at a philosophical level, I would hope that what **(33)** you'd be really proud of is not that we normally walk on two legs, but that we can reason and imagine. Descartes put it succinctly: "I think, therefore I am" although, admittedly, not quite in this context.

This lecture isn't about human behaviour per se, but about primate behaviour in general, and animal behaviour too, since just as we can use the physical characteristics of living primates to give us clues and insights into the physical characteristics of human ancestors, so we hope that the behaviours of non-human primates will be similarly enlightening for the behaviour of our ancestors.

To begin, let's talk a bit about primate cognitive abilities. I don't want to mention a lot of different behaviours without first mentioning cognition. **(34)** Cognition is the amount of thought that goes into a behaviour. There is a world of difference between an animal hitting a nut with a rock and cracking it by accident, and an animal thinking to itself: "I can't bite into this nut. I know, I need something to use as a hammer to crack it." However, **(35)** it can be very difficult coming up with experiments to differentiate these two.

....
Pause (4 seconds)

We can easily test mental skills, such as recall and discrimination, using methods such as the Wisconsin general test apparatus and various training experiments. But it's much harder to work out the degree of thought required. This is still a big problem in evaluating the status **(36)** of great apes. Just how nearly "sentient" are they? Sentient, for those of you who don't remember, **(37)** means there is the presence of conscious thought.

There are various behaviours that could be seen to support the presence of conscious thought in primates. **(38)** Various sorts of altruism, or helping others without directly benefiting, can be found in certain great apes. The animals team up to achieve various goals: for example, hunting, in chimps. This would seem to require a degree of cognition. Another feature that has come to light recently is **(39)** "Machiavellian Intelligence". Work, especially with baboons, seems to indicate that there is a lot of deliberate social deception going on: sneaky mating; passing the blame onto others; using infants for defence. At first glance, this seems very complicated behaviourally, but again, it can, just about, be explained in a fairly minimally cognitive way. Highly trained chimps, such as the signing chimp, Washoe, and the computer-aided communication of Kanzi also indicate a high level of intelligence. An interesting fact is that these language-trained chimps do much better in the standardised intelligence tests too, indicating that we probably underestimate primate intelligence in our traditional experiments. It seems that primates are not all that interested in the colour of pencils; they want to know the latest gossip about their friends - sound familiar?

And of course, cognition and intelligence in primates is a thorny **(40)** problem, with deep moral and political ramifications.

That is the end of section four. You now have half a minute to check your answers.
(Pause the recording for 30 seconds)
That is the end of the listening test. In the IELTS test you would now have ten minutes to transfer your answers to the listening answer sheet.

TEST 4

You will hear a number of different recordings and you will have to answer questions on what you hear. There will be time for you to read the instructions and questions and you will have a chance to check your work.
All the recordings will be played once only. The test is in four sections. At the end of the test you will be given ten minutes to transfer your answers to an answer sheet.
Now turn to section one.

SECTION 1

You will hear two dialogues: the first between two friends at university, the second between one of these people and a university clerk. First you have some time to look at questions 1 to 4. *(Pause the recording for 30 seconds)*
You will see that there is an example that has been done for you. On this occasion only, the conversation relating to this will be played first.

V =Vicky J =Julie C =Clerk
V: Hi, Julie. You look flustered. What's wrong?
J: I left my car parked in the underground parking (lot) and now it's gone.
V: Gone? What do you mean? Do you think it's been stolen?
J: I think so. I'm just so flustered. It's such a big place and I'm not sure. I just can't remember where I left it, or if someone took it.
V: Was it locked?
J: Well, I think I locked it. You know, I was thinking of my class at the time because I was running late, so I'm not one hundred percent sure.

The correct answer is "A". Now we shall begin. You should answer the questions as you listen because you will not hear the recording a second time. Listen carefully and answer questions 1 to 4.

[REPEAT]

V: Where did you leave it?

J: Underground. It was Level 1.

V: Don't you know **(1)** <u>that area is for postgraduate students</u> and not for undergraduate students? Did you get a parking permit from Student Services?

J: No, I didn't. So what does that mean?

V: It means that it's **(2)** <u>probably been towed away.</u>

J: Oh, no. It's the first time I've brought my car. I **(3)** <u>usually catch the train in.</u>

V: How long has it been parked for?

J: Probably around four hours. Is there anything I can do?

V: Yes. Go to the clerk at Student Services and ask what you have to do to get your car back. You'll probably have to get your car out of the compound, and also pay a fine.

J: I don't believe it!

V: I know it's ridiculous, but it's the only way the university can control how many people park on the grounds. There's just not enough parking to accommodate all the students.

J: They could at least have clamped the wheel. Oh, well. How do I get to Student Services?

V: You go towards the Science Department, which is opposite the football field and next to the cafeteria. It's in the building in between.

J: Okay, so **(4)** <u>it's in the building in between the Science Department and cafeteria,</u> which is opposite the football field.

V: That's right. Good luck.

Before you hear the rest of the conversation, you have some time to look at questions 5 to 10.
(Pause the recording for 30 seconds)
Now listen and answer questions 5 to 10.

C: Good morning. Can I help you?

J: Yes, I was told to come here because I seem to have lost my car.

C: What do you mean?

J: Well, it's the first time I've brought my car and I didn't realise there were restrictions, and I think it might have been towed.

C: I see. Are you a postgraduate student?

J: No, undergraduate.

C: Did you get a parking permit?

J: No. I didn't know about the permit.

C: Okay, we'll have to fill out a release form for the compound company where your car has been taken. I'll just need to get some details. Your name?

J: **(5)** <u>Julie Karas</u> - that's spelt K-A-R-A-S.

C: Julie K-A-R-A-S. And your address?

J: **(6)** <u>15 Fremont Avenue.</u>

C: How do you spell Fremont?

J: F-R-E-M-O-N-T, and the district is **(7)** <u>Hawkesley.</u>

C: How do you spell that?

J: H-A-W-K-E-S-L-E-Y.

C: Faculty?

J: I'm in Political Science.

C: So that's the **(8)** <u>Science faculty?</u>

J: Yes.

C: What's the car registration number?

J: It's KIE 6... No, sorry, I always get that wrong. It's I K E 6 1 4 T.

C: **(9)** <u>IKE 614T.</u> What make is the car?

J: It's a **(10)** <u>Fiat Panda.</u>

C: Do you know the model?

J: The model?

C: Yes, what year was it made?

J: Oh, um, 1998, I think, and it's white. Well, actually it's cream.

C: A cream 1988 Fiat Panda.

J: No, 1998.

C: 1998. What I'll do is give the car compound a call, and see if they have it in their possession.

J: Okay, so what should I do?

C: Take a seat in the green room. I won't be long.

That is the end of section one. You now have half a minute to check your answers.
(Pause the recording for 30 seconds)
Now turn to section two.

SECTION 2

You will hear a ranger from the Nitmiluk National Park speaking on a radio programme about hiking in Australia. First you have some time to look at questions 11 to 14.
(Pause the recording for 30 seconds)
Now listen and answer questions 11 to 14.

The Jatbula Trail, located within Nitmiluk National Park, is a four-to-five day trek in Australia's Northern Territory. It follows an ancient Aboriginal song line, and the boulders along the way are scattered with rock paintings. There are five campsites along the trail, first, Biddlecombe Cascade, then Crystal Falls, 17 Mile Falls, Edith River Crossing, and finally Sandy Camp Pool. Only ten people at a time are allowed in each campsite, so you must book in advance, although usually you will not see another person on the trail. Every campsite has a source of permanent water, but otherwise, facilities at each campsite vary. Your first stop, **(11)** <u>Biddlecombe Cascades, has toilets</u> and an emergency call device. **(12, 13)** <u>The next two stops, Crystal Falls and 17 Mile Falls are the most developed campsites; both offer toilets, an emergency call device, and a checkpoint</u> where you must sign in to help rangers locate you in case of an emergency. **(14)** <u>Edith River Crossing also has a checkpoint and an emergency call device, but no organised toilets are provided.</u> Sandy Camp Pool is the most primitive site of all; there is nothing there other than a beautiful sandy beach where you can pitch your tent.

Before you hear the rest of the talk, you have some time to look at questions 15 to 20.
(Pause the recording for 30 seconds)
Now listen and answer questions 15 to 20.

The trail begins at Nitmiluk Centre, where you must register and pay a deposit of 50 dollars. After registering, you may begin your trek. You'll follow the trail overlooking 17 Mile Creek on your left for 8 kilometres until you reach the **(15)** <u>first campsite, Biddlecombe Cascades,</u> where you'll stop for the night.

On the second day, the track leads north from camp. After you have walked for about 5 hours and 10.5 kilometres, you'll reach Crystal Falls campsite located at a sharp bend in the trail. **(16)** <u>There's a marked trail from the campsite to the Crystal Fall viewpoint.</u> Crystal Falls is 30 metres high, and it's breathtaking, so be sure to have a look.

The next day you'll change direction and head west across a valley and then northwest again for about 9.5 kilometres. The track is quite even and flat for the first part of the day, which is a welcome break from the rocky ground of previous days. **(17)** <u>Before you reach the next campsite, you will pass 'The Amphitheatre'</u> - a butterfly and frog filled canyon that's important to the aboriginal people who have left intricate rock paintings on the rock walls. **(18)** <u>A few kilometres further you'll come to 17 Mile Falls campsite beside a series of rock pools and small cascades above 17 Mile Falls Creek.</u> There is a lookout over the falls that shouldn't be missed, and is particularly beautiful at sunset.

On day four you'll take your longest hike, 15 and a half kilometres, going to the west. You'll cross a boggy area as you approach the Edith River. **(19)** <u>If you're tired you may camp here, where you first cross Edith River, or instead follow the river south, crossing it several more times before you reach the campsite at Sandy Camp Pool,</u> where you can spend the last night of your adventure camping on a sandy beach beside a tranquil waterhole.

Leaving Sandy Camp Pool, the track continues through woodland until you pass a checkpoint at Edith River South. From here the trail is lined with the river on the left-hand side and high rocks on the right. **(20)** <u>One last stop is a must at Sweetwater Pool.</u> This is a large waterhole surrounded by rocky ledges that is perfect for a picnic before you return to civilisation. Day trippers can access this point from Edith Falls so it may be your first encounter with another person since leaving Nitmiluk. After a swim make your way to Edith Falls, where your adventure ends. Make sure you deregister at the Edith Kiosk, and then take a hot shower.

That is the end of section two. You now have half a minute to check your answers.
(Pause the recording for 30 seconds)
Now turn to section three.

SECTION 3

You will hear Laura, a laboratory technician, talking to Jamie and Denise, two students, about the procedure to get their final year chemistry projects approved. First you have some time to look at questions 21-25.
(Pause the recording for 30 seconds)
Now listen and answer questions 21-25.

L= Laura, laboratory technician   J=Jamie, student
D= Denise, student
L: Hi there, I'm Laura. I'm the laboratory technician for these chemistry labs, and Professor Mills has asked me to explain the procedure that you'll all have to go through to get your final year projects approved. Most of the procedure involves safety concerns, which we take very very seriously. We don't want any uncontrolled explosions, no fires, and definitely no incidents with toxic gases.
D: You mean like what happened in 2008 when the whole science block had to be evacuated?
L: Yes, exactly! So you've heard about that already, Denise?
D: Professor Mills told us about it on the first day of class. **(21)** It was hilarious!
J: (22) Yeah, but I reckon some people must have gotten into a lot of trouble.
L: (23) To be honest it was mortifyingly embarrassing for the chemistry department, because, not only could no one identify what the toxic substance was, but also at the time of the incident, no one was actually authorized to be carrying out experiments with any toxic substances whatsoever. It turned out a student had got a bit bored and had decided to do some spontaneous experimentation by mixing up some random powders that were lying around. This is actually incredibly foolish, because there are some extremely dangerous substances in the laboratory stores, and everyone was utterly shocked that someone of college age would do something **(24)** so childish and irresponsible. And, in effect, this incident was the reason we developed the safety procedure that each of you must now go through before we let you loose in the laboratory to do your final year project. The procedure will force you to really be aware of safety issues, so just in case, at the moment, any of you think it would be a laugh to mix up some colourful substances or light things on fire for no reason, by the time you've worked your way through the procedure, you'll at least pause for a second thought; at least, we would hope so!
J: So, uh, can I ask something?
L: Yes, Jamie?
J: So, **(25)** we're basically being punished because some other student was irresponsible?
L: Actually, the approval process isn't as bad as that. We can't really call it a punishment! It seems really very long and cumbersome at first, because you'll have to get a lot of different tasks stamped for approval by a lot of different staff members, and I'm sure most of them will have various concerns and suggestions. But my aim today is to break down the process, and explain all the different steps to you, so that it doesn't seem quite so bad.

Before you hear the rest of the talk, you have some time to look at questions 26-30.
(Pause the recording for 30 seconds)
Now listen and answer questions 26-30.

L: All right, let's get started. As I said before, a number of different staff members will be giving you suggestions, and they may not always agree, so just to keep things clear, you should remember that the laboratory supervisor has the final say about whether or not an experiment may be done here, in our laboratory. Your professor has the final say on whether you can do a particular experiment for your project, provided it's approved by the laboratory, and I've got the final say on **how** it may be done.
So, the first step is that you will fill out this safety assessment form. You will have to have a fairly clear idea of your experiment, because you'll need to list all the chemicals you'll be using, the quantities you'll be using for each one, and the nature of the reactions that you'll carry out. You'll also be required to provide a week-by-week schedule so that we can be sure that whatever substances you're working with won't prove to be incendiary if they get mixed up with whatever the person next to you on the bench is getting up to. Really, for most of you this assessment form will be quite straightforward because you're simply not going to be working with anything very dangerous. But for some of you, particularly if you are working with any volatile substances, it could be a bit more complicated. You might have to justify the use of certain substances, or only be allowed to use them on particular days.
Now then, after you've filled out your safety assessment form, and given a copy to your professor, you will submit it to the laboratory supervisor, and he'll review it. This could take a couple of weeks so do it early, don't leave it to the last minute; he's a busy man. **(26)** The laboratory supervisor will eventually make a recommendation to your professor about whether the experiment can go ahead, requires modifications, or may not be done. **(27)** Next, your professor will either approve the project, or not. **(28)** If your professor does not approve the project due to safety concerns, then you, the student, will be notified and you'll begin the process over again by submitting a new safety assessment form that takes into account those troublesome safety issues. Is everyone with me so far?
J: Uh….. I have a question.
L: Yes, Jamie?
J: Er, so if we have to wait weeks for the laboratory supervisor to give his approval, and then we have to re-do the form, uh, we're going to be quite behind our classmates who got approval on their first go. That's a bit unfair, isn't it? I mean, some people are going to have an advantage of several weeks over other people.
L: Well, you needn't really worry about getting behind at this stage; after all, you'll have six months to work on your final project. And you'll only get a two-week block of laboratory time, anyway, so there's time to wait for the laboratory supervisor, provided you get started promptly and don't leave it all to the last two months! Also, don't forget that this is only one step; there are plenty of other steps for other students to get hung up on farther down the line. It will all balance out.
D: But, um, Laura, what if our projects aren't approved?
L: Then you'll come up with another one. Don't get too attached to your project in the beginning. Projects get turned down. Let's see, last year I think only 15 projects got approval on their first go.
J: Out of how many?
L: Out of …. about …… 45, I think; there are less of you this year. But still, be prepared to come up with an alternative project. There are plenty of people to help you if you need ideas; your professor, his RAs, even your fellow students. And don't forget that in the first months of your project the library will be your second home, and the librarians will be your greatest friends.
D: Laura, what's an RA?
L: RA stands for research assistant, like Jess, over there, in the lab coat. Hi, Jess! Now, once your professor has approved your project, you will need to write up a set of experiment safety procedure guidelines. This will include all the practical steps you'll take to keep safe, and exactly what you'll do if you have a spill or some such thing.
D: How will we know all this? We've got no experience in the laboratory.
L: Well, after your professor approves your project, **(29)** he'll assign an RA to help you write the experimental safety procedure guidelines.

You won't be on your own. Finally, **(30)** <u>once that's written, you'll give it to the laboratory technician, that's me, for approval.</u> If I approve it, then you can begin your experiment. If there are problems, we'll sit down together and talk about it, then you and your assigned RA will come up with a way of making your experiment completely safe to conduct, you'll re-do the guidelines, and give it to me again, until it's approved. But the RAs know what they're doing so I don't expect there will be too many problems. Ok? Any questions?

That is the end of section three. You now have half a minute to check your answers.
(Pause the recording for 30 seconds)
Now turn to section four.

SECTION 4

You will hear part of a lecture about the different biomes that are present in Brazil, given as an introduction to a course about sustainable development in South America. First you have some time to look at questions 31-40.
(Pause the recording for 1 minute)
Now listen and answer questions 31-40.

To begin our topic on sustainable development in South America, I would like to briefly acquaint you with the 6 biomes present in the country. Each of these biomes has its own geographic and environmental features, has unique resources that people may exploit, and indeed, each is facing different threats from human development.

Biomes, if you recall, are regions that are climatically and geographically defined and contain distinct communities of plants and animals. They are sometimes named for* the plant communities that occur such as forest, savannah, and grassland; whether these plants are evergreen or deciduous; and climatic factors as well, for example, tropical, temperate, etc.

All right, let's take a look at this map of Brazil. **(31)** <u>The largest biome in Brazil is the Amazonian Rainforest Biome, which you can see located in the north of the country.</u> It's one of two rainforest biomes in Brazil; the second being **(32)** <u>the Atlantic rainforest Biome, which is located in a relatively narrow strip running up the eastern Atlantic coast.</u> **(33)** <u>In the very southernmost part of Brazil, bordered by the Atlantic rainforest, lies the very small and relatively unstudied Pampas biome,</u> which is grassland. Finally, stretching like a belt across the middle of the country, between the two rainforest biomes, lie the Pantanal, the Cerrado, and the Caatinga. **(34)** <u>Starting at the left of the map, you can see the smallest of the three, which is the Pantanal Biome</u> a unique seasonally flooded wetland area. **(35)** <u>In the centre of the country is the Cerrado,</u> the second largest biome in Brazil. Cerrado is tropical savannah - a scattering of grassland and deciduous forest that experiences a short dry season. Finally, **(36)** <u>the last biome, called Caatinga, is located</u> between the Cerrado and the Atlantic forest <u>in the north east of the country.</u> The Caatinga has a very long dry season, lasting 8 to 9 months, and is covered in deciduous scrub.

So, let's begin with the Amazonian Rainforest Biome. As I mentioned previously, it's rainforest, and it's incredibly diverse. It contains the largest single reserve of biological organisms in the world. No one really knows how many species occur in the Amazon forest, but scientists estimate that there could be as many as 5 million. Recently this biome has been under a great deal of pressure from agriculture, with large swathes being cleared and burned to create pasture for the 19 million cattle that the area supports. However, the soils are acidic with very low levels of certain important minerals, and are quickly degraded when heavily grazed, which necessitates more clearing and burning of forest. The rainforest is further disturbed by selective logging of valuable tree species.

....
Pause (4 seconds)

The second largest biome in Brazil is the Cerrado, which is a tropical savannah environment made up of sparse trees and drought resistant grasses. The Cerrado also contains a huge biodiversity; it's estimated that one third of Brazil's plant and animal species are

located in this region. But since 1995, the cultivated pasture area in the Cerrado has increased by almost 70%. It is a common practice to use newly cleared land for the cultivation of crops for a few years, and then when it starts to degrade, to use it for pasture for cattle. **(37)** <u>The Cerrado now supports 72.3 million cattle,</u> which amounts to 41 percent of the cattle in Brazil.

Next, we have the biome called the Caatinga, which is a tropical dryland with a dry season that lasts 8 or 9 months of the year. Vegetation is deciduous, sparse and thorny, and contains a high number of species endemic to Brazil. Agriculture is limited by the lack of water but this biome supports 8.8 million goats and **(38)** <u>8.1 million sheep,</u> besides 23.9 million cattle.

The Pantanal Biome, a wetland formed by the flooding of the rivers of the Paraguay basin, is the world's biggest flooded plain. Vegetation is patchy and variable; it consists of tall grasses, bushes, and widely dispersed trees similar to those of the Cerrado, except that in the Pantanal they are partially submerged for a portion of the year. **(39)** <u>Three million cattle are raised in this biome,</u> however the available grazing area is limited by flooding so large areas can sustain only low numbers of animals. UNESCO recognizes it as a "World Biosphere Reserve" and also as a "World Natural Heritage Site." Ecotourism is becoming important in this region, which diversifies the economic activity.

The Atlantic Rain Forest is the most endangered biome in Brazil and also its most affluent region. It's the most important agricultural and industrial area of the country. It supports 36 million cattle, and most of the country's dairy production takes place there. More than 70% of the Brazilian population, the largest Brazilian cities and the production of about 80% of Brazil's gross domestic product are all located in what used to be the Atlantic Forest. Today, as a result, less than 10 per cent of the Atlantic forest is left. The Biome is also beginning to be recognised as ecologically very important; in the state of Bahia, for example, international researchers have identified a world record of 458 tree species in a single hectare of Atlantic Forest. That is even more diverse than the Amazon rain forest. At the moment, less than 2% of the remaining Atlantic forest is under protected status, and the scientific community is scrambling to secure what little undisturbed forest still remains.

Finally, the Brazilian Pampas Biome has a temperate climate — it's the only biome in Brazil that is not tropical. Grasslands scattered with shrubs and trees are the dominant vegetation. The shallow soil, originating from sedimentary rocks, often has an extremely sandy texture that makes it fragile and highly prone to water and wind erosion. **(40)** <u>The Pampas supports 26 million cattle and 6 million sheep, in mostly natural unmodified pastures;</u> however this biome is being threatened with rapid conversion to the agriculture of cash crops.

All right, so, next week we will go into more detail about the economic policies of the Brazilian government in relation to the development of each of these biomes.

That is the end of section four. You now have half a minute to check your answers.
(Pause the recording for 30 seconds)
That is the end of the listening test. In the IELTS test you would now have ten minutes to transfer your answers to the listening answer sheet.

named for* [*in AmE *'named for'* is used almost as often as *'named after'* and has an identical meaning]

TEST 5

You will hear a number of different recordings and you will have to answer questions on what you hear. There will be time for you to read the instructions and questions and you will have a chance to check your work.

All the recordings will be played once only. The test is in four sections. At the end of the test you will be given ten minutes to transfer your answers to an answer sheet.

Now turn to section one.

SECTION 1

You will hear a telephone conversation between a student and an employee at a university sports facility.

First you have some time to look at questions 1 to 5.

(Pause the recording for 30 seconds)

You will see that there is an example that has been done for you. On this occasion only, the conversation relating to this will be played first.

FS = Former student, Shannon Fleet   E = Employee

E: Hello, Ratner Athletics Centre; how can I help you?

S: Yes, hi. I'm interested in finding out some information about membership.

E: Certainly. Are you a student?

S: No. Is that a problem? I was a student here two years ago . . . .

E: Alright, that's no problem. Current students get membership for no charge, but recreational memberships are also available for purchase for university faculty, staff, alumni, and retirees, as well as their spouses and children.

The answer is "no charge" so this has been filled in for you. Now we shall begin. You should answer the questions as you listen because you will not hear the recording a second time. Listen carefully and answer questions 1 to 5.

[REPEAT]

FS: Ok, good. How much does it cost?

E: **(1)** For an alumnus, that's two hundred and forty pounds annually, or one hundred pounds for a month.

FS: Oh. That's quite expensive. It's a shame I didn't take advantage of the athletics facility when I was a student here. I'll have to think about this.

E: Well, we do offer a really excellent facility. For the cost, members have access to the **(2)** Emily Pankhurst Fitness Centre, which is a beautiful exercise space - open and full of light. The fitness centre includes two weight circuits, free weights, rowing machines, elliptical trainers, recumbent and upright bicycles, step mills, and treadmills [exercise machines] - and many many other activities. But the most prominent, and I'd have to say popular, feature of the Ratner Centre is the **(3)** Dalton swimming pool. It's 50 metres by 25 metres and includes up to 20 lanes in the 25-metre dimension and nine lanes in the 50-metre dimension, and also has two one-metre diving boards available. What activities, specifically, are you interested in?

FS: Yes, well, I'm interested in swimming, and also in getting started with some weight training, although I've never tried it before in my life. I feel rather intimidated, actually. Is there instruction available? You know, someone to teach me to use the machines and maybe help me figure out a training programme to reach my goals?

E: Yes, we have **(4)** personal trainers available for an additional cost. We also offer fitness evaluation, which by the way I highly recommend for someone just starting out with weight training, and you would be orientated to the machines as part of this.

FS: Oh, one more thing. What are the opening hours?

E: We're open **(5)** from six in the morning to midnight on weekdays and from six in the morning to nine p.m. on weekends.

FS: Oh, that's good. Alright, well, I guess I'd like to join.

Before you hear the second conversation, you have some time to look at questions 6 to 10.

(Pause the recording for 30 seconds)

Now listen and answer questions 6 to 10.

E: Very well. Can I have your name please?

S: That's **(6)** Shannon Fleet. S-H-A-N-N-O-N F-L-E-E-T.

E: Ok, and your address?

S: **(7)** Twenty-four Whitehall Close, Newcastle . . . .

E: Sorry, can you please spell the street name for me?

S: Yes, of course. That's W-H-I-T-E-H-A-L-L- C-L-O-S-E- .

E: Got it. And your post code?

S: **(8)** N-E zero, one - E - N

E: N as in night and E as in England?

S: Yes, that's correct.

E: I'll need a phone number.

S: **(9)** Ok, it's 9-7-6-5 4-8-4 4-9-3

E: That's 9-7-6-5 4-8-4 9-4-3

S: No, sorry. The last three numbers are 4-9-3, not 9-4-3.

E: Ok. Now, you'll need to pay when you come for the first time, and you can either pay by cash or credit card.

P: I'll pay cash.

C: Fine. And be sure to bring some sort of proof of address, like a bill or driver's licence.

P: I don't drive. **(10)** Will my electricity bill do?

C: Yes, that's fine. And also bring a passport-sized photo so we can make up your membership card.

P: Ok, thanks. I'll come by this afternoon.

That is the end of section one. You now have half a minute to check your answers. *(Pause the recording for 30 seconds)*

Now turn to section two.

SECTION 2

You will now hear a speaker talking to a group of students planning to study in South America next year.

First you have some time to look at questions 11 to 15

(Pause the recording for 30 seconds)

Now listen carefully and answer questions 11 to 15.

Hello there; good afternoon! Thank you for finding the time in your busy schedules to come to the international student office's first orientation meeting for students going abroad, to South America next autumn. By the way, if you haven't already signed next to your name on our attendance lists - they're located on the table at the entrance of the auditorium - be sure to do it on your way out. Remember, this orientation meeting is obligatory, so you need to make sure we know that you're here.

Alright, to begin, we're going to be talking about health, and specifically the procedures that you have to go through in order to get your student visas for your host country. **(11)** For all of you, this will entail gathering a folder of health information, such as vaccination records and proof from your doctors that **(12)** you're not suffering from any serious contagious diseases. For many of you, this will also entail getting some extra vaccinations, depending on your destination country. All the specifics that each of you will need are to be found in your host country handbook that you received when you were accepted into the programme.

Also each one of you is required to **(13)** attend a consultation with a doctor at the student health centre who is specialised in travel medicine. The health centre can give you details about appointment times, but be sure to book your appointment early, because the specialist is only at the heath centre at certain times; to have the most benefit, you should have your meeting at least 4-6 weeks before your trip, to allow time for your vaccines to take effect. Now, at this consultation, you will be given all the latest information about what vaccines you'll need and any other health considerations you need to be aware of - if **(14)** you'll need to take medication for malaria, for example - or **(15)** what to expect in case of any existing health issues.

Before you hear the rest of the lecture you have some time to look at questions 16 to 20.
(Pause the recording for 30 seconds)
Now listen carefully and answer questions 16 to 20.

Now, I want to talk in a bit more detail about some important health issues that many of you will face. First of all I want to say a few things about Malaria, which will apply to most of you with South American destinations. **(16)** In most South American countries, malaria is present in some areas, but not in others. In Brazil, for example, the Amazon basin is a high-risk area, while the costal cities, such as Rio de Janeiro and Sao Paulo, have a very low risk of malaria. So, if you will be studying in Sao Paulo, you will not need to take medication for malaria. However, if you are studying in Sao Paulo and doing fieldwork somewhere in the Amazon basin, then you will need medication. Likewise, if you plan to travel into rural regions, then you will need medication. You should be realistic about what your plans are, and **(17)** if you decide not to take malaria medication, keep informed and don't travel to a high-risk area. We've had two instances of students returning with malaria in the last 5 years, and both cases had to do with spontaneous travel after their studies to areas with a high risk of malaria.

Of course, there are quite a few other insect-born illnesses that can be caught, so it's essential to avoid being bitten as much as possible, even if you are taking malaria medication. **(18)** To prevent insect bites, you should wear long-sleeved shirts and long trousers whenever possible, and **(19)** use an insect repellent on any bare skin. You should also bring a flying-insect spray to help clear rooms of mosquitoes. The product should contain a pyrethroid insecticide. Bed nets treated with permethrin, if you will not be sleeping in an air-conditioned or well-screened room are also a very good idea. Although it's not always possible, it's best to remain indoors in a screened or air-conditioned area **(20)** during the peak biting periods of dusk and dawn.

Finally, in much of South America, there is a risk of Schistosomiasis - a rather nasty parasitic infection that can be contracted in fresh water. So do not swim in fresh water, except in well-chlorinated swimming pools. Any questions so far?

That is the end of section two. You now have half a minute to check your answers.
(Pause the recording for 30 seconds)
Now turn to section three.

SECTION 3

You will hear a group of students filling out an evaluation form for one of their classes.
First you have some time to look at questions 21 to 23.
(Pause the recording for 30 seconds)
Now listen carefully and answer questions 21 to 23.

E = Ethan   L = Lily   J = Joshua

L: Joshua! Ethan! Wait; don't leave yet. We have to fill in an evaluation form to hand in with our final project.
E: Not another one! We've done one of these forms after each project all term! It's a bit of a waste of time, if you ask me.
L: They just want to give us a chance to have our say about the project.
E: But I haven't much of an opinion about it either way. It's just a project.
J: Yeah, but if you did?
E: Then it wouldn't be a waste of time I suppose; what's your point?
J: **(21)** Just say you have no opinion; what's the problem with that?
E: You're right; I'll do that. And it'll be easier than making something up! But even if we had issues and wrote them down, **(22)** do you think anyone reads them? I rather doubt it.
L: Of course they do! Remember in the first term, when there were

some problems with people in some groups not doing their fair share of the work? There were lots of comments about this on the evaluation forms, and **(23)** so Dr. Smith came and talked to us about it, and decided to add the individual evaluation forms so we could each evaluate our other group members' effort. That was a really important outcome.
J: See, Ethan, without the evaluation forms, we wouldn't have the opportunity to report what a slacker you are!
E: Come on! I've done as much work as anyone!
L: Yeah, it's easy to joke around because we're a good team. My last team wasn't so good though, and I was really grateful for those forms.
E: Ok - let's get it done so we can go.

Before you hear the rest of the conversation, you have some time to look at questions 24 to 30.
(Pause the recording for 30 seconds)
Now listen and answer questions 24 to 30.

L: Okay, first we have to rate the project from one to five, and comment on any good or bad points.
J: We do this part together?
L: Yeah. **(24)** What do you think? Four?
E: Yeah, why not?
J: Um… **(25)** Why four and not five? I don't really think there was much wrong with it. It was a good project. The tasks were well thought out. Not like the last one where one of the tasks was impossible because there was no research on the subject.
L: I agree with you, Josh. There weren't technically any problems with the project. It's just that I like projects to have a sort of practical point, you know, we should see some sort of reason for doing it. Other than the grade, of course. If it had some sort of real-world application, it would have been perfect. What do you think Ethan?
E: I don't know. **(26)** Why don't we give it a four point five?
L: That's a good idea. Can we do that?
J: I don't see why not. And I agree. Four point five.
L: So what about good points? **(27)** Josh said it's well thought out; anything else?
E: **(28)** I liked having a choice between two topics. I mean, some topics just don't interest some people.
L: Yes, you're right. Unfortunately **(29)** I thought they were both boring! I'm sounding a bit negative, aren't I? I can't think of any specific good points.
E: That's alright. Let's move on to the bad points.
L: You're eager to go, aren't you?
E: Yeah. I'm going camping tomorrow and I have to pack! But back to the topic. I haven't got an opinion about bad points; Lily's already said her share, what about you Joshua? Any complaints?
J: No, I think it was a good project. Um… If I had to say something I guess it would be the time scale. **(30)** I think they should have given us more time to do this final project since it was a larger part of our grade. But I don't think that's a big deal.
L: Ok. I think we're done. We just have to do the individual evaluation forms and that's it.

That is the end of section three. You now have half a minute to check your answers.
(Pause the recording for 30 seconds)
Now turn to section four.

SECTION 4

You will hear part of a lecture in a marketing course.
First you have some time to look at questions 31-40.
(Pause the recording for 1 minute)
Now listen carefully and answer questions 31-40.

Lecturer: Today we're going to look at marketing over the life-time of a product and how the different phases in the product life cycle impact on the kinds of marketing decisions we make and influence the marketing strategies we employ.

Of course, the first stage in the product life cycle is known as the Market Introduction Stage. At this point, **(31)** costs are very high indeed, and, since the product is fresh to the market, **(32)** sales volumes can be low to start as the product has yet to take off. What the marketing department must do therefore is get as much publicity as possible for the product and begin to develop brand awareness and loyalty. Think of the process as little steps. **(33)** The first step is to get the brand noticed by your target market. This will require aggressive advertising using mediums which are likely to expose the product to, and, just as importantly, appeal to the target customer. **(34)** The next step would be to encourage the target market to try the product. Promotions, free trials and other special offers all play a role in enticing new customers over to your brand.

Don't expect to make money during the Market Introduction Stage. The focus should be solely on creating brand awareness.

....

Pause (4 seconds)

Then we move into the Growth phase. Now here costs will reduce dramatically as sales rise **(35)** and economies of scale in production begin to kick in. Public awareness of the product has increased and the focus of the marketing campaign will now switch more from creating awareness to generating customer loy-alty and brand recognition. The first step for the marketing gurus **(36)** is to find a way to reward return customers for their loyalty - in other words, provide them with an incentive to continue com-ing back.

During the growth phase, several new competitors are likely to emerge as tangible threats to the business. The next step for the marketing team, then, **(37)** is to differentiate their brand from the alternatives on the market. Unless customers see your product as distinct from the competitors', they really have no reason to remain loyal to it; therefore, this brand differentiation that I have just spoken of is vital.

So, you've grown your business, now it's time to sit back and reap the rewards. We're into the Maturity Stage. During this peri-od, **(38)** sales will peak as the saturation point is reached. **(39)** Competition will be intense, however, the work you have done on developing brand loyalty and differentiating your product from that of competitors will really pay off now. The marketing depart-ment must continue to differentiate the brand from competitors', and, if possible, diversify the product features; that is, **(40)** find new applications for the product in order to open up potential new markets and prolong the Maturity Stage.

The final stage in the product life cycle is Saturation and Decline. Some would argue that reaching this stage is a natural progres-sion for every product. However, there is a growing belief that, should the marketing department do its job properly, the product should stabilise and never really fall into decline. We'll examine this debate a little more closely next time.

That is the end of section four. You now have half a minute to check your answers.

(Pause the recording for 30 seconds)

That is the end of the listening test. In the IELTS test you would now have ten minutes to transfer your answers to the listening answer sheet.

TEST 6

SECTION 1

You will hear a telephone conversation between a recep-tionist and a customer. First you have some time to look at questions 1 to 8. *(Pause the recording for 30 seconds)*
You will see that there is an example that has been done for you. On this occasion only, the conversation relating to this will be played first.

R= Receptionist C= Customer

R: *Good morning, Fairview Lake Camping Centre. Can I help you?*

C: *Oh yes. I'm interested in bringing a group of schoolchildren to your centre for a week's stay this summer, and I'd like some information. Could you tell me something about your organisation?*

R: *Certainly, sir. We have three main functions, really. We are a con-ference centre, an educational institution, and simply a place where you can come and have a fun-filled weekend. Whatever your goal is, our professional staff are on hand to help you.*

The answer is "an educational institution" so this has been filled in for you. Now we shall begin. You should answer the questions as you listen because you will not hear the recording a second time. Listen carefully and answer ques-tions 1 to 8.

[REPEAT]

C: I think we'd like to have an educational visit and some fun at the same time. I was thinking particularly of some of our children who have **(1)** failed exams, and need to retake them next year.

R: I see. Well, we offer coaching in various subjects at most levels; you know, Maths, Sciences, Geography, languages. We adjust the courses according to the needs of your pupils. As for the recre-ational side of the centre, we offer sailing, windsurfing, volleyball, rowing, athletics and quite a few other sports. Most children have never tried **(2)** archery, so we offer courses in that, too. It's very popular.

C: That sounds good. I'll see if there is any interest. And where would the children stay?

R: Well, we have the **(3)** Birch Unit that sleeps 8 people, and Greenback Row which sleeps the same number. Cabins 1-3 each sleep ten people. **(4)** Cabins 5 and 6 sleep twelve people each. How many young people are you thinking of bringing?

C: **(5)** 22. Twelve girls and ten boys.

R: Perfect, then I suggest Cabin 3 for the boys, and Cabin 5 for the girls. How long would you want to stay? Ah, yes, I remember, you said a week, didn't you, Mr...?

C: Bryson, Mike Bryson. Yes, that's right, a week.

R: Good. Groups arrive on a Saturday evening, and leave the follow-ing Sunday morning.

C: That would be fine. Now, when are your courses?

R: Tell me the dates that would suit you, and we'll see what we can do.

C: The end of June would be perfect for us.

R: End of June. Let me see... How about the week starting Sunday, **(6)** June 24th. The week starting Sunday 30th is pretty much booked up.

C: Yes, the 24th would suit us fine. Now, about prices?

R: For one week, including lessons, food, accommodation and all sporting activities, the cost would be **(7)** £425 per child, and £480 per adult. Could I have your school's telephone number, please, Mr Bryson?

C: Yes, certainly. **(8)** It's 647864.

R: 647864. And the code?

C: Em, 4304. Sorry, no. 1304. By the way, are you open in the winter? And if so, what do you offer sports-wise?

R: Yes, we certainly are, Mr Bryson, and we offer ice fishing, cross-country skiing and animal tracking. It's actually very popular in the winter.

Before you hear the rest of the conversation, you have some time to look at questions 9 and 10.
(Pause the recording for 30 seconds)
Now listen and answer questions 9 and 10.

C: Interesting. Perhaps I'll bring a group then, too. Oh, I almost forgot to ask. What are the eating arrangements?

R: We have an enormous amount of space for dining. We can divide the dining area into several separate rooms, if necessary. If you really want your privacy we can give you a separate room, but **(9)** actually we find that mealtimes give you the opportunity to meet people from other groups. There's no difference in price, whatever you choose.

C: Right. What if we want to cook our own meals now and again?

R: Yes, that can be arranged. All of the units have their own tiny kitchens, but there are also many outdoor areas where you can cook over an open fire. We try and have several barbecues too, which are very popular.

C: That all sounds very satisfactory. I know the kids will be enthusiastic, and the prices sound fair enough, **(10)** so I'll speak to my headmaster and get back to you as soon as possible.

R: Good, Mr Bryson. I look forward to hearing from you.

That is the end of section one. You now have half a minute to check your answers. *(Pause the recording for 30 seconds)*
Now turn to section two.

SECTION 2
You will hear a staff member brief a group of mothers on the attractions at the Children's Grand Forest Play Centre. First you will have time to look at questions 11 to 15.
(Pause the recording for 30 seconds)
Now listen carefully and answer questions 11 to 15.

Staff member:

I'm delighted to welcome you all here to our magical little outdoor play centre. We feel very privileged and excited today to have our first customers here to attend the official opening. But before we let you, and more importantly your kids, get down to the business of enjoying themselves, I just wanted to make everyone familiar with the centre's main attractions.

If you look at the map I've given you, **(11)** let's start by following the entrance road straight through the centre to the attraction on the right of the bridge. That is the Petting Zoo; a lovely little area where children can spend time in the company of our very friendly farm animals. **(12)** Continuing left past the bridge will take you to the Toddler's Play Pool. Alternatively, **(13)** taking a right at the Petting Zoo will bring you down to the Bouncy Castle and Fairy Palace. If I can draw your attention to the Waterfall and Frog Pond, you'll notice that there are two attractions close by. **(14)** Following the road that leads to a dead end takes you to Winter Wonderland. Here, we use snow machines to create a magical world of winter delights. We think this will be a big favourite. On the other side of the map, just down from the Fairy Palace,

there's another kind of wonderland-Waterworld. Waterworld is for the older kids; a place where they can have fun on the slides and tubes and play about in the water to their heart's content. Jumping back now to the other side of the map again, you'll see not so much an attraction as a service for you poor tired mums; this is the Babysitting Area. You can leave your little ones in the safe hands of our professional carers should you need a rest. **(15)** The last attraction I've to show you then is the Craft Zone, which is on the right-hand side, down a little closer to the entrance than Waterworld. Here the kiddies can learn how to make all sorts of beautiful things like shiny jewellery and sparkly cards.

Before you hear the rest of the discussion you have some time to look at questions 16 to 20.
(Pause the recording for 30 seconds)
Now listen and answer questions 16 to 20.

That's pretty much everything you need to know, but before I finish, let me just tell you a little more information about the wonderful animals of the Petting Zoo. The Petting Zoo is divided into three areas. **(16)** The area on the left hand side is where children can go on rides; hence the name Ride Zone. We have a friendly donkey called Dan, and a gorgeous little pony called Polly. Dan the Donkey and Polly the Pony are joined for this week only by a very special guest; Larry the Lama. **(17)** Queue for rides at the entrance to the inner circle and pay at the Pay Station located in front of the parents' sit-and-watch stand.

The centre area is known as the Mini Farm Zone. Here the children can see lots of different farm animals living just as they would on a real farm. Join Farmer Tom as he gives half-hourly tours of the farm and shows the little ones how to milk the cows and goats and how to feed the grumpy old pigs.

(18) Zone three is an area we are very excited about. We call it the Performance Zone. **(19)** Inside the Arena, some of our brightest animals will perform a series of tricks for the children, who'll also be entertained by Cluxy the Clown and his show band, the Racketeers. **(20)** The Racketeers will perform on the Main Stage at the centre of the Arena on the hour, every hour. That concludes my little introduction. I hope you have a tremendous day.

That is the end of section two. You now have half a minute to check your answers.
(Pause the recording for 30 seconds)
Now turn to section three.

SECTION 3
You will hear a dialogue between a PE teacher and an administrator at a summer school. First you have some time to look at questions 21 to 27.
(Pause the recording for 30 seconds)
Now listen carefully and answer questions 21 to 27.

P = Paddy   K = Kate

P: Excuse me, I've come to enquire about your summer school courses. My name's Paddy Deans. Please call me Paddy.

K: OK, Paddy, I'm at your disposal. Are you talking about concentrating on one subject or do you want to study a number of different subjects? **(21)** And are we talking about graduate studies or **(22)** preparation for graduate studies? We can also give you advice on a new career, but we're not in the field of Business Management or anything like that.

P: No, nothing like that. I was more interested in your sports programmes. You see, I'm a PE teacher, and I've just got a new post. There's no compulsion to do this, but **(23)** I really want to improve on my teaching and coaching techniques, if you see what I mean. I believe you have an excellent swimming programme, for example.

K: That's right. Most of our instructors reached international level. **(24)** Our course is designed to enhance the technical aspects of stroke, training and the strategy for each participant. Technical instruction, stretching and dry land training, training principles and stroke development are integral parts of the programme, so it's for someone who has reached a good standard of swimming. Each athlete will be videotaped and receive a DVD with stroke analysis.

P: That sounds like just what I'm looking for. What will I need for the course?

K: Swimming trunks, towel, swim cap, flippers, goggles and a pillow and bed linen for the week.

P: Right, I understand. **(25)** Now, would there be any chance of taking part in equestrian events? My new school is horse-riding mad, and to be honest I've never sat on a horse in my life, although I like horses.

K: Well, you've come to the right place, Paddy, and naturally we can provide a horse for you. We have a very well-respected equestrian camp, and don't worry if you're a complete beginner - there are no end of other people in your shoes this year for some reason.

P: What sort of things would I do?

K: **(26)** Well, the beginners would start off with basic horsemanship, how to sit on a horse, how to make it obey simple instructions, you know. But don't worry. One of our instructors will have a long chat with you and define realistic goals. Are you interested in dressage, flat work or show jumping?

P: To be honest I haven't the faintest idea.

K: That's fine. You can watch the experienced riders and try a bit of everything. I'm sure something will grab your fancy.

P: Great. By the way, what's the enrolment deadline for all this?

K: **(27)** Well, we've just extended it by a week, so it's now May 2nd.

P: Fine.

Before you hear the rest of the conversation, you have some time to look at questions 28 to 30.
(Pause the recording for 30 seconds)
Now listen and answer questions 28-30.

K: You arrive on Sunday and leave after lunch on Thursday. The cost is £500. This covers room and board from dinner on the first day to lunch on the last, tuition, programme materials, evening recreational activities and use of one of our horses.

P: So could I do the swimming course, followed immediately by the equestrian course?

K: Oh, yes. They fit in quite nicely, one straight after the other. Now, was there anything else, Paddy?

P: Well, actually yes, now that I'm here. In my new school I'm having to teach girls for the first time in my life, and they're also big on **(28)** rhythmic gymnastics. Now, although I've got lots of experience with Olympic gymnastics, I don't feel at all qualified to teach rhythmic.

K: We do run a course in rhythmic gymnastics, but it's in September. Would you be able to come back?

P: But I'll be back at school then.

K: We've thought of that, and that's **(29)** why it's a weekend course. Three weekends to be exact - first three in September.

P: Put me down for that one then. Any idea what the course involves?

K: Well, I know you study the different events like hoop, ribbon, ball, Indian clubs and so on, **(30)** and you take a dance course.

P: A dance course! But I'm the world's worst dancer. You should see me do the tango.

K: No, Paddy, it's not that type of dancing. It's called educational dance, and teaches you to be aware of your body, and to interpret music. Very important if you want to teach rhythmic gymnastics.

P: Well, I suppose I'd better try that, too. All right, give me the details.

That is the end of section three. You now have half a minute to check your answers.

(Pause the recording for 30 seconds)
Now turn to section four.

SECTION 4
You will hear someone giving a talk to parents on planning further education for their children.
First you have some time to look at questions 31 to 40.
(Pause the recording for 1 minute)
Now listen carefully and answer questions 31 to 40.

Tonight, I'd like to address myself to parents who are planning to send their children to university, but who might be concerned about the cost. There's no doubt that university education is a great asset. Not only will your children learn and grow but, **(31)** according to the Department of Skills figures, on average someone with higher education earns 50% more in a lifetime than someone without. But in the last decade or so, the cost of getting a degree has more than doubled – and it looks as if things are going to get worse. **(32)** Maintenance grants were abolished in 1997 and tuition fees introduced for students in England, Wales and Northern Ireland. **(33)** University fees are rising steadily, some of them more than 6,000 pounds a year. If you thought funding a university education was beyond your reach, think again. With sound planning, you can provide your children with this opportunity of a lifetime. If you're a new parent, remember that the earlier you start saving, the less you have to pay every month and the greater your return. Money will give you flexibility over where your children study and the course they choose. But how should you invest? There's no simple answer, but there are a number of options.

(34) The National Union of Students estimates that the average undergraduate needs about £25,000 to finance three years at university. Based on these figures, it is projected that when someone is at university in 20 years' time, the cost will be approaching £40,000, but this is assuming the university fees will only increase with the rate of inflation. It could, of course, be more.

Parents can save money by encouraging their children to study locally and live at home. **(35)** Almost 80% of the costs students incur are living expenses (rent, food bills, travel, laundry, etc). If your child is already 13 years old, and you haven't started to save yet, there's no time to waste.

....

Pause (4 seconds)

(36) If the young person is interested in joining the armed forces, for example the Royal Air Force, he can get the RAF to sponsor him throughout university; then he'll fly fighter jets and after that work in the public sector as a commercial pilot. Sponsorship from the armed forces is an option hundreds of students take every year. The RAF, for example, will sponsor students for at least £4,000 a year. **(37)** But this involves a minimum service commitment; for the RAF, it's at least 4 years.

If your child likes the idea of engineering or law, he could consider a 'sandwich' course. These normally involve a paid, year-long placement in the industry that he's studying, plus the normal time at university. You get experience in your chosen field - plus a year's salary.

When your child is 16, you should start putting aside what you can, but there's no way you'll be able to fund a degree on savings alone. **(38)** If your child is a gifted sportsman, you may be able to secure a sports scholarship.

Scholarships and bursaries come in all sizes, are awarded for a variety of reasons and may be a one-off or annual payment. You may be eligible to apply simply because of where you come from or for a specific course you are attending. They are seldom advertised and many go unclaimed every year.

The Internet is a great way to start looking. There is a searchable database at www.studentmoney.org and while you're at the computer, go to www.google.co.uk and type in some key words. If you're a keen cricketer, for example, put in 'university bursary sport cricket', for instance. **(39)** Top of the results page is the University of Kent, which gives a £1,500 cricket bursary to talented players.

If you haven't put any money aside, your teenager will almost certainly need to get a student loan - by far the best way for him or her to borrow. **(40)** <u>The maximum yearly loan is about £5,000.</u> There are two reasons why the loan is so attractive; firstly, the index-linked interest rate is very low, far lower than you'd get from the bank. Secondly, you don't have to start paying it back until you've left university and you start earning a decent salary. Now, a few more things to look at...

That is the end of section four. You now have half a minute to check your answers. *(Pause the recording for 30 seconds)*
That is the end of the listening test. In the IELTS test you would now have ten minutes to transfer your answers to the listening answer sheet.

TEST 7

You will hear a number of different recordings and you will have to answer questions on what you hear. There will be time for you to read the instructions and questions and you will have a chance to check your work. All the recordings will be played once only. The test is in four sections. At the end of the test you will be given ten minutes to transfer your answers to an answer sheet.
Now turn to section one.

SECTION 1

You will hear a telephone conversation between a travel agent and a school principal who is organising a school tour for a group of third year students. First you have some time to look at questions 1-3.
(Pause the recording for 30 seconds)
You will see that there is an example that has been done for you. On this occasion only, the conversation relating to this will be played first.

James: Hello. McFadden's Travel! James speaking; how may I help you?
Jonathon: Hi there; my name's Jonathon Presley, principal of Sainsbury Secondary School. I am calling to ask about your early bird tour offer. I saw it advertised in the Evening Herald yesterday.
James: Certainly, Mr. Presley; what would you like to know?
Jonathon: Oh, please, Jonathon will be fine.
James: Of course, Jonathon. How can I help you?
Jonathon: Well, the first thing I'd like to know is how long is your offer valid for? My third-year students are planning a holiday in early April; will they qualify for the discount?
James: The good news is our special offer runs <u>until the end of May.</u>
Jonathon: Oh dear, oh dear, March! That's terrible, we've just missed out.
James: On the contrary, Jonathon. It's May not March; you WILL qualify for the discount.
Jonathon: Oh, fantastic.

Narrator: The offer finishes at the end of May so the answer is (C). Now we shall begin. You should answer the questions as you listen because you will not hear the recording a second time.
Listen carefully and answer questions 1-3.

[REPEAT]
James: And I'm only just getting started; the best news is yet to come.
Jonathon: What do you mean?
James: Well, tell me now ..., how many students are you planning to take on this tour?
Jonathon: I expect there'll be about 45 students and 3 teachers

accompanying them. Why? Are there any further discounts?
James: There are indeed. We do a 25% discount on groups of up to 40 people. For you, we can offer an even better rate; a 50% discount.
Jonathon: Wow, is that on top of the 15% early bird discount?
James: It most certainly is, which **(1)** <u>makes your total tour discount, hmmmmm, fifty plus fifteen, sixty-five percent</u>.
Jonathon: Surely there's a catch, this is too good to be true.
James: Well, there is a condition that you must choose your destination from a list we have selected. You can't book a tour to just anywhere in the world with this discount rate.
Jonathon: I see, and **(2)** <u>would Madrid be on that list by any chance?</u>
James: I am sorry to disappoint you but we do not offer this rate on tours to Madrid. However, we have an excellent all-inclusive 7-day Barcelona tour which is available. How does that sound?
Jonathon: Sounds interesting. What is the total cost per student?
James: Let's see ... It works out at £679 per person with the discount. **(3)** <u>The normal price is £1940</u> so you are saving £1261 per person.
Jonathon: Hold on a moment, let me get a pen to write some of this down; it's getting complicated. Okay, how much will it cost per student?
James: £679
Jonathon: And how much of a saving is that?
James: £1261
Jonathon: Barcelona sounds very good indeed! Tell me, what do you mean by all-inclusive? What does £679 get us?

Before you hear the rest of the conversation, you have some time to look at questions 4-10.
(Pause the recording for 30 seconds)
Now listen and answer questions 4-10.

James: Well, **(4)** <u>that price covers flights,</u> **(5)** <u>3-star hotel accommodation</u> and extras.
Jonathon: James, I must say, I'm very glad I called you this morning. This is a fantastic deal. It covers flights, accommodation and what else?
James: Plus airport taxis, **(6)** <u>breakfast every morning,</u> a city tour and **(7)** <u>theatre tickets</u>.
Jonathon: Great !..... and what about the teachers?
James: The teachers can travel free of charge with the students.
Jonathon: Well I might just go on this tour myself, I've always fancied a trip to Barcelona ...... ehhhh, ehh but for the children's sake, of course.
James: Of course. Now, let's get to work on the booking. Exactly when were you planning to leave?
Jonathon: The 7th of April, if possible.
James: Yes, that's available. And, can you confirm the exact number of students please?
Jonathon: It's either 44 or 45, let me see... Yes, 45, exactly 45 students. No, sorry, in fact that's 46. I forgot about Jenny McCarthy; she sent her application in late so it's not in the same pile as the rest.
James: So that's the 7th of April and 46 students, correct?
Jonathon: Yes, perfect, and three teachers. Is there a morning flight?
James: Yes, your flight is at 7 a.m. on Monday the 7th of April. Arrive at the airport two hours before departure. The flight will take about two and a half hours and you'll land at 10.30 a.m. local time. How does that sound?
Jonathon: Sounds great. Can I give you my e-mail address to confirm the rest of the details?
James: Of course.
Jonathon: (8) <u>It's jonathon.presley@sainsbury.com.</u> That's j-o-n-a-t-h-o-n dot p-r-e-s-l-e-y at s-a-i-n-s-b-u-r-y dot com. And we'll pay by credit card if possible.
James: That'll be perfect. What's your card number?
Jonathon: It's **(9)** <u>6676 6654 9743 1251</u>, expiry date 01 Jan 2015.

James: And the name on the credit card?

Jonathon: That's my own, Jonathon Presley

James: So, £679 times 46 students, I'm going to charge **(10)**£31,234 to your credit card, that's the total cost.

Jonathon: Sounds fine.

James: Great! Well, I think that's all we need for now, Jonathon. It's been a pleasure doing business with you. If you have any questions please don't hesitate to give me a call. We'll be in touch next week to confirm the booking details.

Jonathon: Okay, and thank you very much for your help, James. Bye for now.

James: Bye bye Jonathon! Speak soon.

That is the end of section one. You now have half a minute to check your answers.
(Pause the recording for 30 seconds)
Now turn to section two.

SECTION 2

You will hear an extract from a talk about the history of motor racing. First you will have time to look at questions 11 and 12. *(Pause the recording for 30 seconds)*
Now listen carefully and answer questions 11 and 12.

Presenter: Good morning and welcome to the programme. This week we're continuing our series of features on motor racing and I am delighted to welcome to the show, David McWilliams, widely recognised as the most knowledgeable motor racing historian in England. We've invited David in to talk to us about what is probably the most famous and prestigious motor racing championship in existence today; that is, of course, Formula One. David, Formula One is now a massive racing franchise, but how did it all begin?

David: Well, Formula One has its roots in the European Grand Prix Motor Racing championship which began in the 1920s. After World War Two, the Grand Prix was transformed into a new championship format, the one we are familiar with today, Formula One. The **(11)** 'Formula' stands for the rules which all the drivers and manufacturers must respect. The 'One' signifies that this racing championship is regarded as the best in the world. **(12)** The first world championship race was held in 1950 at Silverstone in England. It was won by Italian Guiseppe Farina, in his Alfa Romeo. Farina narrowly beat his teammate Juan Manuel Fangio of Argentina to the title, yet it was Fangio who would go on to dominate the sport for the rest of the decade winning five world championships. As the years went by, the sport became a global phenomenon and grew from strength to strength, becoming the biggest commercial sport on the planet.

Before you hear the rest of the conversation, you have some time to look at questions 13-20.
(Pause the recording for 30 seconds)
Now listen and answer questions 13-20.

Presenter: There's no doubt that Formula One is big business today David, but what about the real heroes, the great drivers of Formula One, past and present? Who stands out as the best, in your opinion?

David: That's an almost impossible question to answer, but I could narrow it down to three or four amazing drivers; take your pick from any one of them. I'll start with the grand master of Formula One, the great Fangio who I've already mentioned. He dominated the sport throughout the 1950s, **(13)** winning 5 titles in all, his first in 1951, his last in '57, **(14)** a record that stood for 46 years. Indeed, **(15)** he was the first multiple championship winner. Fangio was a fiery and spirited Argentinian who never gave up. His greatest moment came in winning the 1957 championship when he came back from a disastrous pit stop to recover a 30-second deficit and take the championship on the last lap of the last race of the season. That was, of course, to be the last time he'd win the title.

Another undoubted great is Brazilian, Ayrton Senna. Senna won the world title three times, the first being in 1988, the last in 1991. Tragically, he died in a race crash the year after to the dismay of millions of fans watching the race unfold live on T.V. Senna was best known for his skills driving in the wet and **(16)** he won the Monaco Grand Prix, on what is regarded as the most difficult race course in Formula One, more times than any other driver. Perhaps because of this, **(17)** he is regarded as the most naturally-gifted driver to have ever sat behind the wheel.

Another very talented driver was Frenchman, Alain Prost. Prost won the drivers' title four times during his career. His first title victory came in 1985 and his last arrived in 1993. Of course, **(18)** Prost will always be remembered as the driver with the third highest number of championship victories, and, perhaps, even more for the fact that **(19)** he was a great rival of Ayrton Senna. Those two had many great battles.

Last but not, by any means, least, Michael Schumacher is the most recent of these driving greats who deserves a mention. His first title was won in 1994, and he continued to dominate Formula One until he won his last title in 2004. Schumacher holds many driving records including most drivers' championships, race victories, fastest laps, pole positions, points scored and most races won in a single season. **(20)** He is also regarded as the greatest driver on paper having won seven world titles.

Presenter: It sounds like Schumacher is in a league of his own; is he not clearly the best then, David, based on his record?

David: It's not that simple unfortunately. These drivers all raced in different eras with different cars and under different circumstances. I don't believe we can say one was the out and out best but rather that each was the best of his time. That's praise enough.

That is the end of section two. You now have half a minute to check your answers.
(Pause the recording for 30 seconds)
Now turn to section three.

SECTION 3

You will hear four business colleagues discussing a takeover proposal. First you have some time to look at questions 21 to 27. *(Pause the recording for 30 seconds)*
Now listen carefully and answer questions 21 to 27.

Mary: So ... let's go over this again. We don't want to make any mistakes and we all need to agree we're making the right decision.

John: Absolutely; we'd have to spend a lot of money to buy Bizz-Educators Inc.; almost £10 million. So let's get this right, otherwise it'll be our necks on the line.

Dave: Well, I for one think this is an excellent opportunity for our company to expand and break into a new market. I say we should go ahead with the takeover. At £10 million, Bizz-educators is good value for money.

Mary: Ok Dave, I know you're very much in favour of the acquisition. How about you summarise the plus points of this venture for us. Mark, you're less certain and you've highlighted some issues already. Will you summarise the downsides?

Mark: I'd be only too happy to.

John: Right then, Dave, let's start with you. Why is this proposal so attractive? What are the upsides?

Dave: It's simple economics. **(21)** Bizz-educators has a proven track-record and is an industry leader. It is a well-respected company with a great name, has generated excellent goodwill, **(22)** and has consistently made a gross profit of more than £500,000 per annum with a great shareholder return.

Mark: Yeah, but what about the net profit, that's not nearly as high. In fact, last year it made a net loss of £100,000.

Dave: Mark, that's only because it invested in a new manufacturing plant. That's a long-term investment to secure the company's future.

In fact, it's a good thing, not a bad thing. It shows that **(23)** the company has a clear and ambitious strategy going forward. Besides, a £100,000 loss is very small in real terms. It's hardly worth being concerned about. That loss will be clawed back within two years if the **(24)** projected profits for 2012 and 2013 materialise. The forecast is for a net profit of £500,000 in 2012 and £1,000,000 in 2013. The figures speak for themselves. This is a sound investment.

John: I have to agree with Dave. Why are you so sceptical Mark?

Mark: I see where Dave is coming from, but we're overlooking some vital facts. **(25)** First of all, this company wants to remain an independent entity. Hostile takeover bids are fraught with danger. We know from experience; remember Davidsville Inc.? We spent a fortune researching that company and creating a workable business plan only for the merger to fall through.

Mary: Mark's right, it is always difficult to buy a company that doesn't want to be sold. Davidsville was a disaster. Continue Mark.

Mark: That's not my only concern. I am also worried that Bizz-Educators is a production-based company. We have no experience running companies like that. Our market is investment banking and trading. We would have to hire outside managers to run Bizz-Educators for us. That's going to cost more money. Look, I'm not saying it can't be done; **(26)** I'm just saying this is a high-risk venture. Plus there's no synergy. Our business is totally different, so we can't save costs by combining departments.

John: Well, we can certainly see that this decision is not straightforward, by any means.

Mary: Maybe, but we have to come to a conclusion soon; it's almost five o'clock.

Mark: What's the hurry? Can't we postpone our decision and discuss the takeover proposal again tomorrow?

Mary: Mark, have you forgotten that **(27)** we have to have our conclusions ready for tomorrow's board meeting? That's when the official decision will be made.

Before you hear the rest of the conversation, you have some time to look at questions 28 to 30.
(Pause the recording for 30 seconds)
Now listen and answer questions 28 to 30.

Dave: Goodness, it almost slipped my mind. Well, we'd best move on. Mary, John, you were uncertain before. Now that you've listened to the pros and cons of the proposal, what do you think?

John: I think it's a great opportunity for our business. Bizz-Educators is definitely profitable and it is a business on the up, it's growing and is a very attractive takeover proposition for that reason.

Mary: No-one doubts that it's a very successful business, but the question is should we invest? I say we should, provided we can guarantee the following: First of all, I would like assurances that **(28)** the management of Bizz-Educators won't oppose us outright. That would make the bid too difficult. Secondly, I think **(29)** we need to ask an independent mediator to broker the deal on our behalf. Last time we tried to negotiate our own takeover it was a disaster, as Mark said.

John: I agree Mary. I'd also like us to carry out another audit of the company's books.

Mark: In fairness John, I don't think that's necessary. We've done a thorough audit already. It'll just cost more money. **(30)** We must keep the deal secret until it goes through though; if this gets leaked to the press, Bizz-Educators won't be happy. That will make the management even more hostile towards us.

Dave: Good point, agreed. I don't think we need to be concerned about projected profit margins, goodwill or accounting issues. Bizz-Educators has kept very up-to-date account books.

Mary: Great, then we're all agreed, the takeover should go ahead provided we proceed cautiously.

That is the end of section three. You now have half a minute to check your answers.

(Pause the recording for 30 seconds)
Now turn to section four.

SECTION 4

You will hear part of a lecture about conserving energy. First you have some time to look at questions 31 to 40.
(Pause the recording for 1 minute)
Now listen carefully and answer questions 31 to 40.

Tutor: I'd like you to give a warm welcome to our guest speaker today, Dr. Sophia Martin from the Faculty of Science. Dr. Martin is an expert in energy conservation and she's going to talk to us about ways we can conserve energy in the home. This is a very important subject as the world we live in is facing dramatic and potentially destructive climate change as a result of our excessive wastefulness and aggressive exploitation of natural resources.

Dr. Martin: Thank you for the kind words Alice. You are quite right, we face an unprecedented climate crisis and it is up to each and every one of us to do our bit to help stop global warming. Believe it or not, if we all took some simple steps, we could dramatically reduce our carbon footprint and help protect the environment. It is not a cliche, it is not silly nonsense talk, one person really can make a difference and I hope that after my speech today, you will understand how.

But first, what exactly is your carbon footprint? Basically, it's how much you pollute the environment as an individual, or rather **(31)** what volume of greenhouse gas is emitted into the atmosphere because of your day-to-day activities. The key to stopping global warming is for each of us to reduce our carbon footprint, and if we conserve energy in the home, we can achieve some truly dramatic results.

Our homes are actually very inefficient from an energy conservation perspective. **(32)** Indeed, more than 65% of all homes aren't insulated enough. This means that they lose heat and that homeowners waste a lot of energy, not to mention money, on heating during winter. So the first step is **(33)** to fit adequate insulation in the attic and outer walls of your home. This can reduce your heating bills by as much as 25%. What's more, **(34)** the government offers grants to people who want to have their homes reinsulated, so it isn't a very expensive process, and you will probably recoup your investment within a couple of years. I would encourage everyone to consider this course of action; both your wallet and the environment will thank you.

....

Pause (4 seconds)

Believe it or not, there are even simpler things we can do. For a start, **(35)** never paint your interior walls in dark colours. **(36)** Dark colours absorb heat; therefore, you will waste more energy trying to keep your home warm. Always use light colours on interior walls.

Did you know, a dishwasher that is 50% full uses almost the same energy as one that is 90% full? The moral of the story is to wait until your dishwasher is packed before switching it on; it'll save you and the environment. The same is true of most household appliances, so try to use them only when necessary. Another startling fact is **(37)** that replacing just one normal light bulb with an energy efficient light bulb will save you £25 over the lifetime of the bulb. Now just imagine the savings if you replaced all the bulbs in your house.

Having large windows seems to be in fashion right now, yet it makes no sense whatsoever from an energy saving perspective. Windows are one of the biggest causes of heat loss. If you have large windows at home, my advice would be **(38)** to close the curtains and blinds as often as possible. This will help your rooms retain heat. Another simple way to retain heat is to close all inside doors, especially ones which lead into cooler parts of the house. Carpets and rugs are great floor insulators. It's a good idea to have these fitted in rooms where heat retention is an issue.

(39) I would strongly advise people to consider erecting solar panels on their roofs. You don't need to live in a constantly sunny place to reap the benefits of these; even our English weather will suffice. Solar panels can generate enough energy to heat your entire hot water supply, which is fantastic when you think how much you pay for this service at the moment. And, of course, I would encourage people to continue recycling and **(40)** composting waste. The next generation will thank us if we act now and rightfully condemn us for failing to.

Well, I can only hope you have found this speech informative and that I have highlighted the importance of the individual to the cause of environmental protection. Thank you for your attention, I'll hand you back to Alice now....

That is the end of section four. You now have half a minute to check your answers.

(Pause the recording for 30 seconds)

That is the end of the listening test. In the IELTS test you would now have ten minutes to transfer your answers to the listening answer sheet.

TEST 8

You will hear a number of different recordings and you will have to answer questions on what you hear. There will be time for you to read the instructions and questions and you will have a chance to check your work.

All the recordings will be played once only. The test is in four sections. At the end of the test you will be given ten minutes to transfer your answers to an answer sheet. Now turn to section one.

SECTION 1

You will hear a telephone conversation between the owner of a restaurant and a customer who is calling to find out information about food and prices at the restaurant. First you have some time to look at questions 1 to 3.

(Pause the recording for 30 seconds)

You will see that there is an example that has been done for you. On this occasion only, the conversation relating to this will be played first.

Sam: *Hello. Bellucci's Restaurant, Sam speaking. How may I help you?*

David: *Hi, my name's David Marsden, and I'm calling to ask about the offers I saw on the website for your restaurant. I am thinking about organising a party for a friend's birthday.*

Sam: *Yes, Mr Marsden, what information would you like to know?*

David: *You can call me David.*

Sam: *OK, great. So, David, what can I help you with?*

David: *Well, first of all, I wanted to know if the 50% offer that you have on for certain dishes is valid for week nights as well as on the weekend. The party may take place during the week, you see.*

Sam: *Well, there are many dishes that are 50% off on weekends and only a small number of dishes are 50% off during the week. For example, the Spaghetti Bolognaise is 50% off on whatever day you come in during this month, and Lasagna and steaks are 50% off on our most busy days, which are Saturday and Sunday.*

David: *Would you be able to do a discount on the Lasagna if there was a large group of people coming in during the week?*

Sam: *We can only do a 25% discount, but we can do a 50% discount for large groups on any dessert you have with the Lasagna.*

David: *Well, that sounds like a good deal.*

The 50% discount on Lasagna is on the weekends only so the answer is (C). Now we shall begin. You should answer the questions as you listen because you will not hear the recording a second time. Listen carefully and answer questions 1-3.

[REPEAT]

Sam: There are many other offers that we have on, at the moment, as well.

David: What about drinks? Are there any discounts on drinks?

Sam: Yes, of course. **(1)** For every three bottles of house red or white wine ordered, you will get a bottle free. So that is four bottles of wine for only about £25. If you order two bottles of champagne you will get half a bottle free of charge as well.

David: That sounds like a really good offer. Which house wine do you stock? Most restaurants have French house wine and sometimes Spanish but I think **(2)** most of my friends will want to drink Italian wine.

Sam: We normally serve French as the house wine but we will be able to find a nice Italian one instead, if you prefer.

David: That would be great. What about Champagne? We will probably order at least two really good bottles. How much would a good bottle cost?

Sam: Well, you are in luck because the Champagne used to cost £25 per bottle **(3)** but now it's only £20 per bottle so you'll save £5.

Before you hear the rest of the conversation, you have some time to look at questions 4 to 10.

(Pause the recording for 30 seconds)

Now listen and answer questions 4 to 10.

David: That sounds like a good price based on my experience. Now, what side dishes are on the menu that could be ordered with the Lasagna?

Sam: Well, we have a range of side dishes, some go better with the Lasagna than others but of course it's your choice. The chef's special side dish is a chicken and cheese dish. This may be too heavy to have with Lasagna but we have a selection of salads such as a **(4)** mixed salad and a **(5)** Greek salad. They would be the best option with that main course. Some other side dishes that are popular are **(6)** tomato bread with herbs and **(7)** Italian cheese with peppers.

David: That all sounds very tasty and I'm sure all the people who are coming to the party will like these types of dishes. I might come in during the week to try out some of your food before the party.

Sam: So, would you like to reserve the table then for your party?

David: Yes. I was wondering if you have any tables free for the 20th of August?

Sam: I'm afraid we are all booked up on that date but we can **(8)** reserve a table for you for the week after on the 27th of August. Is that OK?

David: Yes, that will be fine.

Sam: How many people will there be?

David: **(9)** Fifteen. Can we have the table for 7:00 o'clock on that evening?

Sam: Yes, that can be arranged. Please, can I take your phone number for the booking?

David: Yes, it's 01445 333 6451

Sam: OK, that's great. Can I also take your email address to send you information about the restaurant and update you about offers and evening entertainment?

David: Sure, it's **(10)** david.hamill@worthing.com, d a v i d (dot) h a m i l l @ w o r t h i n g (dot) c o m

Sam: Great! Well, I think that's all I need for the moment. We will be in touch closer to the date when you'll be coming to the restaurant. If you want to ask anything or order anything special we can cater for most requests.

David: Yes, that would be good as I'm sure I'll think of something.

Sam: Bye Bye David. Speak soon.

That is the end of section one. You now have half a minute to check your answers. *(Pause the recording for 30 seconds)* **Now turn to section two.**

SECTION 2

You will hear an extract from a talk about the history of Tennis. First you will have time to look at questions 11 and 12. *(Pause the recording for 30 seconds)*
Now listen carefully and answer questions 11 and 12.

Presenter: Good afternoon and welcome to the programme. Today we have a special programme about the history of tennis in this country and we also have Steve Mackay in the studio, the all-time great British tennis player, to give us the lowdown on some interesting facts about the sport and other great tennis players. Steve, obviously tennis is one of the most popular sports broadcast on T.V today. Can you tell us about the early days of tennis?

Steve: Well, the medieval form of tennis is known as 'real tennis' and eventually became 'lawn tennis' which is what we know today. 'Real tennis' changed over three centuries from an earlier ball game played around the 12th century in France. This had some similarities to handball. **(11)** <u>People would hit a ball with a bare hand</u> and later with a glove. People say this game was played by monks in monasteries. By the 16th century, the glove had become a racquet. **(12)** <u>'Real tennis' spread in popularity throughout royalty in Europe and was the most popular in the 16th century.</u>

Before you hear the rest of the conversation, you have some time to look at questions 13 to 20.
(Pause the recording for 30 seconds)
Now listen and answer questions 13-20.

Presenter: It's amazing how the sport has changed then over time and how technology has helped to advance it with the state-of-the-art tennis racquets that we have today. So, what about the players who will go down in history as the best at this sport? Who do you think will be remembered on the Wall of Fame?

Steve: Well, obviously I have many favourites and all tennis players have different styles and will be remembered for different aspects of their game. The first player though that has to be mentioned is the great Bjorn Borg. He will go down in history due to the fact that **(14)** <u>he won 11 Grand Slam singles titles</u> between 1974 and 1981, five at Wimbledon and six at the French Open. **(13)** <u>Born in '56</u> in Sweden, Borg became the youngest winner of the Italian Championship just before his 18th birthday, and two weeks later he was the youngest winner of the French Championship. Borg is the only player in the open era to **(15)** <u>have won both Wimbledon and the French Open in the same year</u> more than once.

Another very important tennis player is Boris Becker. He was born in 1967 in Leimen, West Germany, and **(16)** <u>he is a six-time Grand Slam singles champion</u>. Since he retired in 1999 from the professional tour, media work and his personal life have kept him in the headlines. An interesting aspect of his career is the fact that **(17)** <u>he was the youngest ever male Grand Slam singles champion, winning Wimbledon at 17 years, 7 months.</u>

Moving on to our next great player, we have Pete Sampras. He was born on August 12, 1971 in Washington D.C and during his 15-year career **(18)** <u>he won 14 Grand Slam men's singles titles</u>. His flair for the game was evident at age 3 when he discovered a tennis racquet in the basement of his home and spent hours hitting balls against the wall. His parents are of Greek origin. He has given some truly unforgettable performances on the court over the years.

The final player I will mention is the great Andre Agassi. **(19)** <u>He was born on April 29, in 1970</u> in Las Vegas, Nevada. During his career he won 4 Australian Open titles, 1 French Open, 1 Wimbledon and 2 US Open which gives a total of eight Grand Slam titles. An interesting aspect of his career was that he turned professional at the age of 16 and **(20)** <u>his first tournament was in La Quinta</u>, California. He won his first match against John Austin 6-4, 6-2 but then lost his second

match to Mats Wilander 6-1, 6-1. By the end of the year, Agassi was ranked World No. 91.

Presenter: These players really have achieved a great amount in their lives and they will be talked about for years to come, especially when the Wimbledon Championships come round in June. Steve, which one is your ultimate favourite?

Steve: I just can't answer that; they all evoke great memories in the world of tennis and they have all contributed so much to the game. Their names will always be inscribed on the wall of champions!

That is the end of section two. You now have half a minute to check your answers.
(Pause the recording for 30 seconds)
Now turn to section three.

SECTION 3

You will hear four students discussing a conference they want to organise at their college.
First you have some time to look at questions 21 to 27.
(Pause the recording for 30 seconds)
Now listen carefully and answer questions 21 to 27.

Sam: So .... Mr Peters has finally agreed that we can organise this year's college conference, so we need to really go through all the most important items in order to establish a general schedule for the conference and how we are going to put it all together.

Kate: Yes, I agree. We can't leave things to the last minute and there are quite a lot of good speakers who have offered their services for this conference.

Dave: It's important that things go smoothly. Don't forget that Mr Peters has been against the idea of this conference for the last two years so we need to make it worthwhile and get at least 100 students to attend, so that we can prove this is an event that students can benefit from.

Lucy: The most important thing we need to consider is the range of speakers who we will invite to the conference. If they are well-respected in their different fields then the students will be very keen to come and hear the talks. We don't have a massive budget either, so we have to negotiate on the fees that the speakers will charge.

Kate: Sam, you mentioned before this meeting, that you have had some calls from some interesting potential speakers. Can you give us the lowdown on the rough list that you have at the moment?

Sam: Yes, the main person on my list, who is an expert in the field of Business Management, is **(21)** <u>Professor Harman. He would be good at running workshops</u> where students can discuss how to start a business and he likes to include role-plays, which make the sessions more interesting.

Kate: Yes, I've heard of him and people have told me that he is dynamic and interesting. He doesn't like just giving lectures; he likes to get the students involved more in the discussion. We should definitely send him a formal invitation. What about another area of study such as Maths?

Sam: Well, I have done some research on Mr Steve Bishop. I heard about him because my brother went to see him give a lecture at a University in his area. Apparently, **(22)** <u>he is well-respected among many Universities in England</u> for his knowledge in the field of Maths. He's even done some research with some famous Mathematicians.

Lucy: My sister studies Maths at University and I think he came to her University, too, to give some extra lectures. He would be a good one to keep on the list. I could send the invitation to him if you want, Sam.

Sam: That would be great, thanks. We have speakers now to talk about business and mathematics so it would be a good idea to invite someone who is an expert in an Arts subject, like English or Drama. I haven't actually got any ideas for Arts subjects.

Kate: Well, I'm planning to do Drama at University and I know of a lady who is the head of Drama at a well-known University. Her name is **(23)** Sandra Bolton. She would give some Drama seminars where students can discuss aspects of theatre and production in smaller groups. I also know a professor called Mr Max Wallington. He is a Professor of English Literature and he would come and give a lecture about Shakespeare. I'll send invitations to Ms Bolton and Mr Wallington then.

Sam: Great! That's two Arts subjects covered then. The final main subject area we need to think about is Science. Dave, you want to study Biology at University, don't you? Do you know of any Professors we can contact?

Dave: (24) Well, there's the famous Professor Sean O'Brien. He's done quite a lot of work in the field of genetics. I'm sure all the budding scientists will really want to come and hear him speak. As well as this, there's the 'mad scientist', Geoff O'Hara who is very knowledgeable about Albert Einstein and he can come and talk about his famous theories.

Sam: Perfect. Now that we have some speakers in mind to cover the main areas of study we need to think about the administration and organisation of the conference. To start with, we need to send the invitations out to all the speakers we have agreed on, on school-headed paper. Kate, Lucy and I will take care of that. Dave, would you be able to **(25)** contact a photographer to come and take pictures for the newsletter that will be printed after the conference?

Dave: Yes, I know a good photographer who has come to the college for some other events. I will contact him as his photos were of really good quality.

Sam: Lucy, would you be able to order the food and drinks? Which caterers do you think we should use? We don't want to spend too much money. We have about £400 to cover food and drink for 100 students. We need a selection of finger food and soft drinks.

Lucy: (26) I will contact Flying Fish. They are quite cheap and they will do some discounts for us as we have used them before at the college. Don't worry Sam, I'll sort all that out.

Sam: Excellent. We have covered a lot for today. I will book the main college hall and rooms 10, 11, 12 and 13 this week. I think we need to have about two more meetings before the conference. **(27)** The next one we'll schedule for Wednesday 6th June. Can everyone do that or would Thursday 7th June be better?

Kate: The first date you said is fine with me.

Dave: Me too.

Lucy: Yes that's fine with me as well.

Before you hear the rest of the discussion you have some time to look at questions 28 to 30.
(Pause the recording for 30 seconds)
Now listen and answer questions 28-30.

Sam: Last thing to mention before we finish up for today is some things that Mr Peters, our lovely headmaster, has said. As we said at the beginning, he hasn't been so enthusiastic about this conference and he has given us some rules we have to stick to during the conference. I've made a photocopy of them for everyone. I think we should just go through them now to get them out of the way.

Lucy: Good idea.

Sam: Well, the first thing Mr Peters said is that **(29)** we have to make a record of all the students who attend the conference as he wants those figures after the event to check that the money he gave us to organise it was worth it. **(28)** He also wants to know which subject each of the students who attended is going to study at University to show that we have provided suitable speakers at the conference. He said that he doesn't mind how many speakers we invite as long as the lectures are well-attended. The last requirement was that **(30)** we help organise the travel arrangements for the speakers. We can discuss the details of this in the next meeting.

Kate: That all sounds fairly easy to manage. Did Mr Peters not say anything about tidying up the hall and the rooms after? I would have

thought that he would have said something about that.

Sam: That wasn't something on the list. I could check with him but the cleaners who clean the college on a regular basis might tidy everything up. They would just have to be paid a bit more. I don't think the conference will produce too much mess anyway.

Dave: It would be good to get some help with all that anyway.

Sam: Yes. So, that's everything then. Let's go for lunch now, I'm starving. We can speak about the next lot of things at the next meeting.

That is the end of section three. Now you have half a minute to check your answers.
(Pause the recording for 30 seconds)
Now turn to section four.

SECTION 4

You will hear part of a lecture about healthy eating. First you have some time to look at questions 31-40.
(Pause the recording for 1 minute)
Now listen carefully and answer questions 31 to 40.

Professor: I'd like to introduce our speaker today who has come all the way from Manchester. Dr Paul Harold, the Head of Research in Nutrition at Manchester University. He is going to talk to us about ways we can improve our lifestyle and fitness. This will include watching what we eat and being more careful about our calorie intake as well as taking regular exercise. This is an important current issue as many people eat too much junk food and the nation as a whole is fatter than it was one hundred years ago.

Dr Harold: Thank you, James, for your introduction. You are absolutely right; statistics show that the nation is heavier than it used to be and this is due to the long hours that we work and the lack of time we have to prepare healthy meals that are low in fat and sugar. There are some simple steps everyone can take to help improve their general health; maybe lose some weight first; in the long run, it could lower your cholesterol and blood pressure.

The first thing to do in order to check that your weight is healthy is to work out your Body Mass Index or BMI. This is a tool that can help you find out if you are a healthy weight for your height. Obviously the height of a person will affect what weight they should be. **(31)** To work out your BMI you should take your weight in kilograms and divide it by your height in metres. Then you divide the results by your height in metres again. The results you come up with can be checked on a chart to see if your BMI is too high, too low or about right.

Even if your BMI is about where it should be it is still important to eat a healthy and well-balanced diet. A healthy diet involves consuming appropriate amounts of all the food groups, including an adequate amount of water. Nutrients can be obtained from many different foods, so there are a wide variety of healthy diets.

To start with, it is important to eat starchy foods such as bread, cereals, potatoes, rice, and pasta, together with fruit and vegetables and this should provide the bulk of most meals. **(32)** Some people wrongly think that starchy foods are 'fattening'. In fact, they contain about half the calories of the same weight of fat. Also, starchy foods often contain a lot of fibre. When you eat starchy foods, you get a feeling of fullness which helps to control appetite. **(33)** It is also important to eat at least 5 portions, and ideally 7 to 9 portions, of a variety of fruit or vegetables each day. If you eat a lot of 'fruit and vegetables', then your chances of developing heart disease, a stroke, or bowel cancer are reduced. **(34)** You also need a certain amount of protein to keep healthy. However, most people eat more protein than is necessary. You should choose poultry such as chicken or lean meat. There is evidence that **(35)** eating oily fish helps to protect against heart disease. It is probably the 'omega-3 fatty acids' in the fish oil that helps to reduce build-up in the arteries. Aim to eat at least two portions of fish per week, one of which should be oily.

Obviously what we eat is highly important but it is also crucial to do regular exercise as it strengthens the heart, **(36)** <u>tones our muscles</u> and is also good for the mind. We're increasingly living in a world where physical activity has stopped being a day-to-day part of our lives. **(37)** <u>We have domestic appliances</u> to wash and dry for us and cars to get us around and with the decline in manual labour many of us spend our working day sitting at desks. **(38)** <u>Adults should do a minimum of 30 minutes moderate-intensity physical activity</u>, five days a week. You don't have to do the whole 30 minutes in one go. Your half-hour could be made up of three ten-minute bursts of activity spread through the day, if you prefer. **(39)** <u>The activity can be a 'lifestyle activity' such as walking to the shops or taking the dog out or structured exercise</u> or sport, or a combination of these. But it does need to be of at least moderate intensity. For bone health, **(40)** <u>activities that produce high physical stresses on the bones are necessary.</u>

Well, I hope you have learned some interesting facts from this talk and that it will help you to change your lifestyles for the better. Thank you for your attention and I believe that James has some handouts to give you on this subject, James....

That is the end of section four. You now have half a minute to check your answers. *(Pause the recording for 30 seconds)*
That is the end of the listening test. In the IELTS test you would now have ten minutes to transfer your answers to the listening answer sheet.

TEST 9

You will hear a number of different recordings and you will have to answer questions on what you hear. There will be time for you to read the instructions and questions and you will have a chance to check your work. All the recordings will be played once only. The test is in four sections. At the end of the test you will be given ten minutes to transfer your answers to an answer sheet.
Now turn to section one.

SECTION 1

You will hear a telephone conversation between a customer and an overseas shipping agent. First you have some time to look at questions 1-8.
(Pause the recording for 30 seconds)
You will see that there is an example that has been done for you. On this occasion only, the conversation relating to this will be played first.

Jackie: Good afternoon. Denham's Shipping. How can I be of service?
Tim: Well, I wish to enquire about sending a container of personal items from the UK to <u>Ireland</u>.

The customer wants to send his container to Ireland, so the *Country of destination* is Ireland. You should answer the questions as you listen because you will not hear the recording a second time. Listen carefully and answer questions 1-8.

[REPEAT]
Jackie: No problem, would you like me to give you an estimate of the cost?
Tim: Yes, please.
Jackie: Well, first of all, may I take your details?
Tim: Of course. My name's Tim Lafferty.

Jackie: Could you spell your surname for me, please, Tim?
Tim: Yes, **(1)** <u>it's Lafferty</u>; L – a – f – f – e – r –t –y
Jackie: Thank you, Tim. Now, where would you like us to pick your container up from?
Tim: My university, if possible.
Jackie: Okay, let me make a note of the address.
Tim: It's **(2)** <u>Abbeyfield University</u>.
Jackie: Is that A-B-B-E-Y-F-I-E-L-D?
Tim: That's right. Park Street, Brighton.
Jackie: Perfect. And may I take down your postcode, too?
Tim: It's **(3)** <u>BR8 9P3</u>.
Jackie: Great. Thank you, Tim. Have you the container's measurements?
Tim: I do. It's approximately 2.5 metres long by **(4)** <u>1.25 metres wide</u>.
Jackie: I see. Quite a big one then!
Tim: Indeed!
Jackie: And the height?
Tim: **(5)** <u>I make it a metre and twenty centimetres deep.</u>
Jackie: So that's 2.5 by 1.25 by 1.2.
Tim: Right.
Jackie: And what will actually be in the box, Tim?
Tim: Oh, mostly old uni books.
Jackie: Okay
Tim: And some **(6)** <u>music albums.</u>
Jackie: Anything else?
Tim: Yes, a little bit of **(7)** <u>stationery.</u>
Jackie: I see. And could you put an estimate on the value of the items?
Tim: The books are quite valuable; **(8)** <u>they're worth around £1800. The music albums, maybe half that, say £900, and you can put the stationery down as £300.</u>

Before listening to the rest of the conversation you have some time to look at questions 9 and 10.
(Pause the recording for 30 seconds)
Now listen and answer questions 9 and 10.

Jackie: Okay. And will you be purchasing contents cover from us also?
Tim: Eh, I'm not sure what you mean.
Jackie: Sorry, let me explain; because your items are worth more than £2,000, we recommend that you purchase insurance to cover yourself in the event of damage or loss.
Tim: Makes sense. What are my options?
Jackie: Well, we offer three insurance deals — the premium rate, standard rate and economy rate ones. Premium offers full cover in the event of loss, damage or theft, which means you would be provided with the full cost of replacing your belongings.
Tim: What about standard and economy?
Jackie: Standard will give you today's value — the second-hand value of your belongings - and economy provides you with a fixed payment of £1000 in the event of loss, damage or theft.
Tim: Well, I can afford to live without those books to be honest, so just give me the cheapest option.
Jackie: **(9)** <u>We recommend standard cover for all our customers.</u>
Tim: No, thank you. That won't be necessary. The cheapest option will be fine.
Jackie: No problem. And one last thing; will you be needing delivery at your office, at your house, or do you intend to pick up your container at the port?
Tim: **(10)** <u>Home delivery would suit me best I think.</u>
Jackie: We'll.... *(fading)*

That's the end of Section 1. You have half a minute to check your answers. *(Pause the recording for 30 seconds)*
Now turn to Section 2.

SECTION 2

You will hear a tour guide talking to her tour group. First you will have time to look at questions 11-15.
(Pause the recording for 30 seconds)
Now listen carefully and answer questions 11-15.

Tour guide: Well, we certainly have a busy day ahead of us, so let's get started, shall we? You'll find a map of the museum with the itinerary I've just handed out. The museum's our first port of call, so let's have a look at the map now. **(11)** The door on the right of the entrance hall leads into the Gift Shop and Ticket Centre. Once we pick up our entrance tickets, I'd ask everyone to deposit their bags and coats in the cloakroom which is located towards the back of the Gift Shop and Ticket Centre. If you want to pick up an information leaflet, you can approach the Information Desk situated along the right-hand side.
(12) Now, once you come back into the entrance hall, the door on the opposite side to the Gift Shop leads into the Art Gallery. There is a special exhibition on there at the moment which is not to be missed.
(13) If you continue on up the entrance hallway, that leads into the Main Exhibition Centre. At the back left-hand side there are some toilets.
(14) Beside the toilets, you'll find the 3D Theatre. I strongly recommend that you make time for the 30-minute presentation in the theatre. It is well worth a viewing. **(15)** Running along the right-hand side of the Main Exhibition Centre is the Modern Art Studio. Here, not only can you view some of the most famous works of the 20th century, but you can also sit in on a workshop run by a local artist. So that's the art museum.

Before you hear the rest of the discussion you have some time to look at questions 16-20.
(Pause the recording for 30 seconds)
Now listen and answer questions 16-20.

(16) Next on the itinerary is the Aquarium. Depending on how long we spend at the museum, we might have to give this one a miss. It's not what I'd call a highlight of the day, but it would be a shame if we didn't get to see it, **(17)** as it's on route to the Solheim Country Club, where we're booked in for lunch at 1 o'clock. Originally, **(18)** we had planned to stop off at the Milltown Winery afterwards, but we've had to scrap that plan, otherwise we'd never get to the Zoological Gardens before closing time. **(19)** We have pre-booked the gardens and must be there by 2:30, so no dillydallying please after lunch — straight back onto the bus. The gardens close at 3:30, so we've an hour there which should give us ample time to look around. **(20)** Time allowing, we'll stop off at the famous Stout Brewery after that if traffic isn't too heavy and we're in Lincoln before 5. If not, we'll head straight for the National Concert Hall where you're in for a real treat of an evening with a performance from the world-renowned cellist, Andres Borovski. We have to be in our seats by 6:30 sharp. After that, it's back to the hotel for the night where a buffet meal will be waiting for us at half eight — or whenever we get back.

That is the end of section two. You now have half a minute to check your answers.
(Pause the recording for 30 seconds)
Now turn to section three.

SECTION 3

You will hear a discussion between two design students and their tutor on a practical assignment. First you have some time to look at questions 21-25.
Pause the recording for 30 seconds)
Now listen carefully and answer questions 21-25.

Tutor: So have you chosen a product yet?
Jenny: I think so. We'd like to build a gyroscopic exercise aid.
Tutor: Sounds interesting. Tell me more.
Maeve: Well, we did some research and were amazed to discover the sheer range of applications for gyroscopic technology. **(21)** Gyroscopes are used in laser and optical devices and can be found in many consumer appliances, too.
Tutor: Right, tell me about this product specifically though. The aim of the assignment is to create something **(22)** practical, functional and beneficial for consumers. Justify your decision.
Jenny: Well, we believe we can design and build a cheap and effective muscle-strengthening aid by taking advantage of the inertial forces created by a gyroscope.
Maeve: Yes, what we want to do is design a ball which can be held in the palm. Within the ball, there will be a simple gyroscope. This gyroscope can be set in motion by movements of **(23)** the lower arm and wrist together in synch. The device will not require any external power source because it will be sustained by the movements of the arm and wrist. This will create considerable resistance and an excellent lower-arm strengthening aid. It will be simple to design and cheap to produce, yet extremely effective.
Tutor: This all sounds very good. I'm impressed!
Jenny: Thanks Mark, we're glad you like it. I think we're really onto something here. Our research has told us there's nothing comparable in the market and that a product like this would have multiple uses. Not only could it be used as an everyday **(24)** toning and exercise device, it could also be beneficial to people in rehabilitation who have suffered serious lower-arm injuries. We see the product being marketed towards **(25)** high-performance athletes, like tennis and golf players, for whom lower-arm strength is vital, too.

Narrator: Before you hear the rest of the discussion you have some time to look at questions 26-30.
(Pause the recording for 30 seconds)
Now listen and answer questions 26-30.

Tutor: I've heard enough to give your project the go ahead. Now, let's talk costs.
Maeve: Right, well we estimate that around £3,000 will be required for product development.
Tutor: You mean to build the prototype?
Maeve: Exactly. **(26)** And we'll need half of that again to carry out some product testing.
Tutor: And what's your timeline for the project?
Jenny: **(27)** The prototype should be ready a fortnight after work on the design starts and we'll need another 6 weeks for testing.
Maeve: **(28)** We want to enlist the help of 15 people to test the prototype. Ideally, we want 5 professional athletes to try it out, **(29)** 5 recovery patients and the remainder of the subjects will be **(30)** gym members — our three target markets.
Tutor: Okay. Well, you have a lot of work to do, but you've certainly made a good start. Let's meet again on Monday to get the ball rolling.

That is the end of section three. You now have half a minute to check your answers.
(Pause the recording for 30 seconds)
Now turn to section four.

SECTION 4

You will hear part of a lecture about public speaking. First you have some time to look at questions 31-40.
(Pause the recording for 1 minute)
Now listen carefully and answer questions 31-40.

It is only natural to feel somewhat nervous before giving a speech, and while a few nerves never did any harm — and can in fact prove beneficial — letting your nerves overcome you can be detrimental. Today's presentation will focus on ways to control those butterflies and help you to give better presentations in future.

First and foremost, **(31)** you've got to know your material. I can't stress that enough. If you fail to prepare, you might as well prepare to fail. **(32)** Even the most experienced speakers never turn up unprepared and NEVER try to wing it. Personalise your subject and use humour, anecdotes and conversational language. This will make it easier for you to remember what you want to say.

Secondly, practise, practise, practise! **(33)** Rehearse well in advance, and preferably out loud, and with all the equipment you plan on using. Practise your timing — when to pause and when to breathe — and prepare for the unexpected. Something always goes wrong, especially when you are relying on technology. So always have a back-up plan.

Get to know your audience before you have to stand up in front of them. **(34)** Meet and greet them on the way in, perhaps. It is much easier to talk to a group of friends than a group of strangers. And, just as importantly, know your room as well. Arrive early, pace the speaking area and practice using the microphone and visual aids.

The hardest part is trying to relax. Never rush straight into your speech. Begin slowly and address the audience first. In fact, even **(35)** before you start, take a few deep breaths. You know - one one-thousand, two one-thousand, three one-thousand - this will turn your nervous energy into enthusiasm.

....

Pause (4 seconds)

(36) Visualisation can be a great confidence booster. Visualise yourself making the speech in the way that you intend. Imagine your voice loud and confident, and picture the audience clapping and rooting for you. Remember, people want you to succeed. The audience wants to hear an interesting and insightful speech. They aren't hoping you make a fool of yourself.

(37) Whatever you do, avoid making unnecessary apologies. If you make a mistake or two, forget about it. Few will notice and it will all be forgotten before too long.

(38) People often forget the importance of body language. Don't underestimate this. Your words carry far less meaning than your delivery. Success is defined by your intonation and confidence. If you come across as a confident person, people will listen to you — you will command their attention. Stand tall and proud and deliver with conviction. **(39)** Humans are very bad listeners. We remember less than 25 percent of what is said and place far more emphasis on how it is said.

Last of all, **(40)** be realistic and give yourself a chance. No one becomes the perfect speaker overnight. It takes time to hone your presentation skills.

That is the end of section four. You now have half a minute to check your answers. *(Pause the recording for 30 seconds)*
That is the end of the listening test. In the IELTS test you would now have ten minutes to transfer your answers to the listening answer sheet.

JUSTIFICATIONS OF THE ANSWERS
for the Reading Section

TEST 1
Reading Passage 1
Justification of the Answers

1. C is **True** because the text states that 'Once the basic criteria of adequate shelter and nutrition are satisfied...'

2. E is **True** because a married couple 'live on average three years longer and enjoy greater physical and psychological health than .... couples in a cohabitational relationship'.

3. G is **True** because the text says that 'certain features correlate highly with happiness. These include autonomy over how, where and at what pace work is done'. 'Control of one's life in general is also key'.

4. Paragraph 1: 'And what is true for individuals can be applied on a larger **scale (level)** to the world population.'

5. Paragraph 2: 'Social **interaction** among families, neighbourhoods, workplaces, communities and religious groups correlates strongly with subjective well-being.'

6. Paragraph 3: '... people who are in control of the work they do...' '**Control** of one's life in general is also key. '

7. Paragraph 4: 'Choice, and citizens' belief that they can affect the **political process**, increase subjective well-being' -Paraphrased: if you can affect the political process you change the **course** of politics.

8. NOT GIVEN as although the text implies that underdeveloped nations are not concerned with achieving material wealth, it is not stated in the text that they do or do not try to attain the same standard of living as developed countries.

9. TRUE as the first paragraph explains how the 'obsession with getting rich' is down to 'jealousy, competitiveness or just keeping up with the Joneses'.

10. NOT GIVEN as although the text mentions that 'family life provided the greatest source of satisfaction', it does not say that this increased with the size of the family.

11. FALSE as the text states that poor health **is** determined by one's attitude to life in the fourth paragraph, where it states that 'evidence exists for an association between unhappiness and poor health'. 'Happy people, it seems, are much less likely to fall ill and die than unhappy people'.

12. TRUE as worrying is instinctive and causes unnecessary stress in the modern world. The fifth paragraph details how this 'stems from our cave-dwelling days'.

13. FALSE because both the second and the seventh paragraph state that family is more important than friends in ensuring happiness.

Reading Passage 2
Justification of the Answers

14. Paragraph B is **v** as it outlines how the written work that Zamenhof published became a spoken language.

15. Paragraph C is **viii** as the paragraph discusses the basic structural details of Esperanto and the way that it functions as a language.

16. Paragraph D is **iii** as it explains that some people cannot identify with Esperanto and find it 'artificial'.

17. Paragraph E is **vi** as it says 'to rebut the accusation that it is not a 'real' language, point out that it is frequently used at international meetings.'

18. Paragraph F is **i** as it builds on the previous paragraph and argues that Esperanto allows everyone to learn the language given its structure.

19. Paragraph G is **ii** as this paragraph describes how so many languages are used at the moment and this prevents the optimum results being achieved. Having just the one second language would increase productivity, effectiveness and efficiency immensely.

20. C because paragraph C details how research has been conducted into this.

21. D - 'Esperanto has an artificial feel' and 'by nature of its artificiality it is impossible to become emotionally involved with that language'.

22. B because speaking just Esperanto would save 'billions of dollars which are now being spent on translators and interpreters', which could be spent on 'improving the health of stricken populations of the world'.

23. YES because 'Esperanto does not give advantages to the members of any particular people or culture, but provides an ethos of equality of rights, tolerance and true internationalism'

24. NO because the first paragraph states that it is the 'most widely spoken artificial language', which means that there must be others.

25. NOT GIVEN because the text does not mention self-study courses.

26. YES. Paragraph F describes how Esperanto can be used to make formal presentations and can be used in informal conversations.

Reading Passage 3
Justification of the Answers

27. 'varying rates' - **Paragraph 2:** *This degradation of formerly productive land is a complex process. It involves multiple causes, and it proceeds at **varying rates** in different climates.*

28. 'intensify' - **Paragraph 2:** '*Desertification may **intensify** a general climatic trend, or initiate a change in local climate, both leading towards greater aridity.*'

29. 'initiate' - **Paragraph 2:** '*Desertification may .... **initiate** a change in local climate, both leading towards greater aridity.*'

30. 'aridity' - **Paragraph 2:** '*Desertification may .... initiate a change in local climate, both leading towards greater **aridity**.*'

31. 'vegetation' - **Paragraph 2:** '*The more arid conditions associated with desertification accelerates the depletion of **vegetation** and soils.*'

32. 'soils' - **Paragraph 2:** '*The more arid conditions associated with desertification accelerates the depletion of vegetation and **soils**.*'

33. G - The paragraph suggests that 'drastic cuts in emissions of greenhouse gases are required to stabilise atmospheric concentrations of these gases.'

34. E - 'if current trends in emissions of greenhouse gases continue, global temperatures are expected to rise faster over the next century than over any time in the last 10,000 years.'

35. D - 'Often little or no data is available to indicate the previous state of the ecosystem or the rate of degradation'.

36. B - as the paragraph details how desertification results 'from various factors including climatic variations and human activities'.

37. loss - **Paragraph F** - '*Crop production would be further threatened by increases in competition for water and the prevalence of pests and diseases and **land loss** through desertification and sea-level rise.*'

38. desertification - **Paragraph B** -'*Land degradation occurs all over the world, but it is only referred to as **desertification** when it takes place in drylands.*'

39. drylands - **Paragraph B** - '*....but it is only referred to as desertification when it takes place in **drylands**.*'

40. irrigation - **Paragraph C** - '*In addition, such areas also suffer from land degradation due to over-cultivation, overgrazing, deforestation and poor **irrigation** practices.*'

TEST 2
Reading Passage 1
Justification of the Answers

1. A as the article states that 'some stress can be positive and research has suggested that a moderate level of stress makes us perform better'.

2. G because the article describes an obsessive-compulsive world as one 'filled with dangers from outside and within'.

3. D as schizophrenics 'may lose touch with reality'

4. E as ADHD sufferers 'are not just very active but have a wide range of problem behaviours, which can make them difficult to care for and control'.

5. B as People with ASD 'can be good at creative activities, like art, music and poetry'.

6. 'Creative' Paragraph 1: *'People with Autistic Spectrum Disorder can be good at **creative** activities like art, music and poetry.'*

7. 'Quiet and dreamy' - Paragraph 2: *'ADD can easily be missed because the child is **quiet and dreamy**'.*

8.'unusual ways' - Paragraph 4: *'they may lose touch with reality, see or hear things that are not there and act in **unusual ways** in response to these 'hallucinations'*

9. 'suicide' - Paragraph 5: *'You may even feel that life is not worth living, and plan or attempt **suicide**.'*

10. D - Paragraph 5 - Depression - "reduced or increased appetite or weight".

11. C - Paragraph 4 - Schizophrenia - 'an episode of schizophrenia can last for several weeks'

12. C - Paragraph 2 - Stress - 'stress may be caused either by major upheavals and life events such as divorce, unemployment, moving house and bereavement'.

13. B - Paragraph 8 - '...and the performance of rituals, reaches such an intensity or frequency...'.

Reading Passage 2
Justification of the Answers

14. ii as the paragraph describes how 'third world' countries are following the same path that European countries did when they were developing into the states that they are today.

15. i - 'And despite the poverty of the countryside and the urban shanty towns, the ruling elites of most third world countries are wealthy.'

16. vi - 'This combination of conditions in Asia, Africa Oceania and Latin America is linked to the absorption of the developing world into the international capitalist economy ... the creation of a world market ... led to underdevelopment'.

17. viii - 'The prices of developing-world products are usually determined by large buyers in the economically dominant countries of the West'.

18. iv - as the paragraph outlines how the 'birth rate continues to rise at 'unprecedented levels' and that there are 'worsening poverty and starvation levels'.

19. YES - 'highly dependent economies devoted to producing primary products for the developed world ....traditional rural social structures'.

20. NOT GIVEN - paragraph E discusses population growth but makes no mention of why it is occurring.

21. YES - Paragraph D states: 'terms of trade are set to deteriorate when the cost of imports rises faster than income from exports....'

22. NO as 'only the oil-producing countries - after 1973 - succeeded in escaping the effects of Western domination of the world economy'.

23. D - 'The developing world .... is considered a common entity with common characteristics'.

24. F - 'The third world is nothing and it wants to be something'.

25. A - 'economic dependence on advanced countries'.

26. E - 'The economies of the developing world grew slowly or not at all'.

Reading Passage 3
Justification of the Answers

27. H - 'some believe this technology may cause physical harm...'

28. A - One of the earliest known examples of biometrics in practice was a form of fingerprinting used in China in the 14th century.... to distinguish young children from one another'

29. F - 'The match points are processed using an algorithm'.

30. C - 'Hundreds of companies are involved with new methods'.

31. G - Signature comparison is not as reliable, all by itself as other biometric verification'.

32. Paragraph C - 'As the industry grows, however, so does the public concern over **privacy issues**.'

33. Paragraph E - 'Additionally, it is used for **personal comfort** by identifying a person and changing personal settings accordingly, as in setting car seats by facial recognition.'

34. Paragraph G - 'A record of a person's **unique characteristic** is captured and kept in a database.'

35. Paragraph B - 'In the 1890s, an anthropologist and police desk clerk in Paris named Alphonse Bertillon sought to fix the problem of **identifying** convicted criminals and turned biometrics into a distinct field of study.'

36. Paragraph B - 'After the failure of Bertillonage, the police started using **fingerprinting**, ... '

37. Paragraph G - 'individuals who claim to be someone they are not (**identity** theft).'

38. Paragraph D - '..the **driving force** behind biometric verification..."

39. Paragraph D - 'In addition to security, the driving force behind biometric verification has been **convenience**...'

40. Paragraph H - 'Also, the data obtained using biometrics can be used in unauthorised ways without the individual's **consent**.'

TEST 3
Reading Passage 1
Justification of the Answers

1 E - Paragraph 3: "Britain's 'new Victorian' prisons are designed for security and control rather than for the rehabilitation..."

2 B - Paragraph 3: "...rather than for rehabilitation and education which is increasingly recognised as what prisoners need."

3 G - Paragraph 4: 'concept of the 'Learning prison'.'

4 C - Paragraph 4: 'Any transformation of the penal system must start with the redesign of prison buildings. Prison architecture has a clearly discernible effect on behaviour, operational efficiency, interaction and morale.'

5 A - Paragraph 4: "First, the more compact spatial organisation of the house reduces staff time spent on supervising and escorting prisoners. Second, the system places educational and other facilities at the heart of the building, ..."

6. A - 'last year, architects Buschow Henley were commissioned by a think tank organization working with the Home Office Prison Service to research and develop an alternative prison model' This is clearly a progressive attitude.

7. C - 'Such high rates of recidivism means that the prison population is continuing to grow at an alarming rate'.

8. B - The final paragraph mentions a number of ways that the new layout of prisons helps to educate and rehabilitate prisoners and to boost their self-esteem through social interaction and education within the system.

9. C 'the bed is placed lengthways along the external wall at high level, freeing up space below. Storage is built in....'

10. Paragraph 5: 'each with a **discrete external area** that can be productively used for sport'

11. Paragraph 6: 'the **bed** is placed lengthways along the external wall at high level'

12. Paragraph 6: '**Storage** is built in.'

13. Paragraph 6: 'neighbouring 'buddy' cell linked by **sliding doors**'

Reading Passage 2
Justification of the Answers

14. TRUE - " 'Mental retardation' refers to substantial limitations in present functioning. It is characterised by significantly sub-level intellectual functioning existing concurrently with related limitations in two or more of the following applicable adaptive skill areas."

15. FALSE - 'With appropriate supporters over a sustained period, the life functioning of the person with mental retardation will generally improve'.

16. FALSE - Parental consent is only required 'if the athlete is a minor.'

17. NOT GIVEN - the article does not say that Down Syndrome participants often excel in their chosen sport.

18. FALSE - They cannot take part in some activities, which are listed in B.1.

19. TRUE- '15% of individuals with Down Syndrome have a defect in the cervical vertebrae C-1 and C-2 in the neck.
This condition exposes Down Syndrome individuals to the heightened possibility of a neck injury if they participate in activities that hyperextend or radically flex the neck or upper spine'.

20. NOT GIVEN - Nowhere in the article does it say that participating in sports improves the communication and social skills of those with intellectual disabilities.

21. B - The title 'Conditions of participation' indicates this.

22. C - 'There are well over 350 causes of intellectual disability and in three-quarters of the cases the specific cause is unknown'.

23. D - 'No person shall, on the grounds of gender, race, religion, colour, national origin or financial constraint, be excluded from participation in the Special Olympics.

24. A '15 percent of individuals with Down Syndrome have a defect in the cervical vertebrae C-1 and C-2 in the neck.'

25. C Soccer is listed as one of the high-risk sports and the article states that 'an acknowledgement of the risks signed by the adult athlete or his/her parents/guardian if the athlete is a minor' is necessary to participate in these sports.

26. F - 'Accredited programmes may allow all individuals with Down Syndrome to continue in most Special Olympics sport training and competition activities. However, such individuals shall not be permitted to participate in sport training and competitions, which, by their nature, result in hypertension, radical flexion or direct pressure on the neck or upper spine'.

Reading Passage 3
Justification of the Answers

27. D - Paragraph 3 - is correct because 'there has been a marked increase [upward trend] in discrimination and violence directed against migrants, refugees and other non-nationals by extremist groups in many parts of the world.'

28. F - Paragraph 6 - is correct because: 'Racism is an ideological construct that assigns a certain race and/or ethnic group to a position of power [having a controlling hand] over others [other sections of society] on the basis of physical and cultural attributes'.

29. C - Paragraph 7 - is correct because: 'manifestations of xenophobia occur against people of identical physical characteristics [not physically distinct], even of shared ancestry [not culturally distinct]'.

30. A - Paragraph 6 - is correct because: 'Racism is an ideological construct that assigns a certain race and/or ethnic group to a position of power over others on the basis of physical and cultural attributes"

31. D 'Many of these, 80-97 million, are estimated to be migrant workers with members of their families.' (Paragraph 1)

32. B 'but xenophobia and racism have become manifest in some societies'.

33. A - 'the lack of any systematic documentation or research over time makes it unclear whether there is an increase in the level of abuse'.

34. C 'xenophobia is often played down and sometimes denied by authorities.' (Paragraph 3)

35. NOT GIVEN. Although the article mentions that some immigrants are refugees, it does not say why.

36. TRUE. The article states that there are 'tens of millions more internal immigrants, mainly rural to urban'.

37. TRUE. 'The extent of racial discrimination and xenophobia is often played down and sometimes denied by authorities.'

38. NOT GIVEN. The text states that 'there has been marked discrimination and violence directed against migrants, refugees and other non-nationals by extremist groups' but it does not say that this is because they create a sense of insecurity.

39. NOT GIVEN. There are no links made between education and racism or xenophobia.

40. FALSE. The text mentions 'manifestations of xenophobia occur against people of identical physical characteristics, even of shared ancestry, when such people arrive, return or migrate to states or areas where occupants consider them outsiders.'

TEST 4
Reading Passage 1
Justification of the Answers

1. B 'it is estimated that Biomass will have the largest increase among renewable energy sources, rising by 80 percent and reaching 65.7 billion kw in 2020'.

2. D 'the high cost of manufacturing fuel cells has prevented the mass use of this valuable energy source'.

3. C 'wells are drilled into geothermal reservoirs to bring the hot water or steam to the surface'.

4. D 'fuel cells are electromagnetic devices that produce electricity through a chemical reaction'.

5. NOT GIVEN the energy forms are not compared in terms of efficiency.

6. TRUE 'Wave energy conversion extracts energy from surface waves, from pressure fluctuations below the surface, or from the full wave. Wave energy also exploits the interaction of winds with the ocean surface.

7. TRUE 'not only do they protect against harmful by-products, but using alternative energy helps to preserve many of the natural resources that we currently use as energy'.

8. FALSE alternative energy sources 'are not the result of burning fossil fuels or the splitting of atoms'.

9. Paragraph A 'Alternative, or renewable, energy sources show significant promise in helping to reduce the **amount of toxins** that are by-products of energy use.'

10. Paragraph B 'The use of **renewable energy** is contributing to our energy supply.'

11. Paragraph C 'Biomass is renewable energy that is produced from **organic matter**.'

12. Paragraph D '**Geothermal energy** uses heat from within the earth.'

13. Paragraph H 'The **high cost** of manufacturing fuel cells has prevented the mass use of this valuable energy source.'

Reading Passage 2
Justification of the Answers

14. H 'Most cases of colour blindness, about 99% are hereditary'.

15. F 'colour-blind persons can spot camouflage colours where those with normal colour vision are fooled by it'.

16. B 'inherited colour vision problems cannot be treated or corrected'.

17. C 'Since males have an X-Y pairing and females have X-X, colour blindness can occur much more easily in males'.

18. J 'people with this disorder cannot identify red or green by itself, but can if among a coloured group'.

19. E 'monochromacy, where one can only see grey, or shades of black, grey and white'.

20. G They may not be able to tell which colours are which in the case of warning lights.

21. C 'Colour blindness results from an absence or malfunction of certain colour-sensitive cells in the retina.' These cells are called cone cells.

22 D 'The rarest form of all is total colour blindness, monochromacy' and 'another term for total colour blindness is achromatopsia'.

23. D 'buying clothes that to the 'normal' eye seem positively garish'.

24. *'All of these cells send information about colour to the brain via the* **optic nerve** *which connects to the retina at a point very close to the macula.'*

25. *'The* **retina** *is a neuro-membrane lining the inside back of the eye, behind the lens.'*

26. *'Cone cells, also called photoreceptors, are concentrated mostly in the central part of the retina, in an area called the* **macula***.'*

Reading Passage 3
Justification of the Answers

27. NOT GIVEN - Paragraph F - although less water is used in the production of rice than of grain to feed cattle, it does not state that vegetarians actually drink less water than meat eaters; it would vary from person to person depending on their diet.

28. TRUE - Paragraph F - 'A US diet rich in livestock products requires 800 kilograms of grain per person a year, whereas diets in India, dominated by a starchy food staple such as rice, typically need only 200 kilograms.'

29. FALSE - Paragraph F- 'As people move up the food chain, consuming more beef, pork, poultry, eggs, and dairy products, they use more grain.' and 'Using four times as much grain per person means using four times as much water.'

30. TRUE - Paragraph F -'in addition to population growth, urbanization and industrialization also expand the demand for water. As developing country villagers, traditionally reliant on the village well, move to urban high-rise apartment buildings with indoor plumbing, their residential water use can easily triple.'

31. FALSE - Paragraph K - 'It is now often said that future wars in the region will more likely be fought over water than oil'. - not food

32. NOT GIVEN - Paragraph I - Both countries are mentioned but the text discusses importing grain not oil.

33. C - 'it takes 1,000 tons of water to produce 1 ton of grain.'

34. E there are many references to over-pumping throughout the whole of the paragraph.

35. B this 'population growth is sentencing millions of people to hydrological poverty'.

36. F 'urbanisation and industrialisation also expand the demand for water'.

37. B 'We live in a water-challenged world, one that is becoming more so each year as 80 million additional people make their claims to the Earth's water resources'.

38. A - 'A US diet rich in livestock products requires 800 kilograms of grain per person a year, whereas diets in India, dominated by a starchy food staple such as rice, typically need only 200 kilograms'.

39. D - 'Unless governments in water-short countries act quickly to stabilise their populations and to raise water productivity, their water shortages may soon become food shortages.'

40. B - 'those that are financially strongest'

TEST 5
Reading Passage 1
Justification of the Answers

1. F 'This is an insect that might become more widespread because of climate change' (The House Longhorn Beetle).

2. B 'This problem may be overcome by clogging the suspected holes… '.

3. D 'Contact insecticides might also kill the natural predators' - spiders.

4. A 'Beetle damage in oak timbers is a slow process and if we make it slower through good building maintenance then the beetle population may eventually decline to extinction'.

5. FALSE 'Infestation deep within modified heartwood is more difficult to detect, particularly because the beetles will not necessarily bite their own emergence holes if plenty of other holes are available'.

6. FALSE 'clogging the suspected holes with furniture polish or by covering a group of holes tightly with paper or card. Any emerging beetles will make a hole that should be visible, so that the extent and magnitude of a problem can be assessed'. - so they aren't trapped

7. FALSE they are effective

8. NOT GIVEN - 'Surface spray treatments are generally ineffective' however no mention is made of whether the House Longhorn Beetle is an exception.

9. TRUE 'Heat treatments may be the only way to eradicate a heavy and widespread infestation without causing considerable structural degradation of the building'.

10. C 'good maintenance then the beetle population may eventually decline to extinction.'.

11. D 'The beetles fly to light and some form of light trap may help to deplete a population. The place in which it is used must be dark, so that there is no competing light source'.

12. B 'Surface spray treatments are generally ineffective because they barely penetrate the surface of the timber and the beetles' natural behaviour does not bring it into much contact with the insecticide'.

13. B 'Old damage is, however, frequently found elsewhere, thus indicating a wider distribution in the past, and infested timber is sometimes imported'.

Reading Passage 2
Justification of the Answers

14. Paragraph 1: 'Therapeutic jurisprudence is the study of the role of the law as a therapeutic *agent*.'

15. Paragraph 1: ' …and the therapeutic and *antitherapeutic* consequences of the law'.

16. Paragraph 2: 'The general aim of therapeutic jurisprudence is the *humanising* of the law'

17. Paragraph 2: ' …so long as other values, such as *justice* and due process, can be fully respected… '

18. Paragraph 3: 'therapeutic jurisprudence is especially applicable to this third category' i.e. '(3) the roles of legal *actors*'.

19. Paragraph 4: ' encouraging us to look very hard for *promising* developments… '

20. Paragraph 4: 'It encourages people to think *creatively*… "

21. Paragraph 5: 'One type of cognitive behavioural treatment encourages offenders to prepare *relapse prevention plans* which require…'.

22. Paragraph 5: ' ….which require them to think through the *chain of events* that lead to criminality.'

23. Paragraph 5: 'to anticipate *high-risk situations*, and to learn to avoid or cope with them.'

24. NOT GIVEN - Paragraph 5: Although rehabilitation programs are said to 'look rather promising' no concrete information is given or claim made about how greatly they reduce the chances of criminals re-offending.

25. TRUE - Paragraph 6: 'From a therapeutic jurisprudence standpoint, the question is how these programmes might be brought into

the law .... to make them part of the legal process itself'.
26. FALSE - Paragraph 7: A prisoner does not decide on punishment, but has a 'voice in his rehabilitation'.

Reading Passage 3
Justification of the Answers
27. D - 'Sleep may be a way of recharging the brain.'
28. A - 'Whereby metabolic rate drops significantly for a few hours.'
29. C - 'there is only a modest further energy saving to be gained by sleeping.'
30. B - 'When a person enters stage 3, extremely slow brain waves called delta waves are interspersed with smaller, faster waves.'

31. Paragraph 3 - '*Stage 1 is **light sleep** where you drift in and out of sleep and can be awakened easily.*'
32. Paragraph 3 - '*In stage 2, eye movement stops and **brain waves become slower**...*'
33. Paragraph 3 - '*When a person enters stage 3, extremely slow brain waves called delta waves are interspersed with **smaller, faster waves**.*'
34. Paragraph 3 - '*Stages 3 and 4 are referred to as **deep sleep**, ...*'
35. Paragraph 4 - '*In the REM period, **breathing** becomes more rapid, irregular and shallow..*'

36. Paragraph 2 - '*..... to exercise important neuronal connections that might otherwise **deteriorate** due to lack of activity.*'
37. Paragraph 2 - '*Sleep lowers a person's **metabolic rate**...*'
38. Paragraph 3 - '*We do not enter **torpor**, ...*'
39 - 40. Paragraph 4 - '*When a person falls asleep and wakes up is largely determined by his or her **circadian rhythm**, a **day-night cycle** of about 24 hours.*'

TEST 6
Reading Passage 1
Justification of the Answers
1. A - is **x** as the paragraph describes the ancient origins of the term graffiti and then moves on to discuss the modern use of the term.
2. B - is **viii** because the paragraph discusses another graffiti artist who is considered to have revolutionised the art form.
3. C - is **ii** as the paragraph details the lifestyle, values and traditions of the graffiti artists.
4. D - is **iii** because it discusses the equipment that is used by graffiti artists; the tools of their trade.
5. E - is **v** because it describes how graffiti is no longer restricted to the lower classes, but has transcended class and race boundaries.
6. F - is **vi** because it highlights how many shops have exploited the graffiti industry for commercial gain.
7. G - is **i** because this paragraph discusses how graffiti is now acknowledged as a valid art form.

8. NOT GIVEN as the article mentions the laws, but not how effective they were.
9. TRUE - Paragraph **A** states 'as hip hop music emerged so did a new outlet for artistic visibility'
10. FALSE - not hostility, it just wasn't recognised as high art at first.

11. F - as 'what began as an urban, lower-income protest, graffiti now spans all racial and economic groups'.
12. C - this is stated in paragraph **E**.
13. E - 'shoe polish, deodorant roll-ons and other seemingly innocent containers were emptied and filled with paint.'

Reading Passage 2
Justification of the Answers
14. B the paragraph details many different teaching methods and locations including study trips.
15. A the paragraph details how distance learning courses are just as successful as those courses taught on-site.
16. E 'distance learning is not meant to replace a face-to-face classroom, but is one major way to make education more accessible to society'.
17. E 'as advances in communication and digital technology continue, residential or demonstration labs may someday be replaced with comparable experiences provided through distance education'.
18. B as students can 'undertake lab work using more sophisticated equipment, or equipment too expensive to provide at home.

19. B as students 'undertake assessed lab work' at residential or summer schools.
20. D - 'they advise the faculty, for example, on how information is presented on a website or the format in which the information is presented'.
21. C - as 'staff tutors are responsible for the selection, monitoring and development of part-time Associate Lecturers.'
22. C - because the paragraph mentions 'Quality issues are a major concern for those who intend to pursue degree programmes via distance learning, especially with the proliferation of distance learning programmes.'

23. NOT GIVEN as the text makes no reference to this although paragraph A does say that universities try to overcome this lack of interaction.
24. YES - 'residential and summer schools serve a similar purpose; the difference is the duration'.
25. NO. The article devotes a whole paragraph (C) to describing demonstration lessons.
26. NOT GIVEN - paragraph D states that instructional designers play a 'significant role' , however salaries are not mentioned.

Reading Passage 3
Justification of the Answers
27. A - second paragraph: 'Latchkey children were once found only among the lower classes, but the situation has gradually spread to the middle and upper classes. The same is true of adolescent violence.' - 'However, in recent times, the "teen violence" epidemic has penetrated society at every economic level.'
28. F - the seventh paragraph states: 'They are also more likely to be the victims of crimes.'
29. H - 'has courage enough to resist pressure from friends and others'.

30. A - the first paragraph details how 'programmes were set up in factories, in schools and community centres to gather in all the children'
31. C - 76% were left alone after school.

32. TRUE 'because they are raised in dysfunctional families, are taught by example to be manipulative, secretive and unpredictable'.
33. NOT GIVEN - no mention of the age that they leave home
34. FALSE - seventh paragraph: 'While there are certainly genetic and biological factors involved in the development of an adolescent's propensity towards acting out their feelings of rage and isolation, environment also plays a key role in this arena.'
35. TRUE - 'talks about his or her feelings and thoughts easily with parents and others'.

36. Paragraph 1 - '...when fathers had gone off to war, and mothers had gone into **industry**'
37. Paragraph 1 - 'The country's **response** was prompt and comprehensive.'

38. Paragraph 2 - 'Sadly, finding young children at home without **adult supervision** has become much too commonplace.'
39. Paragraph 7 - 'Adolescents who fall under the classification of latchkey children are more likely than others of the same age group to experience feelings of rage and isolation and to express those emotions in a **physically aggressive** manner.'
40. Paragraph 8 - '**Personality** characteristics, skills, and maturity are useful criteria for determining a child's readiness to be home alone.'

TEST 7
Reading Passage 1
Justification of the Answers

1. vi. "humankind has always looked towards the stars and dreamt of one day making the voyage into the unknown and exploring outer space".
2. ii. "it has been a long time since the last moon landing, almost 40 years ..... According to NASA, plans are afoot for a manned mission to Mars at some point after 2020".
3. vii. "Denis Tito, became the first space tourist ... A year later, South African millionaire Mark Shuttleworth followed in his footsteps".
4. v. "At present, space tourism is undoubtedly reserved for an elite and wealthy few, but what of the future".
5. viii. "Even the Hilton group wants to get in on the act with talk of plans to build a Hilton on the moon".

6. C. Paragraph C. "Denis Tito, became the first space tourist, spending ten days on the International Space Station".
7. D. Paragraph C. "Mark Shuttleworth followed in his (Denis Tito's) footsteps".
8. B. Paragraph D. "If Eric Anderson, president of Space Adventures, the company that organised Tito and Shuttleworth's trips, is to be believed, it will be the next big thing".
9. E. Paragraph D. "Gene Meyers, the company's president, predicts that in 2020 a five-day holiday at the hotel will cost less than $25,000".

10. F Paragraph E. "The spaceship will be able to hold 100 guests, each with a private room offering 'truly unique views' of the **Earth's** sunset".
11. NG Paragraph E. "plans to build a Hilton 'on the moon'.
12. T Paragraph B. "According to NASA, plans are afoot for a planned mission to Mars at some point after 2020. A return to the moon has been scheduled sooner"
13. T Paragraph D. "At present, space tourism is undoubtedly reserved for an elite and wealthy few".

Reading Passage 2
Justification of the Answers

14. A. Paragraph 2. "And yet there are animals here, animals that exhibit a remarkable tolerance of the most inhospitable conditions on the planet".
15. D. Paragraph 2. "Less than half a metre beneath the surface of the snow, a furry white creature scurries ... along a tunnel. It is a collared lemming. It and other members of its family have excavated a complex home".
16. A. Paragraph 3. "Fur is comprised of dense layers of hair follicles"
17. C. Paragraph 4. "Air is an extremely effective insulator .... i.e. it has a very limited ability to conduct heat away from a warm surface".
18. C. Paragraph 4. "If an arctic fox or wolf is exposed to an air temperature of about minus ten degrees, the temperature near the 'tips of the fur' will match the air temperature, but at the surface of the skin it will be closer to thirty degrees".
19. A. Paragraph 5. "they are endotherms, meaning they can generate their own body heat".

20. B. Paragraph 5. "Together, thermoregulation and fur make arctic mammals perfectly equipped to face the toughest conditions the arctic can throw at them".

21. Paragraph 2 - 'Nor can reptiles withstand the extreme cold. And yet there are animals here, animals that exhibit a remarkable **tolerance** of the most inhospitable conditions on the planet.'
22. Paragraph 3 - 'They pay by using some of their precious and scarce food supply to generate heat within their bodies so that their **biochemical processes** can continue to function efficiently.'
23. Paragraph 3 - 'A thick insulating coat of fine **fur** covering all but the lemmings' eyes achieves this.'
24. 'Paragraph 3 - Fur is the **life preserver** of the Arctic.'
25. Paragraph 5 - 'Air is an extremely effective insulator, which is the same as saying it is a **poor conductor**, i.e. it has a very limited ability to conduct heat away from a warm surface.'
26. Paragraph 6 - 'When arctic mammals are cold, they raise their **metabolic rate** and produce more heat. When they are warm, the reverse happens.'

Reading Passage 3
Justification of the Answers

27. A. Paragraph 2. "steering Germany to reunification. And by defeating Austria and France in quick succession...".
28. A. Paragraph 3. "Bismark was forced to make a political U-turn" but "even managed to win over the church whose support he now needed".
29. C. Paragraph 4. "despite his attempts to destroy the socialist movement, its popularity had trebled by 1890".
30. B. Paragraph 5. "Bismark now believed that his ambitions were best served by peace. His plan to isolate a hostile France...".
31. D. Paragraph 6. 'His political and diplomatic juggling, therefore, simply cannot be considered a total success.'

32. True. Paragraph 5. "Congress of Berlin which he hosted was an outstanding success".
33. False. Paragraph 5. "He built up strategic alliances with the big powers, Russia, Italy and Austria-Hungary".
34. Not Given. Bismark's opinion about his reign is not expressed in the passage.

35. ii. The paragraph describes his rise up the 'political ladder' until he became Prussian Chancellor.
36. viii. "despite maintaining a veneer of democracy, the German parliament was effectively powerless to oppose him".
37. ix. "Bismark was forced to make a political U-turn".
38. vi. "Bismark viewed the growing popularity of the Socialist Democratic Party as a serious threat".
39. iii. "after 1871, Bismark devoted a lot of his time to foreign policy".
40. i. The paragraph comments on his reign as chancellor and analyses his legacy in terms of his successes and failures.

TEST 8
Reading Passage 1
Justification of the Answers

1. B. "The greenhouse effect is very important when we talk about climate change... the greenhouse effect is a naturally occurring phenomenon".
2. E. The paragraph discusses use of renewable energy, using less fossil fuels and recycling as examples of actions that can be taken.

3. A. The paragraph defines climate change as "changes in our climate which have been identified since the early part of the twentieth century".
4. D. "There are many institutions around the world whose sole priority is to take action against these environmental problems".

5. C. "looking at the knock-on effects of potential changes. For example are we likely to see an increase in precipitation and sea levels?".

6. D. Paragraph C. "Professor Max Leonard has suggested, 'while it may be controversial some would argue that climate change could bring with it positive effects as well as negative ones'".

7. C. Paragraph B. "such as Dr Michael Crawley, argue: 'even though this natural phenomenon does exist it is without a doubt human activity that has worsened its effect...".

8. A. Paragraph E. "with all this information and the possible action we can take, it isn't too late to save our planet".

9. B. Paragraph B. "Dr Ray Ellis suggests: 'human activity may be contributing a small amount to climate change but this increase in temperature is an unavoidable fact".

10. Yes. Paragraph B. "Although the greenhouse effect is a naturally occurring phenomenon, it is believed that the effect could be intensified by human activity and the emission of gases into the atmosphere.
11. Not Given. There is no mention about nuclear energy.
12. Yes. Paragraph D. "Greenpeace is an organisation that .... exposes the companies and governments that are blocking action".
13. No. Paragraph E. "Fortunately, the regular use of renewable energy is becoming increasingly popular".

Reading Passage 2
Justification of the Answers
14. C. Paragraph 1. "dozens of schools which are known as private schools ... perpetuate privilege and social division".
15. D. Paragraph 2. "Private schools therefore have an advantage ... as they are entirely 'middle class' and this positive attitude creates an environment of success".
16. C. Paragraph 3. *'If my son gets a five-percent-better chance of going to University then that may be the difference between success and failure."*
17. A. Paragraph 4. "the real reason that parents fork out the cash is prejudice" and the desire to conform to dinner party conventions.
18. C. Paragraph 5. "Private schools spend £300 per pupil a year on investment in buildings and facilities; the state system spends less than £50".
19. A. Paragraph 6. "Most private schools that you will find are set in beautiful, well-kept country houses, with extensive grounds and gardens".
20. B. Paragraph 1. Private schools 'perpetuate social division' and in Paragraph 5. the writer describes facilities such as laboratories, music rooms, squash courts etc.

21. Paragraph 1: *'The English education system is **unique** due to the fact .... as private schools'*
22. Paragraph 1: *'The overwhelming majority of students ... come from **middle-class** families.'*
23. Paragraph 2: *'However, statistics such as these can be **deceptive**...'*
24. Paragraph 2: *'**apply** themselves more diligently to their school work.'*
25. Paragraph 3: *'There are many parents .... children's **schooling**.'*
26. Paragraph 6: *'Many may ... is just about on the level of an industrial **shed**.'*

Reading Passage 3
Justification of the Answers
27. B. Paragraph 1. "If a black family wanted to eat at a restaurant, they had to sit in a separate section of the restaurant ... He could never understand this".
28. A. Paragraph 2. "King first achieved national renown when he helped mobilise the black boycott of the Montgomery bus system?".
29. D. Paragraph 3. "He advocated non-violent direct action based on the methods of Gandhi".
30. A. Paragraph 4. "In 1965, he led a campaign to register blacks to vote".

31. D. Paragraph 5. "King found that his message of peaceful protest was not shared by many in the younger generation".

32. Yes. Paragraph 2. "The 382-day boycott led the bus company to change its regulations, and the Supreme Court declared such segregation unconstitutional".
33. No. Paragraph 3. '...in Birmingham, Alabama, where the white population were violently resisting desegregation.'
34. Not Given. Paragraph 5. We only know he began to protest about the Vietnam war but there is no information about the outcome of the protest.

35. v. Paragraph A. describes his birthplace, family and education, comprising his background.
36. iv. Paragraph B. gives details about the protest and boycott of the Montgomery bus system.
37. ii. Paragraph C. "He advocated non-violent direct action".
38. i. Paragraph D. "in August 1963, and delivered his famous 'I have a dream' speech".
39. vi. Paragraph E. "King began to protest against the Vietnam war".
40. iii. Paragraph F. "in room 306 at the Lorraine motel ..... King was shot at 6:01p.m.".

TEST 9
Reading Passage 1
Justification of the Answers
1. The correct answer is **B**: "...and taking its name from its two founding members ..."
2. The correct answer is **E**: " ...Having sold more than 100 million albums worldwide, 46 million in the States alone..."
3. The correct answer is **G**: "the band that came to symbolise the hedonistic rebelliousness of the 1980s and 90s punk-rock period..."
4. Paragraph 2: *"Founding member Tracii Guns' failure to attend **rehearsals** led to him being replaced as lead guitarist by Slash."*
5. Paragraph 2: *"It was here on the road that the band established its **chemistry** and though it only managed to release one four-track EP..."*
6. Paragraph 3: *".... the song and its accompanying music video received regular **airplay** and shot to the top of the US charts"*
7. Paragraph 6: *"But when all's said and done, there's no denying the enduring **appeal** of GNR."*
8. The correct answer is **D**: "...the band went on a hiatus, not recording or touring together for the best part of two years, before Slash officially quit in 1996. Most of the other band members followed Slash out..."
9. The correct answer is **D**: "The band's promised new album, *Chinese Democracy*, never materialised ... It wasn't until 2008, with Rose now the only remaining member of the original band, that *Chinese Democracy* was finally released."
10. The correct answer is **A**: "It was here on the road that the band established its chemistry...". Chemistry between people is a positive way of interacting.
11. The correct answer is **C**: "unfortunately, drummer Adler's lifestyle got the better of him. The extent of his dependence on drugs was so bad that he could no longer perform with the band and was fired in July, 1990"
12. The correct answer is **C**: "A sixth member of the group was also added as Dizzy Reed became the band's keyboardist"
13. The correct answer is **B**: "...the song and its accompanying music video received regular airplay and shot to the top of the US charts..."

Reading Passage 2
Justification of the Answers

14. The correct answer is **D**; "Nowadays, they are more commonly constructed out of polyurethane foam making them much lighter...." A and B are incorrect because they were true in the past; not today. C is true only for long boards.

15. The correct answer is **D**; "surfing was first observed being enjoyed by native Tahitians ... Later travellers also reported seeing naked locals ... amusing themselves in the surf off the coast of Hawaii. Perhaps this is one of the reasons why the sport is synonymous with the South Pacific and Hawaii in particular." The first two locations are both in the South Pacific.

16. The correct answer is **D**; "Today, however, the popularity of surfing is such that surf clubs have popped up almost everywhere, from the windy West Coast of Ireland, to the ultra-chic Californian beaches."

17. The correct answer is **D**; "The prospective surfer would be well-advised to consider the dangers associated with the sport before he takes to the waves."

18. The correct answer is **A**; "Although the board itself offers buoyancy, it can also be a hindrance, and a deadly one at that if its leash becomes entangled in a reef, holding the surfer underwater."

19. The correct answer is **C**; "Collisions ... can also be extremely hazardous and can lead to concussion – a death sentence if the surfer is not rescued from the water quickly."

20-21. The correct answers are **B** and **D**; "Ideal water conditions for surfing can be extremely demanding on the body," and "Although more rare, attacks by marine animals are not uncommon, with sharks, rays, seals and jellyfish posing the greatest threats". A is incorrect because technically it is the leash holding surfers underwater, and C is incorrect because the encounters are rare.

22-23. The correct answers are **B** and **C**. For B - "it can also ... be extremely rewarding, and there are few feelings to compare with the exhilaration of riding out your first wave", and for C - "So for those of you daredevil adrenalin junkies who fancy having a go..."

24. "surfing carries with it the inherent danger of **drowning**..."

25. "Five-day courses start from as little as **£100**..."

26. 'all-inclusive' means that everything is included - "there are **all-inclusive camps**, too, which cover accommodation, meals, lessons and equipment."

Reading Passage 3
Justification of the Answers

27. "As investors tire of **stock market instability**..."

28. "Here are some tips from successful **real estate** mogul, Janet Anderson..."

29. "According to Janet, one of the best ways to identify a bargain is to **hunt for foreclosures**."

30. "Foreclosures are properties banks have repossessed because their owners were unable to meet the **mortgage repayments**."

31. "Banks want a quick sell ... They want to cut their losses and get **their money back** as quickly as possible."

32. "Developing a network ... can be an excellent way to identify such **bargains**."

33. "the biggest mistake you can make is to **borrow too much** or **over-borrow**"

34. The correct answer is **Yes**; "For first-time investors, lenders usually demand bigger down payments".

35. The correct answer is **No**; it is the opposite - "That's more of your money on the table and, therefore, should anything go wrong you're in for a big financial hit."

36. The correct answer is **Yes**; "mortgage payments and deposits are only part of the long-term cost of buying a rental property. There is also the cost of repairs, administration and maintenance, rental manager's fees, insurance... "

37. The correct answer is **No**; "...all of which require you to hold a significant amount of money in reserve" so it is implied that it is necessary, but banks do not require it.

38. The correct answer is **Yes**; "One of the biggest traps for first-time-investors ... is the temptation to pay over the odds to get the property you desire."

39. The correct answer is **No**; "...the housing market is not very hot at the moment, which means the danger of overpaying is not so great"

40. The correct answer is **Not Given**; The areas earmarked by the government are separate to the areas of urban renewal • we know nothing about the relationship, if any, between these two.

ANSWER KEY
IELTS Practice Tests 1 - 9

TEST 1

Listening - Section 1
1. faster   2. more affordable   3. luggage
4. 92.4 percent   5. 186   6. 11:46
7. 22:25   8. overnight   9. half (of)   10. 2 hours

Listening - Section 2
11. 142 weeks   12. 2-3 weeks
13. February   14. summer   15. early autumn
16.C   17.E   18.F   19.B   20.A

Listening - Section 3
21.D   22.B   23.C   24.A   25.D
26. tease   27. so nervous   28. individually
29. different side   30. teacher

Listening - Section 4
31. AIDS epidemic   32. better nutrition   33. developing countries
34. Eastern Europe   35. three million
36. one third   37. drug addiction
38. large cities   39. to cure   40. (serious) threat

Reading - Passage 1
1-3. C/E/G
4.F   5.B   6.D   7.G
8.NG   9.T   10.NG   11.F   12.T   13.F

Reading - Passage 2
14.v   15.viii   16.iii   17.vi   18.i   19.ii
20.C   21.D   22.B
23. YES   24. NO   25. NG   26. YES

Reading - Passage 3
27. varying rates   28. intensify
29. initiate   30. aridity   31. vegetation 32. soils
33.G   34.E   35.D   36.B
37.E   38.G   39.C   40.A

TEST 2

Listening - Section 1
1. 11.30   2. 12.15   3. tube
4. ticket office   5. £15   6. £10   7. van
8. 6   9. 83   10. Alexandra

Listening - Section 2
11.B   12.H   13.C   14.D   15.F   16.E
17. limited   18. lottery   19. October   20. guest

Listening - Section 3
21.C   22.C   23.A   24.B
25. 20/twenty minutes   26. butter
27. 100 grammes/a small quantity
28. organic yogurt   29. town hall   30. alcohol, coffee

Listening - Section 4
31. film   32. inbuilt   33. settings
34. hole   35. described   36. crucial
37. instant   38. speed   39. more light   40. shadows

Reading - Passage 1
1.A   2.G   3.D   4.E   5.B
6. creative   7. quiet and dreamy   8. unusual ways   9. suicide
10.D   11.C   12.C   13.B

Reading - Passage 2
14.ii   15.i   16.vi   17.viii   18.iv
19. YES   20. NG   21. YES   22. NO
23.D   24.F   25.A   26.E

Reading - Passage 3
27.H   28.A   29.F   30.C   31.G
32. privacy issues
33. personal comfort/car seats
34. unique characteristic
35. identification
36. fingerprinting
37. identity   38. factor   39. convenience   40. approval

TEST 3

Listening - Section 1
1. went blank   2. plugged in   3. on the/using the internet
4. not sure   5. Morningside (area)
6. 7:45   7. Branston   8. Sarrencen   9. £60   10. half an hour

Listening - Section 2
11.B   12.A   13.C   14.A   15.A   16.B   17.B   18-20. C/D/E

Listening - Section 3
21. an article   22. puzzled   23. record   24. 50 references
25. (the) requests   26. telephone call   27. course
28. information   29. email   30. meeting

Listening - Section 4
31. the fossil record   32. changed physically
33. reason and/or imagine   34. thought
35. experiments   36. great apes
37. presence of   38. altruism
39. social deception   40. moral and political

Reading - Passage 1
1.E   2.B   3.G   4.C   5.A   6.A   7.C   8.B   9.C
10. (discrete) external area   11. bed   12. storage   13. sliding doors

Reading - Passage 2
14.T   15.F   16.F   17.NG   18.F   19.T   20.NG
21.B   22.C   23.D   24-26.A/C/F

Reading - Passage 3
27.D   28.F   29.C   30.A
31.D   32.B   33.A   34.C
35.NG   36.T   37.T   38.NG   39.NG   40.F

TEST 4

Listening - Section 1
1.B   2.C   3.B   4.C
5. Julie Karas   6. 15 Fremont Avenue   7. Hawkesley   8. Science
9. IKE 614T   10. Fiat Panda

Listening - Section 2
11.B   12.C   13.C   14.A   15.C   16.E   17.H   18.I   19.D   20.F

Listening - Section 3
21.C   22.B   23.A   24.A   25.B
26.G   27.B   28.F   29.C   30.D

Listening - Section 4
31.B   32.A   33.H   34.G   35.E   36.D
37. 72.3   38. 8.1   39. 3   40. none

Reading - Passage 1
1-2. B/D   3.C   4.D   5.NG   6.T   7.T   8.F
9. amount of toxins   10. renewable energy
11. organic matter   12. geothermal energy   13. (high) cost

Reading - Passage 2
14.H   15.F   16.B   17.C   18.J   19.E   20.G
21.C   22.D   23.D
24. optic nerve   25. retina   26. macula

Reading - Passage 3
27.NG   28.T   29.F   30.T   31.F   32.NG
33.C   34.E   35.B   36.F
37.B   38.A   39.D   40.B

TEST 5
Listening - Section 1
1. £240   2. fitness centre   3. swimming pool   4. trainers
5. midnight/24.00   6. Fleet   7. 24 Whitehall Close
8. NE0 1EN   9. 9765 484 493   10. electricity bill

Listening - Section 2
11. records   12. contagious disease   13. travel medicine
14. medication   15. health issues   16. present
17. keep informed   18. long trousers   19. bare skin
20. dusk ... dawn

Listening - Section 3
21.D   22.E   23.B
24. 4   25. 5   26. 4.5
27. well thought out   28. two topics   29. boring   30. more time

Listening - Section 4
31. very high   32. low   33. target market   34. try the product
35. of scale   36. reward   37. brand   38. peak   39. intense
40. applications

Reading - Passage 1
1.F   2.B   3.D   4.A
5.F   6.F   7.F   8.NG   9.T
10.C   11.D   12.B   13.B

Reading - Passage 2
14. agent   15. antitherapeutic   16. humanising   17. justice
18. actors   19. promising   20. creatively
21. relapse prevention plans   22. chain of events
23. high-risk situations
24.NG   25.T   26.F

Reading - Passage 3
27.D   28.A   29.C   30.B
31. light sleep   32. brain   33. smaller, faster waves
34. deep sleep   35. breathing   36. deteriorate   37. metabolic rate
38. torpor   39. day-night cycle   40. circadian rhythm

TEST 6
Listening - Section 1
1. failed exams   2. archery   3. 8 people
4. 5, 6 / (5 and 6)   5. 22   6. June 24th
7. £425   8. 1304 647864   9.B   10.A

Listening - Section 2
11.C   12.B   13.A   14.G   15.D
16. Ride   17. Pay Station   18. Performance   19. Arena   20. Main

Listening - Section 3
21-22. A/D   23.B   24.C   25.B   26.A   27.C
28. rhythmic gymnastics   29. weekend course
30. dance course

Listening - Section 4
31. 50%   32. tuition fees
33. £6,000   34. £25,000
35. living expenses   36. armed forces
37. 4 years   38. (sports) scholarship
39. £1,500   40. yearly loan

Reading - Passage 1
1.x   2.viii   3.ii   4.iii   5.v   6.vi   7.i
8.NG   9.T   10.F   11.F   12.C   13.E

Reading - Passage 2
14.B   15.A   16.E   17.E   18.B   19.B   20.D   21.C   22.C
23.NG   24.YES   25.NO   26.NG

Reading - Passage 3
27-29. A, F, H   30.A   31.C   32.T   33.NG   34.F   35.T
36. industry   37. response   38. adult supervision
39. (physically) aggressive   40. personality

TEST 7
Listening - Section 1
1.C   2.A   3.C
4. flights   5. (hotel) accommodation   6. breakfast (every morning)
7. theatre tickets   8. jonathon.presley@sainsbury.com
9. 6676 6654 9743 1251   10. £31,234

Listening - Section 2
11.A   12.C
13. 1957   14. 46   15. multiple championship   16. Monaco
17. naturally gifted   18. highest   19. great rival   20. greatest driver

Listening - Section 3
21. leader   22. £500,000   23. strategy   24. projected profits
25. takeover (bid)   26. high risk   27. board meeting
28-30. A, B, E

Listening - Section 4
31. amount / volume   32. 65%   33. attic
34. grants/financial aid   35. (the/your) interior   36. absorb
37. £25   38. curtains/blinds   39. solar panels   40. waste

Reading - Passage 1
1.vi   2.ii   3.vii   4.v   5.viii
6.C   7.D   8.B   9.E
10.F   11.NG   12.T   13.T

Reading - Passage 2
14.A   15.D   16.A   17.C   18.C   19.A   20.B
21. tolerance   22. processes   23. fur
24. preserver   25. conductor   26. metabolic

Reading - Passage 3
27.A   28.A   29.C   30.B   31.D
32.T   33.F   34.NG
35.ii   36.viii   37.ix   38.vi   39.iii   40.i

TEST 8

Listening - Section 1
1.B   2.B   3.A
4. Mixed Salad   5. Greek Salad   6. bread (with) herbs
7. cheese with peppers   8. 27th August   9. 15 (fifteen)
10. david.hamill@worthing

Listening - Section 2
11.C   12.A
13. 1956   14. Eleven   15. the same year
16. Six   17. 17 years 7   18. Fourteen
19. 1970   20. tournament

Listening - Section 3
21.workshops   22. well-respected   23. seminars   24. genetics
25. newsletter   26. Flying Fish   27. Wednesday 6th June
28-30. D, F, G

Listening - Section 4
31. your weight   32. (wrongly) think   33. five portions
34. protein   35. oily fish   36. muscles   37. appliances
38. 30 minutes   39. structured   40. high physical stresses

Reading - Passage 1
1.B   2.E   3.A   4.D   5.C
6.D   7.C   8.A   9.B
10.YES   11.NG   12.YES   13.NO

Reading - Passage 2
14.C   15.D   16.C   17.A   18.C   19.A   20.B
21. unique   22. middle-class   23. deceptive
24. apply   25. schooling   26. shed

Reading - Passage 3
27.B   28.A   29.D   30.A   31.D
32.YES   33.NO   34.NG
35.v   36.iv   37.ii   38.i   39.vi   40.iii

TEST 9

Listening - Section 1
1. Lafferty   2. Abbeyfield   3. BR8 9P3   4. 1.25   5. 1.20
6. Music albums   7. Stationery   8. £3000
9.B   10.B

Listening - Section 2
11. Gift Shop   12. Art Gallery   13. Main Exhibition Centre
14. 3D Theatre   15. Modern Art Studio
16.B   17.A   18.C   19.A   20.B

Listening - Section 3
21. appliances   22. practical   23. lower arm   24. rehabilitation
25. high-performance athletes   26. £1,500   27. 2   28. 15
29. 5 recovery patients   30. gym members

Listening - Section 4
31.A   32.B   33.B   34.C   35.C
36. visualise   37. apologies
38. body language   39. 25%   40. realistic

Reading - Passage 1
1.B   2.E   3.G
4. rehearsals   5. chemistry   6. airplay   7. appeal
8.D   9.D   10.A   11.C   12.C   13.B

Reading - Passage 2
14.D   15.D   16.D   17.D   18.A   19.C
20-21. B, D   22-23. B, C
24. drowning   25. £100   26. All-inclusive camps

Reading - Passage 3
27. stock market instability   28. real estate
29. hunt for foreclosures   30. mortgage repayments
31. their money   32. bargains/bargain properties
33. borrow too much / over-borrow
34.YES   35.NO   36.YES   37.NO   38.YES   39.NO   40.NG

Succeed in IELTS

9 Practice Tests

The **Self-study** Guide includes:

- a Writing Supplement with **model Compositions** marked according to IELTS guidelines
- detailed **JUSTIFICATION** of the Answers for **all** the key parts of each practice test
- Audioscripts & Key

Published by GLOBAL ELT LTD
www.globalelt.co.uk
Copyright © **GLOBAL ELT LTD, 2011**

Every effort has been made to trace the copyright holders and we apologize in advance for any unintentional omission. We will be happy to insert the appropriate acknowledgements in any subsequent editions.

British Library Cataloguing-in-Publication Data

A catalogue record of this book is available from the British Library.

Succeed in IELTS - Self-Study Guide - ISBN: 978-1-904663-36-2

TASK TYPES: (2) MULTIPLE CHOICE

Remember...

1. The questions will follow the order of the recording.
2. You will be told either to choose ONE option from A, B and C, or TWO options from A, B, C, D and E.
3. Always read the questions before you start. This will give you an idea of what the recording is about and what to listen for.
4. Listen carefully to the narrator's introduction to find out what the recording is about.
5. As soon as you've finished one question, listen out for the answer to the next (do not dwell on questions you aren't sure of as you only hear the recording once; quickly move on or risk missing another answer).

EXAMPLE: TEST 3 - SECTION 2

Read the instructions carefully to see whether you have to select one or two of the options. The most common MCQ question is the select-one-option type.

Although the questions will be in the order they appear on the recording, the options, A, B and C, will not necessarily be in the order they are heard.

As with all tasks, do not always expect the questions to be worded in the exact same way as the information on the recording. Often, the correct answer will be paraphrased.

SECTION 2   *Questions 11 - 20*

Questions 11 - 17
Choose the correct letter, A, B or C.

11   The speaker's job requires
   A   a great deal of walking.
   B   extensive travel.
   C   clean water.

12   Why is this story being told?
   A   to promote Charity-Water
   B   for entertainment purposes
   C   to encourage Helen

15   Helen is feeling
   A   ecstatic about her new life.
   B   curious about the charity workers.
   C   nostalgic about her old life.

16   What did the speaker notice about Helen?
   A   that she had bathed recently
   B   the care she took with her appearance
   C   that she was wearing a green uniform

TASK TYPES: (3) FORM COMPLETION

N.B. Form completion tasks are very similar to note completion exercises.

EXAMPLE: TEST 3 - SECTION 1

You don't have to write the same number of words in each space; you can write up to the maximum number of words allowed, so, in this case, one, two or three.

The importance of not going over the word limit cannot be stressed enough. If you write too many words you will not receive any marks for that question.

Do not expect the information around the gap to appear in exactly the way it is heard on the recording; it may be paraphrased, or the word order may be modified. However, the missing word(s) itself will always be found on listening to the recording.

Look how we can predict what type of word to write:
5 = noun
6 = number
7 = noun

Remember that your spelling must be accurate. For names, places etc. you will hear the missing word(s) spelt on the recording.

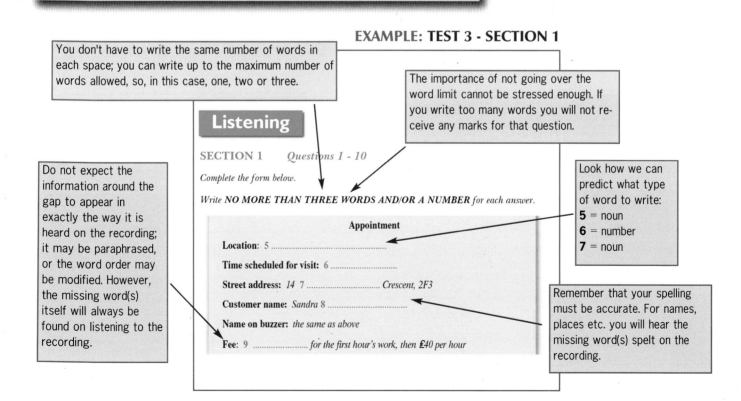

Listening

SECTION 1   *Questions 1 - 10*

Complete the form below.

*Write **NO MORE THAN THREE WORDS AND/OR A NUMBER** for each answer.*

Appointment

Location: 5 ....

Time scheduled for visit: 6 ....

Street address: *14* 7 .... *Crescent, 2F3*

Customer name: *Sandra* 8 ....

Name on buzzer: *the same as above*

Fee: 9 .... *for the first hour's work, then £40 per hour*

TASK TYPES: (4) TABLE COMPLETION

N.B. Table completion tasks are very similar to note completion exercises.

EXAMPLE: TEST 5 - SECTION 3

You will hear the exact word you need to write, though the information around it may be phrased differently.

The questions are in the same order as the information on the recording, so, if they go across the table row-by-row, then the information on the recording follows in the same way, with each row being discussed in turn. If they go down column-by-column, then the recording will discuss each column in turn.

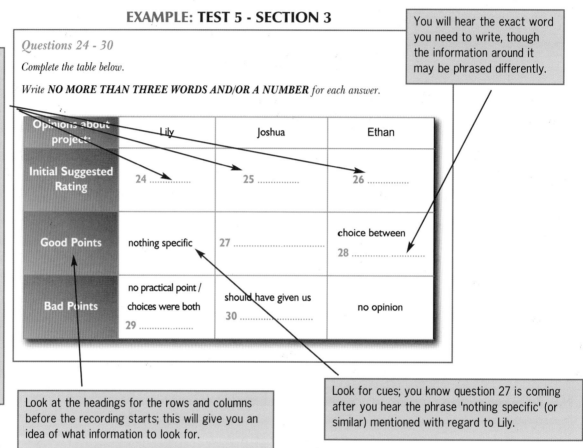

Questions 24 - 30

Complete the table below.

Write **NO MORE THAN THREE WORDS AND/OR A NUMBER** *for each answer.*

Opinions about project:	Lily	Joshua	Ethan
Initial Suggested Rating	24	25	26 ....
Good Points	nothing specific	27	choice between 28 ....
Bad Points	no practical point / choices were both 29	should have given us 30	no opinion

Look at the headings for the rows and columns before the recording starts; this will give you an idea of what information to look for.

Look for cues; you know question 27 is coming after you hear the phrase 'nothing specific' (or similar) mentioned with regard to Lily.

TASK TYPES: (5) FLOW-CHART COMPLETION

Remember...

1. Flow-charts require you to follow the development of a discussion.
2. The steps in the flow-chart will be in the same order as what you hear.
3. Listen carefully to the part of the discussion to which the task relates because you will only hear it once.
4. There are two types of flow-chart task; A and B (see below). A requires you to choose an option (A, B, C etc.) from the box to complete each space. B requires you to write the exact word(s) you hear in the space.

EXAMPLE (TYPE A) TEST 4 - SECTION 3

Look for cues; the answer to question 26 will come shortly after you hear 'laboratory supervisor reviews the application' (or similar).

There will usually be more options than there are spaces, so there are some options you will not need. Do not use any option more than once.

The questions are in the order that you will hear them, so follow the flow-chart in the direction the questions lead you.

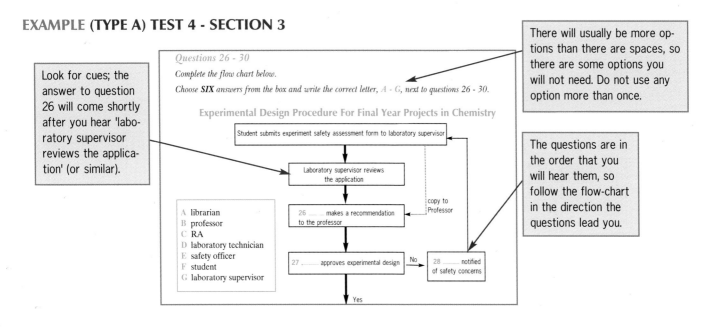

Questions 26 - 30

Complete the flow chart below.

Choose **SIX** answers from the box and write the correct letter, A - G, next to questions 26 - 30.

Experimental Design Procedure For Final Year Projects in Chemistry

Student submits experiment safety assessment form to laboratory supervisor

Laboratory supervisor reviews the application

26 .... makes a recommendation to the professor — copy to Professor

A librarian
B professor
C RA
D laboratory technician
E safety officer
F student
G laboratory supervisor

27 .... approves experimental design — No → 28 .... notified of safety concerns

Yes

EXAMPLE (TYPE B) TEST 5 - SECTION 4

Type B flow-charts are very similar to note completion exercises. Make sure that you always read the instructions and remember the word limit.

Always look for cues to listen out for. Here, obvious ones include 'Stage 2' and 'Features'. After you hear these phrases, you should listen carefully for the answer to question 35.

Remember, you should write down the exact word you hear - and spelling is very important, too. Expect the information around the missing word(s) to be paraphrased; similar in meaning but not exactly the same as what you hear on the recording.

Read the title and the information in the flow-chart itself carefully in the time allowed; this will give you some idea of the subject matter.

Flow-charts can be laid out in either a horizontal or vertical direction, or, in some cases, a combination of both. So as not to get confused, simply follow the questions, which you will always hear in the correct order.

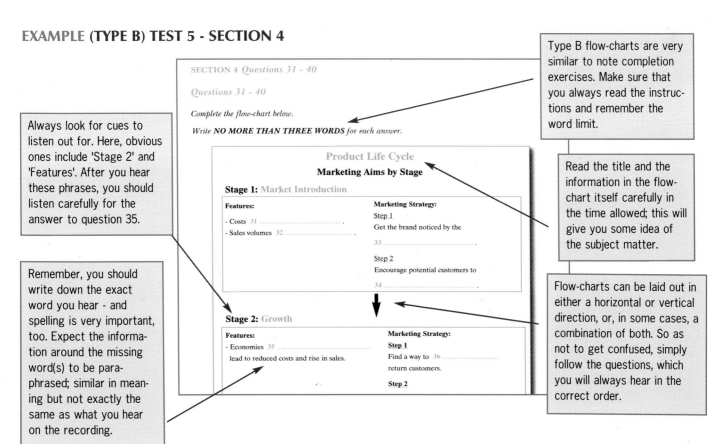

SECTION 4 Questions 31 - 40

Questions 31 - 40

Complete the flow-chart below.

Write **NO MORE THAN THREE WORDS** for each answer.

Product Life Cycle

Marketing Aims by Stage

Stage 1: Market Introduction

Features:
- Costs 31 ....
- Sales volumes 32 ....

Marketing Strategy:
Step 1
Get the brand noticed by the

33 ....

Step 2
Encourage potential customers to

34 ....

Stage 2: Growth

Features:
- Economies 35 ....
  lead to reduced costs and rise in sales.

Marketing Strategy:
Step 1
Find a way to 36 ....
return customers.

Step 2

TASK TYPES: (6) DIAGRAM LABELLING

Remember...

1. You will have to transfer the information you hear to a simple picture or plan of some kind.
2. You will need to be familiar with the kind of language used to express where things are.
3. Listen carefully to the part of the discussion to which this task relates because you will only hear it once.
4. There are three types of diagram labelling tasks. See below for details.

EXAMPLE (TYPE A) TEST 2 - SECTION 2

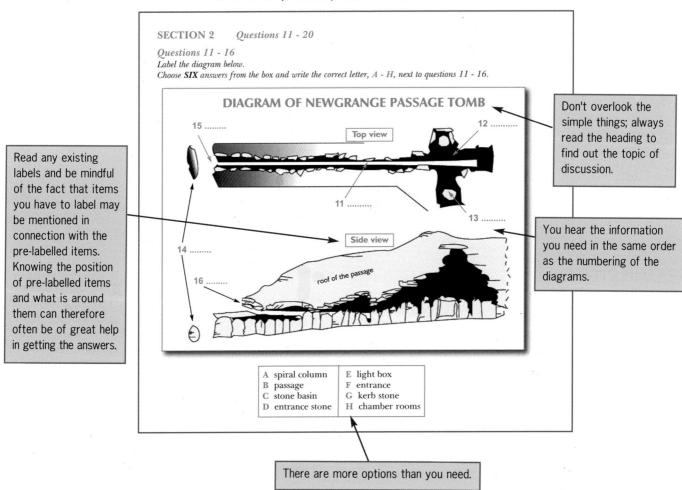

SECTION 2   Questions 11 - 20

Questions 11 - 16
Label the diagram below.
Choose **SIX** answers from the box and write the correct letter, A - H, next to questions 11 - 16.

DIAGRAM OF NEWGRANGE PASSAGE TOMB

Top view

Side view

roof of the passage

15 ....
12 ....
11 ....
13 ....
14 ....
16 ....

A spiral column
B passage
C stone basin
D entrance stone
E light box
F entrance
G kerb stone
H chamber rooms

Don't overlook the simple things; always read the heading to find out the topic of discussion.

Read any existing labels and be mindful of the fact that items you have to label may be mentioned in connection with the pre-labelled items. Knowing the position of pre-labelled items and what is around them can therefore often be of great help in getting the answers.

You hear the information you need in the same order as the numbering of the diagrams.

There are more options than you need.

EXAMPLE (Type B) TEST 1 - SECTION 2

Questions 16 - 20

Label the floor plan below.
Write the correct letter A - G next to the questions below.

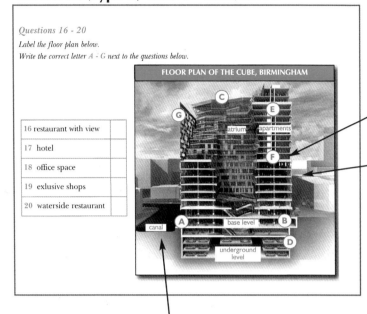

FLOOR PLAN OF THE CUBE, BIRMINGHAM

16 restaurant with view	
17 hotel	
18 office space	
19 exlusive shops	
20 waterside restaurant	

The letters A-G are not in the order they will be discussed in the recording.
The information in the recording will follow the same order as questions 16-20.

Not all the letters will be used.

As always, listen out for cues and use them to help you locate the items you are looking for. Areas such as the rooftop, canal and atrium are great reference points.

EXAMPLE (Type C) TEST 6 - SECTION 2

Questions 16 - 20

*Label the diagram below. Write **NO MORE THAN TWO WORDS** for each answer.*

The third type of diagram labelling is similar to note completion. Listen out for the exact word(s) you need, adhere to the word limit for each space and ensure that you spell your answers correctly.

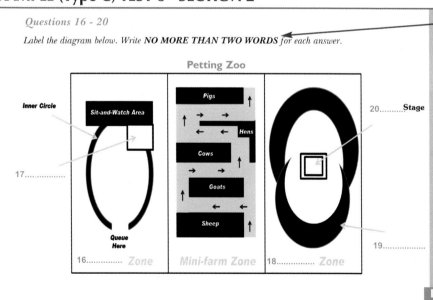

Petting Zoo

141

TASK TYPES: (7) MAP LABELLING

N. B. Map labelling is very similar to diagram labelling. There are three types of map questions and they follow the format of types A, B and C above.

Remember...
1. Read the instructions so you know what to write (e.g. a word or letter).
2. Look at the map and try to understand what it shows and how each location might be described.
3. Use the places already marked on the map to help you follow the recording.

EXAMPLE (MAP 1) TEST 6 - SECTION 2

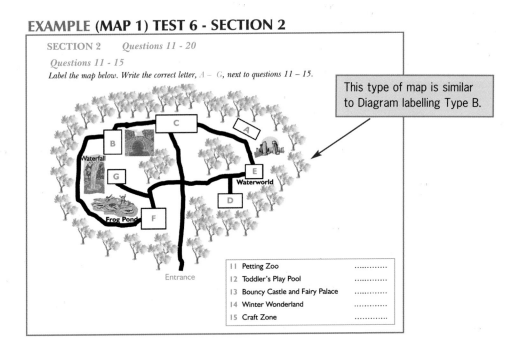

This type of map is similar to Diagram labelling Type B.

EXAMPLE (MAP 2) TEST 9 - SECTION 2

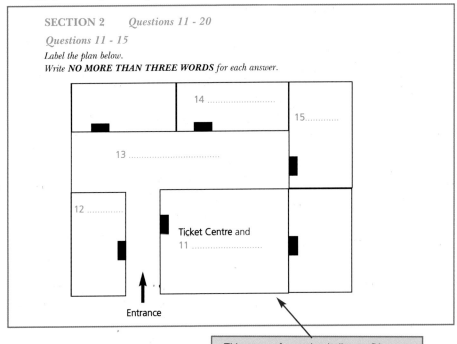

This type of map is similar to Diagram labelling Type C.

TASK TYPES: (8) MATCHING

Remember...
1. Matching requires you to listen to detailed information and connect it to a number of places, people, groups etc.
2. You will only hear the part of the recording related to the matching task ONCE.
3. Match ONE piece of information from the box to each question.

EXAMPLE (Type 1) TEST 9 - SECTION 2

In this matching task you can choose the options more than once.

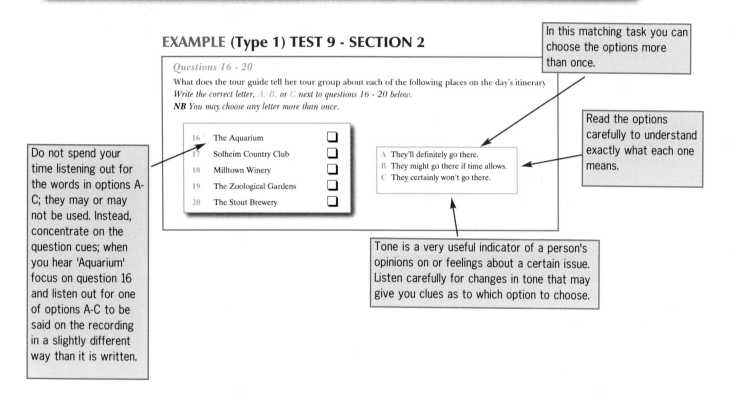

Questions 16 - 20

What does the tour guide tell her tour group about each of the following places on the day's itinerary
Write the correct letter, A, B, or C next to questions 16 - 20 below.
NB *You may choose any letter more than once.*

16	The Aquarium	☐
17	Solheim Country Club	☐
18	Milltown Winery	☐
19	The Zoological Gardens	☐
20	The Stout Brewery	☐

A They'll definitely go there.
B They might go there if time allows.
C They certainly won't go there.

Do not spend your time listening out for the words in options A-C; they may or may not be used. Instead, concentrate on the question cues; when you hear 'Aquarium' focus on question 16 and listen out for one of options A-C to be said on the recording in a slightly different way than it is written.

Read the options carefully to understand exactly what each one means.

Tone is a very useful indicator of a person's opinions on or feelings about a certain issue. Listen carefully for changes in tone that may give you clues as to which option to choose.

EXAMPLE (Type 2) TEST 5 - SECTION 3

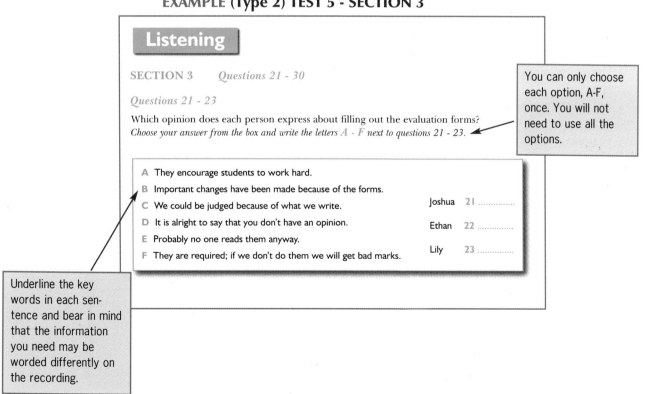

Listening

SECTION 3   *Questions 21 - 30*

Questions 21 - 23

Which opinion does each person express about filling out the evaluation forms?
Choose your answer from the box and write the letters A - F next to questions 21 - 23.

A They encourage students to work hard.
B Important changes have been made because of the forms.
C We could be judged because of what we write.
D It is alright to say that you don't have an opinion.
E Probably no one reads them anyway.
F They are required; if we don't do them we will get bad marks.

Joshua 21 ....
Ethan   22 ....
Lily   23 ....

You can only choose each option, A-F, once. You will not need to use all the options.

Underline the key words in each sentence and bear in mind that the information you need may be worded differently on the recording.

TASK TYPES: (9) SENTENCE COMPLETION

N.B. Sentence completion is similar to note completion.

EXAMPLE: TEST 9 - SECTION 3

SECTION 3   *Questions 21 - 30*

Questions 21 - 25

Complete the sentences below.
*Write **NO MORE THAN TWO WORDS** for each answer.*

> Gyroscopes are used in laser devices and are found in many consumer 21 ....
>
> The purpose of the project is to design a functional, 22 .... and beneficial consumer product.
>
> The gyroscopic exercise ball can be set in motion by movement of the 23 .... and wrist together in synch.
>
> The gyroscopic ball could help people in 24 .... who have lower-arm injuries.
>
> The product could also be aimed at 25 .... for whom lower-arm strength is very important.

Note that for all 'completion' tasks, hyphenated words are counted as one word and contracted words are never tested.

As with all 'completion' tasks, adhere to the word limit for each space.

Identify the key words to listen out for, e.g. 'consumer' and 'laser devices' in question 21. Use these as your cues to tell you when to get ready to hear the answer. Try to pick key words that aren't easily paraphrased (e.g. laser devices) or just think of key concepts, e.g. the concept of movement or motion for question 23.

General Listening Tips

- The listening paper lasts 30 minutes.

- You will be given ten minutes at the end to transfer your answers to your answer sheet.

- The paper is common to both the academic and general modules of the IELTS.

- The level of difficulty increases from Section 1 to Section 4.

- Each section is heard ONCE only.

- The instructions for each task are written on the paper.

- There is a short pause before each section and a short pause before each separate task.

- A brief introduction is heard before each section, outlining the context of the recording. This introduction is not written on the paper itself.

- Correct spelling is absolutely essential.

IELTS

READING SECTION

EXAM GUIDE

This section contains a detailed analysis of the **Reading** section of the exam with Exam Tips and Guidance for all the different Reading tasks that students will encounter taking the IELTS exam, with reference to the tasks included in the Practice Tests.

Reading Section Format

Passage	No. of Questions	Text Type	Task Types
1	13 (2 or 3 tasks)	Texts may be sourced from books, journals, magazines, newspapers or websites. They are suitable for undergraduate and postgraduate level reading, but are general-interest not specialist-interest.	multiple choice matching short-answer choosing True/False/Not given
2	13 (2 or 3 tasks)		choosing Yes/No/Not given diagram labelling summary completion sentence completion
3	14 (2 or 3 tasks)		note/table/flow-chart completion locating information

Time: **60 minutes** (including time to transfer your answers onto the answer sheet)

Marking: **1 mark for each correct answer.**

READING PASSAGE 1

is...
- a text of up to 900 words (usually factual or descriptive)
- made up of two or three tasks and 13 questions in total
- usually slightly easier than passages 2 and 3

tests...
- your understanding of texts which could be included in an academic course
- your ability to follow an argument and/or opinions and/or a series of facts or ideas
- a range of reading skills including **reading for main ideas** and **reading for detail**, as well as understanding the structure of a text at both sentence and paragraph level

READING PASSAGE 2

is...
- a text of up to 900 words
- made up of two or three different tasks and 13 or 14 questions in total
- usually slightly harder than passage 1

for what it tests refer to Passage 1 guidelines

READING PASSAGE 3

is...
- a text of up to 950 words (so can be slightly longer than 1 and 2)
- made up of two or three different tasks and 13 or 14 questions in total
- usually more difficult than passages 1 and 2

for what it tests refer to Passage 1 guidelines

READING TIPS

- there are **40 questions** in total on the reading paper
- no one passage will have more than **14 questions** attached to it
- only answers found in or inferred from the information in the texts are correct; you are not required to use your background knowledge
- attempt all questions; you have nothing to lose by guessing

TASK TYPE: (1) TRUE/FALSE/NOT GIVEN

Task: Compare the information given in each statement with the information found in the text to decide whether or not the information is the same in both.

You must...

1. Read the statements carefully (they will be in the same order as the information in the passage).
2. Scan the text to find the information you need (and read the section carefully if necessary).
3. Decide if the idea expressed in each statement agrees with the text (TRUE) or contradicts the text (FALSE), or, if there is no information about the statement in the text (NOT GIVEN).

EXAMPLE: TEST I - PASSAGE I

Do the following statements agree with the information given in Reading Passage 1?

In spaces 8 - 13 below write

> There is always at least one TRUE, one FALSE and one NOT GIVEN answer in the question set.

TRUE	*if the statement agrees with the information*
FALSE	*if the statement contradicts the information*
NOT GIVEN	*if there is no information on this*

Look at each question in turn and underline the important words. Then scan the text to find the section which mentions the information you need. Read this section carefully.

8   People from <u>underdeveloped nations</u> try to attain the same <u>standard of living</u> as those from <u>developed nations.</u>   ....

9   Seeing what others have makes people want to have it too.   ....

10   The larger the family is, the happier the parents will probably be.   ....

11   One's attitude to life has no influence on one's health.   ....

12   Instinct can be a barrier to happiness.   ....

13   <u>Family and friends</u> rank equally as sources of happiness.   ....

Do not expect the statements to appear in the exact same way in the passage; the information you need will often be reworded or paraphrased. To help you locate where it is, choose words from the statements that are unlikely to have been changed i.e. in the case of question 13 *family and friends*.

Note:

- Remember the questions are in the order the information appears in the text. If you have found 8 and 10, but cannot find the answer to 9, you can therefore narrow your search down to the text between where you found those answers.

- The information you need to find will not necessarily be evenly spaced in the passage. There may even be some paragraphs which do not relate to the questions.

- Always look at the title and the information in the opening few lines of the text before you do anything else. This will give you an idea of what the text might be about.

- Next, read the text quickly (gist-read) in order to get a general understanding of what is being discussed.

TASK TYPE: (2) YES/NO/NOT GIVEN

Task: Compare the information given in each statement with the information found in the text to decide whether or not the information is the same in both. You have to be able to understand the different opinions, ideas and/or attitudes expressed.

You must...

1. Read the statements carefully (they will be in the same order as the information in the passage).
2. Scan the text to find the information you need (and read the relevant section carefully if necessary).
3. Decide if the ideas expressed in each statement agree with the opinions/ideas of the writer (YES) or contradict them (NO), or, if there is no information about the opinion/idea in the text (NOT GIVEN).

> Read the instructions very carefully. Here it talks about the claims in the article generally. If it said 'do the following statements agree with the writer's views?', then it would only be the writer's views you should concern yourself with, even if other views are mentioned in the text.

EXAMPLE: TEST 9 - PASSAGE 3

Questions 34 - 40

Do the following statements agree with the information given in Reading Passage 3?
In spaces 154 - 40 below, write

YES	*if the statement agrees with the information*
NO	*if the statement contradicts the information*
NOT GIVEN	*if there is no information on this*

> This task-type is very similar to Type 1.
> Remember all three options: YES, NO and NO GIVEN, must be used at least once.

> Underline the key word(s) in the statements and scan the passage for them. Be mindful of the fact that the passage may not contain the exact word(s) you are looking for, but a synonym instead.

34	Banks demand larger deposits from first-time property investors.	_____
35	By making a larger deposit, investors can limit their personal financial risk.	_____
36	There are a lot of long-term costs to take into consideration before purchasing a rental property.	_____
37	Banks require you to hold a lot of money in reserve to meet your long-term property maintenance costs.	_____
38	Many investors are tempted to pay more than they should for their investment properties.	_____
39	At the moment, house prices are extremely high in general.	_____
40	There are a lot of urban renewal projects that have been earmarked by the government.	_____

TASK TYPE: (3) DIAGRAM LABELLING

Task: To understand a detailed description, and relate it to information in a diagram. The section of the passage related to the diagram will often be concerned with a process or a description of something.

You must...
1. Scan the text to find specific information.
2. Find the word(s) or number in the text which fits each space and copy it into the gap.

EXAMPLE: TEST 3 - PASSAGE 1

Looking at the heading of the diagram may help you determine the section of the passage to focus on in order to find the answers.

Pay close attention to the word limit and do not exceed it. Here, you can write one, two or three words in each space, whichever is correct.

Examine each space carefully to determine what kind of word is missing i.e. a noun /adjective etc.

Ensure that the answer you write in each space is spelt correctly; otherwise you will lose marks.

The notes in the diagram may use synonyms of the words in the passage rather than the same ones; therefore, look out for words of a similar meaning as well as exact matches.

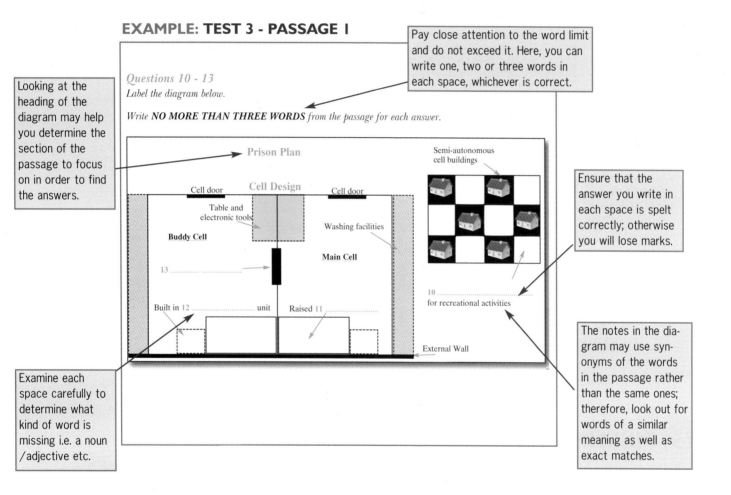

Questions 10 - 13
Label the diagram below.

*Write **NO MORE THAN THREE WORDS** from the passage for each answer.*

Prison Plan

Cell Design

Cell door   Cell door

Table and electronic tools

Buddy Cell

Washing facilities

Main Cell

13 ....

Built in 12 .... unit   Raised 11 ....

External Wall

Semi-autonomous cell buildings

10 ....
for recreational activities

Note:
You must use words copied directly from the passage. The form of the words copied should not be altered. The information in the diagram will not always be numbered/displayed in the same order as it is written about in the passage.

TASK TYPE: (4) MULTIPLE CHOICE 1

Task: To develop a general and detailed understanding of the text.

You must...

1. Read questions or incomplete sentences which focus on ideas and information in the text.
2. Choose the correct option A, B, C or D to answer the question or complete the statement.

EXAMPLE: TEST 6 - PASSAGE 2

In four-option multiple choice questions, there will never be more than one correct option.

Note:
The questions may relate to a small part of the passage, a large section or, occasionally, questions may refer to the passage as a whole.

Questions 19 - 22

Choose the correct letter A, B, C or D.

19 One purpose of the summer school is to

   A encourage students to work individually.
   B enable students to be assessed directly.
   C allow students to undertake simple experiments.
   D familiarise students with laboratory equipment.

Multiple choice questions do follow the order of the text, so the answer to 20 will come before 21.

20 Instructional designers advise faculty on the

   A course content.
   B support services for students.
   C suitability of library material.
   D visual display of coursework.

Careful! Often the incorrect options will use similar words to those in the text to act as a distraction and focus your attention away from the correct answer.

21 Staff tutors are responsible for the

   A monitoring of students' progress.
   B suitability of courses for students' needs.
   C appointment of certain teaching staff.
   D training of all teaching staff.

Make sure you read far enough to cover all four options; then you can make an informed decision as to the right answer.

TASK TYPE:
(5) MULTIPLE CHOICE 2

Multiple choice 2 - select more than one option

EXAMPLE: TEST 9 - PASSAGE 2

1 always read the instructions for every question very carefully

2 don't assume because it is multiple choice that you only have to select one answer

3 for multiple choice questions containing MORE THAN FOUR OPTIONS you will be required to select AT LEAST TWO of them

Questions 20 - 21

*Choose **TWO** letters, A - E.*

Which **TWO** of the following are hazards that surfers face?

   A being held underwater by reefs.
   B the potential for shark attacks.
   C frequent encounters with jellyfish.
   D demanding water conditions.
   E hazardous rescue attempts.

TASK TYPE: (6) MATCHING SENTENCE ENDINGS

Task: To understand a number of significant ideas expressed in the text.

You must...

1. Read the first halves of the sentences.
2. Choose the ending for each half sentence from a number of options so that the complete sentence correctly reflects an idea or opinion that is expressed in the passage.

EXAMPLE: TEST 4 - PASSAGE 2

Questions 14 - 20

Complete each sentence with the correct ending A - K from the box below.

Write the correct letter A - K in spaces 14 - 20 below.

The questions are laid out in the order the information appears in the text.

14   Colour blindness can be caused by a birth defect, or   ....
15   Surprisingly, some people who are colour blind   ....
16   People with hereditary colour blindness   ....
17   Because of our genetic make-up, colour blindness   ....
18   Red-green genetic photoreceptor disorders mean that people ....
19   People with monochromacy   ....
20   The inability to see certain lights   ....

Look out for words/ideas that are hard to rephrase, and scan for these in the text.

Make sure that the option you select for the gap fits grammatically (i.e. the sentence makes sense), as well as reflecting the information expressed in the text.

A   can see better at night than during the day.
B   cannot be treated by surgery.
C   can affect men much more easily than women.
D   can affect their sensitivity to bright lights.
E   can see no colour at all, other than shades of black, grey and white.
F   can see things that people with normal vision cannot.
G   can have very dangerous consequences for colour blind people.
H   can be acquired or inherited.
I   can mean having to wear contact lenses.
J   cannot distinguish certain colours if they stand alone.
K   can match all colours of the spectrum.

There are always more options than needed.
Read carefully as some may have similar meanings but differ on important points.

Note:
As always, start by reading the passage for gist (to get a general idea of what it is about). Then look at the questions, underline the key words and scan for where they appear in the text. Read the section around the key words carefully.

23

TASK TYPE: (7) SENTENCE COMPLETION

Task: To understand key points in the text.

You must...

1. Read each sentence and identify where in the text the information to fill the gap is located.
2. Complete each gap by choosing a word or words from the text.

REMEMBER, FOR ALL COMPLETION EXERCISES...

1 there is a maximum number of words you can use to fill each gap, which is stated in the instructions

2 the information is not necessarily displayed in the order that it appears in the passage

3 you must copy the words from the text exactly as they appear - do not alter their form

EXAMPLE: TEST 5 - PASSAGE 2

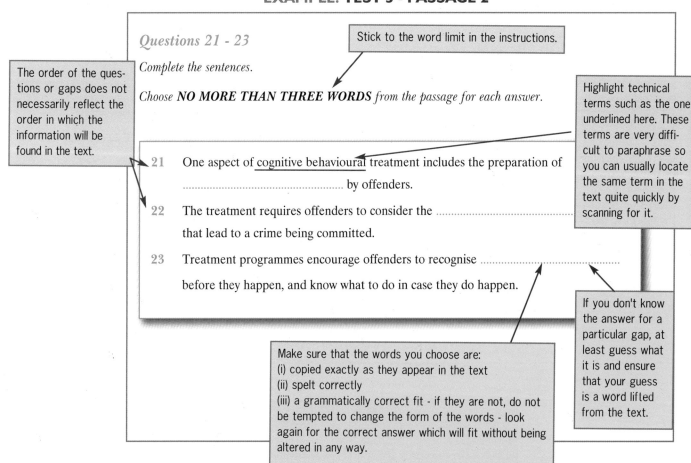

The order of the questions or gaps does not necessarily reflect the order in which the information will be found in the text.

Stick to the word limit in the instructions.

Questions 21 - 23

Complete the sentences.

Choose **NO MORE THAN THREE WORDS** *from the passage for each answer.*

Highlight technical terms such as the one underlined here. These terms are very difficult to paraphrase so you can usually locate the same term in the text quite quickly by scanning for it.

21 One aspect of <u>cognitive behavioural</u> treatment includes the preparation of .... by offenders.

22 The treatment requires offenders to consider the .... that lead to a crime being committed.

23 Treatment programmes encourage offenders to recognise .... before they happen, and know what to do in case they do happen.

Make sure that the words you choose are:
(i) copied exactly as they appear in the text
(ii) spelt correctly
(iii) a grammatically correct fit - if they are not, do not be tempted to change the form of the words - look again for the correct answer which will fit without being altered in any way.

If you don't know the answer for a particular gap, at least guess what it is and ensure that your guess is a word lifted from the text.

TASK TYPE: (8) NOTE COMPLETION

EXAMPLE: TEST 5 - PASSAGE 2

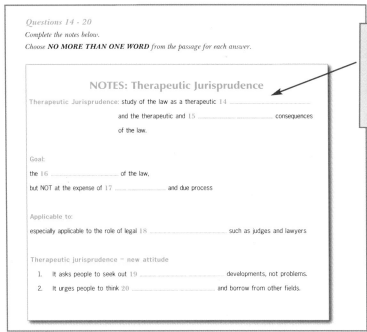

Questions 14 - 20
Complete the notes below.
*Choose **NO MORE THAN ONE WORD** from the passage for each answer.*

NOTES: Therapeutic Jurisprudence

Therapeutic Jurisprudence: study of the law as a therapeutic 14 ....
and the therapeutic and 15 .... consequences
of the law.

Goal:
the 16 .... of the law,
but NOT at the expense of 17 .... and due process

Applicable to:
especially applicable to the role of legal 18 .... such as judges and lawyers

Therapeutic jurisprudence = new attitude
1. It asks people to seek out 19 .... developments, not problems.
2. It urges people to think 20 .... and borrow from other fields.

If a note / table completion or summary type task is the first type of task you must answer for a given passage, it may be helpful to skim over the information in the notes/table/summary before reading the passage as this will give you a good idea of what the passage is about.

NOTE
- all completion tasks are similar: sentence/note/flow-chart/table

- but for note, flow-chart and table completion you must understand a whole section(s) of the text not just key points

TASK TYPE: (9) FLOW-CHART COMPLETION

Task: To understand the description of a process or sequence of events.
You must...

1. Scan the text to find specific information using the key words in the flow-chart to help you locate where the relevant information is in the passage.
2. Find the word(s) or number in the text which fits each space and copy it into the gap.

EXAMPLE: TEST 1 - PASSAGE 3

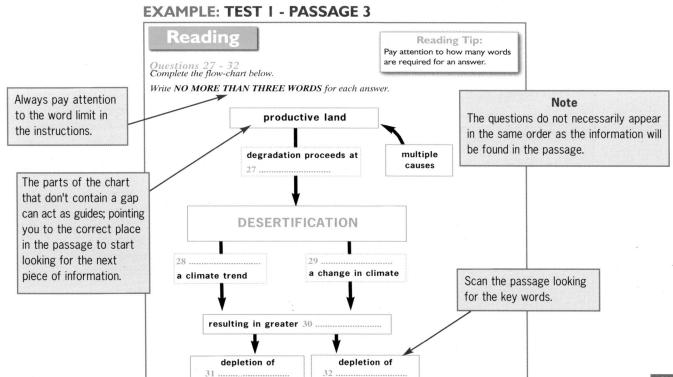

Reading

Reading Tip:
Pay attention to how many words are required for an answer.

Questions 27 - 32
Complete the flow-chart below.
*Write **NO MORE THAN THREE WORDS** for each answer.*

Always pay attention to the word limit in the instructions.

Note
The questions do not necessarily appear in the same order as the information will be found in the passage.

The parts of the chart that don't contain a gap can act as guides; pointing you to the correct place in the passage to start looking for the next piece of information.

Scan the passage looking for the key words.

productive land

degradation proceeds at
27 ....

multiple causes

DESERTIFICATION

28 ....
a climate trend

29 ....
a change in climate

resulting in greater 30 ....

depletion of
31 ....

depletion of
32 ....

TASK TYPE: (10) SUMMARY COMPLETION

Task: To understand the main points of part (or occasionally all) of the text.

You must...

1. Locate the parts of the text to which the summary refers and find the answers to the questions.

> There is another type of **SUMMARY COMPLETION** that does not require you to write words in the gaps; this is outlined below:

EXAMPLE: **TEST 5 - PASSAGE 3**

> **Note:**
> Be aware that the answers might **NOT** be in the same order as they appear in the text. However, the correct answers will be the **exact words** that you find in the text.

Questions 36 - 40

Complete the summary.
*Choose **NO MORE THAN TWO WORDS** from the passage for each answer.*

> Try to predict from context what part of speech the missing word is: e.g. Question **37** must be a noun because of the article 'the' that precedes it.

Sleep is so essential to a person that he can actually go longer without food than without sleep. During sleep, the brain has the chance to close down and do some repair work on neuronal connections which could otherwise 36 .... in a state of inactivity. Sleep also gives the brain the opportunity to organise data, especially newly-learned information.

During this rest period, the 37 .... drops and energy consumption goes down. At the same time, the cardiovascular system has a much-needed rest. While they go into a deep sleep, humans don't fall into 38................................. , unlike some small animals such as rodents. A 39 .... of 24 hours is described as a person's 40 .... , and this greatly influences a person's amount of sleep, and the type of sleep he gets.

TASK TYPE: (11) SUMMARY COMPLETION 2

EXAMPLE: **TEST 1 - PASSAGE 1**

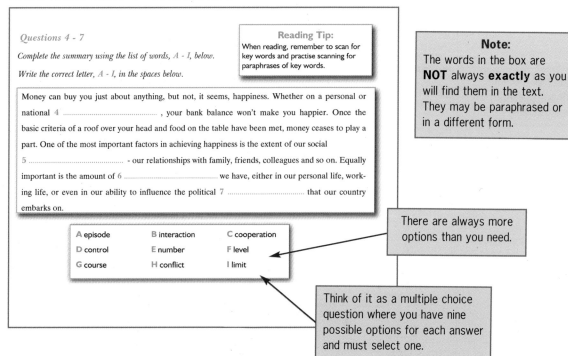

Questions 4 - 7

Complete the summary using the list of words, A - I, below.

Write the correct letter, A - I, in the spaces below.

> **Reading Tip:**
> When reading, remember to scan for key words and practise scanning for paraphrases of key words.

> **Note:**
> The words in the box are **NOT** always **exactly** as you will find them in the text. They may be paraphrased or in a different form.

Money can buy you just about anything, but not, it seems, happiness. Whether on a personal or national 4 .... , your bank balance won't make you happier. Once the basic criteria of a roof over your head and food on the table have been met, money ceases to play a part. One of the most important factors in achieving happiness is the extent of our social 5 .... - our relationships with family, friends, colleagues and so on. Equally important is the amount of 6 .... we have, either in our personal life, working life, or even in our ability to influence the political 7 .... that our country embarks on.

A episode	B interaction	C cooperation
D control	E number	F level
G course	H conflict	I limit

> There are always more options than you need.

> Think of it as a multiple choice question where you have nine possible options for each answer and must select one.

TASK TYPE: (12) TABLE COMPLETION

Task: To understand the way the table is laid out and find specific information in the text.

You must...

1. Locate the part of the text where the answer can be found.
2. Find and copy the exact words from the text which correctly fill the gap.

Use the column and row headings to give you a clue for where you should look in the passage to find the missing information.

EXAMPLE: **TEST 2 - PASSAGE I**

Questions 6 - 9

Complete the table below.

*Write **NO MORE THAN THREE WORDS** from the passage for each answer.*

Disorder	Personality Trait Exhibited by Sufferer
Autism Spectrum Disorder	May excel in activities of a 6 .... nature.
Attention Deficit Disorder	May appear 7 ....
Schizophrenia	May respond to experiencing episodes of the disease by behaving in very 8 ....
Depression	May experience feelings of futility that lead to thoughts of 9 ....
Obsessive Compulsive Disorder	May frequently experience feelings of doubt and anxiety.

TASK TYPE: (13) MATCHING

(A) Matching Names

Task: To relate ideas, information or opinions in the text to a number of people, places, dates etc.

You must...

1. Read a list of statements and match them to a list of options by finding the information in the text.
2. Write the letter of the matching statement in the gap for each question.

(B) Matching Headings

Task: To select an appropriate title for some or all of the paragraphs

You must...

1. Read a list of headings and match them to the lettered paragraphs of the original passage.
2. Write the letter of the matching heading in the gap for each question.

EXAMPLE: (TYPE A) **TEST 2 - PASSAGE I**

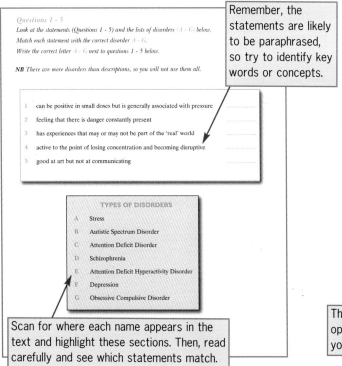

Questions 1 - 5

Look at the statements (Questions 1 - 5) and the lists of disorders (A - G) below.

Match each statement with the correct disorder A - G.

Write the correct letter A - G next to questions 1 - 5 below.

NB *There are more disorders than descriptions, so you will not use them all.*

1	can be positive in small doses but is generally associated with pressure
2	feeling that there is danger constantly present
3	has experiences that may or may not be part of the 'real' world
4	active to the point of losing concentration and becoming disruptive
5	good at art but not at communicating

Remember, the statements are likely to be paraphrased, so try to identify key words or concepts.

TYPES OF DISORDERS

A   Stress
B   Autistic Spectrum Disorder
C   Attention Deficit Disorder
D   Schizophrenia
E   Attention Deficit Hyperactivity Disorder
F   Depression
G   Obsessive Compulsive Disorder

Scan for where each name appears in the text and highlight these sections. Then, read carefully and see which statements match.

EXAMPLE: (TYPE B) **TEST 6 - PASSAGE I**

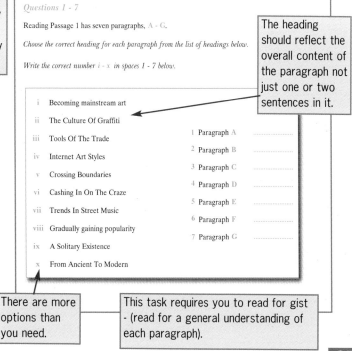

Questions 1 - 7

Reading Passage 1 has seven paragraphs, A - G.

Choose the correct heading for each paragraph from the list of headings below.

Write the correct number i - x in spaces 1 - 7 below.

i	Becoming mainstream art
ii	The Culture Of Graffiti
iii	Tools Of The Trade
iv	Internet Art Styles
v	Crossing Boundaries
vi	Cashing In On The Craze
vii	Trends In Street Music
viii	Gradually gaining popularity
ix	A Solitary Existence
x	From Ancient To Modern

1   Paragraph A   ....
2   Paragraph B   ....
3   Paragraph C   ....
4   Paragraph D   ....
5   Paragraph E   ....
6   Paragraph F   ....
7   Paragraph G   ....

The heading should reflect the overall content of the paragraph not just one or two sentences in it.

There are more options than you need.

This task requires you to read for gist - (read for a general understanding of each paragraph).

TASK TYPE: (14) LOCATING INFORMATION

Task: Scan the passage to find specific information in different paragraphs.

You must...
1. Read a text divided into labelled paragraphs.
2. Read statements which focus on details from individual paragraphs.
3. Find which paragraph contains the information in the statement.

EXAMPLE: TEST 2 - PASSAGE 3

Questions 27 - 31

Reading Passage 3 has eight paragraphs, **A - H.**

Which paragraph contains the following information?

Write the correct letter A - H in spaces 27 - 31 below.

Some sections may contain the answers to more than one question.

27   possible health hazards associated with the use of biometrics   ....

28   convicted criminals were not the first to be identified by the use of biometrics   ....

29   the application of mathematics in assessing biometric data   ....

30   despite its limitations, biometrics has become a commercial field of activity   ....

31   some biometric methods are useful only in conjunction with others   ....

Note:
You should scan the passage for key words/concepts contained in each statement, then read related sections carefully to confirm your answer.

General Reading Tips

1 start each reading section by scanning over the first task (this will give you an idea of what the passage is about)

2 then read the passage for gist (read it to get a general understanding of what is being discussed)

3 finally, adopt the strategy required for each task as outlined in this guide; generally:
(i) scan the passage for key words in the question
(ii) read the section you have identified carefully to confirm the correct answer

IELTS

WRITING SECTION

EXAM GUIDE

This section contains a detailed analysis of the Writing section of the exam with Exam Tips and Guidance with examples from writing tasks included in the Practice Tests.

Writing Section Format

Task	Suggested time and marks	Text type and number of words
1	**20 minutes** one-third of the marks for the writing paper	a summary of the information shown on the graph, chart, table or diagram 150 words minimum
2	**40 minutes** two-thirds of the marks for the writing paper	a discursive essay in response to a statement of opinions or ideas 250 words minimum

TASK 1

is...
- a writing task based on data which is presented in the form of a graph, bar chart or diagram

tests.....
- your ability to write about the information shown in an accurate and concise manner
- your ability to use an appropriate register i.e. formal / neutral
- your ability to write using accurate grammar, spelling and punctuation
- your ability to organise ideas clearly and cohesively

requires you to...
- recognise and select important and relevant data from the graph/chart/diagram
- summarise the data shown in at least 150 words
- plan, write and revise your answer in approximately 20 minutes
- write about the most important parts of the data
- compare and contrast features of the data as appropriate
- draw attention to and interpret any significant or unusual features of the data

TASK 2

is...
- a formal discursive essay

tests...
- how well you can express and evaluate ideas
- whether or not you can use an appropriate style
- your use of grammar and vocabulary, as well as your spelling
- your ability to organise your thoughts into paragraphs which form a cohesive whole

requires you to...
- present arguments in a clear and organised way
- discuss the idea or subject outlined in the task
- write at least 250 words in approximately 40 minutes
- give your opinion and use examples to support it
- conclude your writing with a brief statement making clear your final opinion on the idea/subject being written about

STRATEGY

always...
- read the task (1 or 2 min)
  - highlight the key words in the question
  - try to understand exactly what is being asked
  - make a note of all the points you have to cover in your answer
- [task 1 only] take some time to study the graph/chart/diagram and the kind of data it is presenting (1 min)
- plan your answer (3 or 5 min) and
  - decide what you want to say/put in each paragraph
  - review your work for mistakes at the end (1 min)

TASK ANALYSIS (UNDERSTANDING THE QUESTION)

TASK I WRITING TEST 7

1
Read the first part of the question carefully. It tells you what information is represented on the chart.

2
Identify what you are being asked to do in the question. (For Task 1, this is usually the same three things every time.)
(i) summarise
(ii) report main features
(iii) compare

Writing

WRITING TASK 1
You should spend about 20 minutes on this task.

The chart shows the end of year value for four major international money market indices in 2005, 2006, 2007 and 2008. [FTSE 100 = UK Market Index,   Dow Jones = US Market Index, KOSPI = Korean Market Index,   CAC 40 = French Market Index]

Summarise the information by selecting and reporting the main features, and make comparisons where relevant. **1**   **2**   **3**

Write at least 150 words.

End of Year Index Values

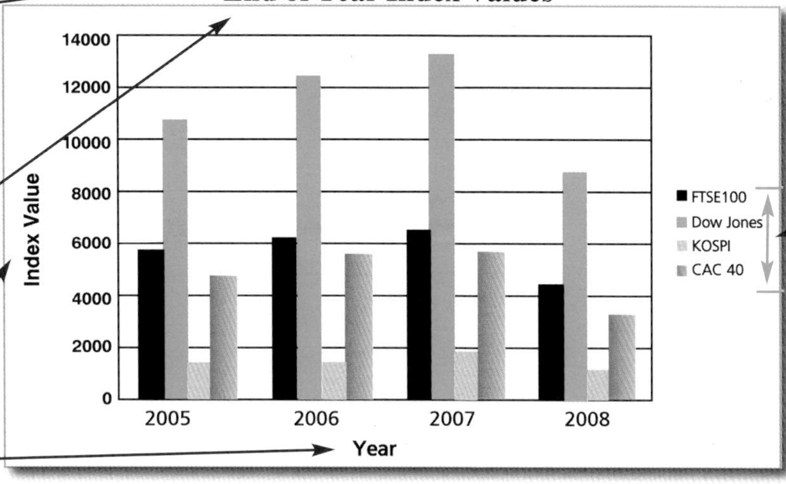

3
Look at the chart itself:
(i) read the main title
(ii) read the axis titles

4
Examine the key (the key tells you what the symbols/shadings/colours represent).

F:
The four indices follow the same overall trend; rising in value from 2005 to 2007, and falling sharply in 2008.

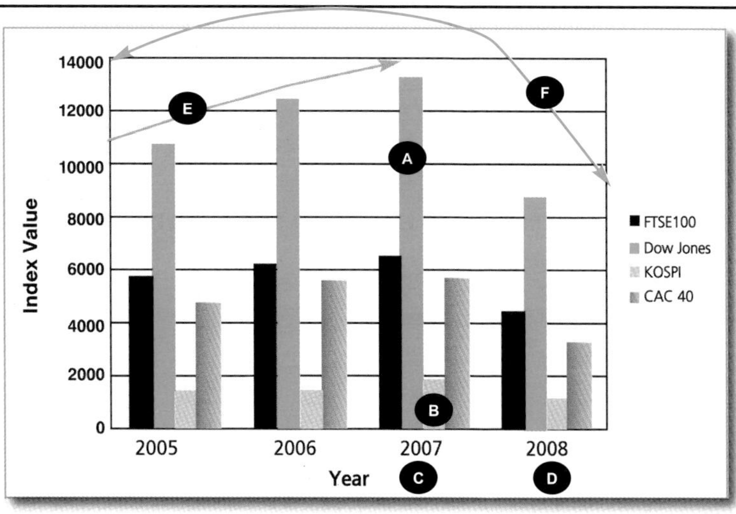

5
Identify the key features by examining the chart more closely.

A:
- The Dow Jones is the consistently highest-valued index.
- Peak value 2007.
- Low 2008.

E:
- From 2005 until 2007, there was an upward trend in the values of the indices.

B:
- The KOSPI is the consistently lowest-valued index.
- same high and low pattern as Dow.

D:
- 2008 was the year in which the four indices had their worst performance.

C:
- 2007 was the year in which all four indices performed best.

F:
The KOSPI is the least volatile index, making the smallest gains and losses.

E:
The Dow Jones is the most volatile index, registering the largest increases and decreases in value.

D:
The KOSPI is by far the lowest-valued index. It is less than half the value of the next-biggest index.

7
Compare the data.

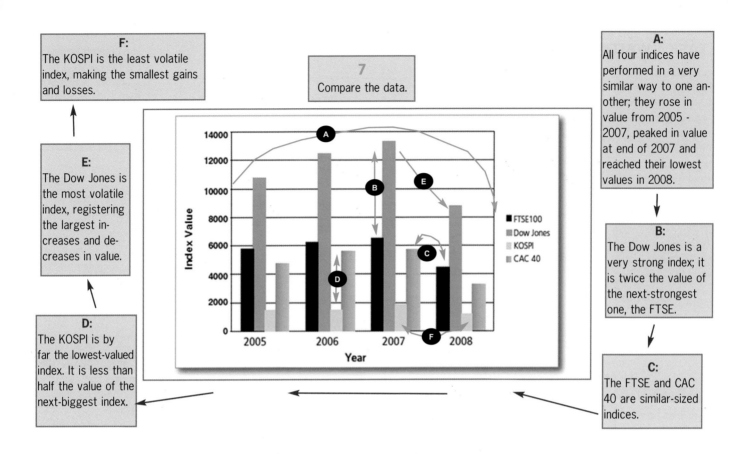

A:
All four indices have performed in a very similar way to one another; they rose in value from 2005 - 2007, peaked in value at end of 2007 and reached their lowest values in 2008.

B:
The Dow Jones is a very strong index; it is twice the value of the next-strongest one, the FTSE.

C:
The FTSE and CAC 40 are similar-sized indices.

TASK ANALYSIS : SUMMARY OF STEPS

1 READ THE FIRST PART OF THE QUESTION CAREFULLY (TELLS YOU ABOUT THE CHART/GRAPH/DIAGRAM)

2 IDENTIFY WHAT YOU MUST DO - HIGHLIGHT KEY POINTS IN THE QUESTION

3 STUDY CHART/GRAPH/DIAGRAM; READ MAIN TITLE AND AXIS TITLES (OR LABELS)

4 EXAMINE KEY; UNDERSTAND WHAT EACH SYMBOL/COLOUR/SHADE REPRESENTS

5 STUDY CHART/DIAGRAM/GRAPH CLOSELY AND IDENTIFY KEY FEATURES

6 COMPARE THE DATA ; NOTE PATTERNS IN DATA AND SIMILARITIES/DIFFERENCES BETWEEN INDIVIDUAL DATA SETS

FORMULATING YOUR ANSWER

Plan:
A simple plan is all that is required for this task-type. You are writing a basic summary, which will typically have three or four paragraphs.

Opening Paragraph: State what is being shown in the chart/diagram/graph. You could also make a general statement of the main overall point.

Main body: This may be one paragraph summarising the main points shown in more detail. However, if the diagram involves more than one main idea, it is fine to make two or more paragraphs - one addressing each main idea.

Conclusion: Briefly state the overall point of the diagram, and if you wish to speculate about reasons for the trends shown, or draw conclusions about what is shown, this is the place to do it.

SAMPLE PLAN

P1: The chart shows ... the value of four international money markets .....

P2: The American index was the strongest....
The British market index was the second-most valuable....
The French and British markets are closely aligned.....
Korean market was the lowest-valued.....

Concluding paragraph: From 2005 until 2007, the graph suggests that .....

SAMPLE ANSWER

Open by explaining what information the chart illustrates.

This chart follows the value of four international money markets over four years. *All four of the market indices rose steadily in value from 2005 to 2007 inclusive, registering a sharp drop in value at the end of 2008. The four markets seem to mirror each other's performance, suggesting that there is a strong correlation in market trends; a rise or fall in one index is reflected in the other indices.*

Be familiar with the kind of language used to describe changes in values.

The American index was the strongest in each of the four years, peaking in value at around 13,000 points in 2007, before dropping off to its lowest level at around 9,000 points in 2008. The British market index was the second-most valuable throughout the four years, peaking in 2007 at about 6,500 points before registering a 2,000 point drop in value by the end of 2008. The French and British markets are closely aligned in terms of value and performance, suggesting their economies may be of similar size, while the Korean market was the lowest-valued in each of the four years, though it exhibited a similar performance trend.

Show that you can read the data by quoting some relevant figures.

From 2005 until 2007, the graph suggests that the global economy may have been performing strongly since all four markets registered steady increases in value. It is also clear that in 2008, the economy contracted, both locally and globally, as is reflected in the significant fall in market value registered across the four indices.

Mention obvious features / patterns / trends.

The section in Italics is known as the main idea; a general summary of the chart's main features.

After opening and stating main idea, compare features in more detail in the second paragraph.

State the overall point of the diagram and draw conclusions about what is shown.

USEFUL LANGUAGE

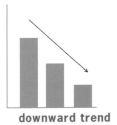

downward trend

upward trend

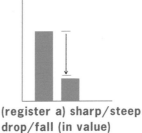

(register a) sharp/steep
drop/fall (in value)

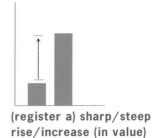

(register a) sharp/steep
rise/increase (in value)

volatile / unstable
performance

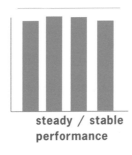

steady / stable
performance

Note:
Briefly check spelling, grammar and length
(150+ words) at the end of the task.

MORE USEFUL LANGUAGE

The Language of Contrast:

On the one hand... + On the other hand...
It is clear that... + whereas/while...
We can see that... + however...
It is clear that... + By contrast,

Describing what you see:
It is clear that...
It can be seen that...
The chart shows...
The chart illustrates...
The chart represents...

**Describing numbers and amounts
as they get bigger/smaller:**

to rise	/	to fall
to increase	/	to decrease
to grow	/	to shrink
to double	/	to halve
to go up	/	to go down
to expand	/	to contract

The language of similarity
It is clear that... + similarly,...
We can see that... + likewise,...

Percentages and proportions:

90%	10%
ninety percent (of)	ten percent (of)
a large/high percentage (of)	a small/low percentage (of)
most (of)	few (of)
the (vast) majority (of)	a (small) minority (of)
nine out of ten	one out of ten
nine in every ten	one in every ten
nine-tenths (of)	one-tenth (of)
nearly all (of)	barely any (of)

TASK ANALYSIS (UNDERSTANDING THE QUESTION)
TASK 2 WRITING TEST I

1
The first bold section will inform you about the subject matter of your composition. Highlight the key words before going any further.

2
The second bold section tells you what you must write i.e. in this case you must express your personal view on the subject.

WRITING TASK 2

You should spend about 40 minutes on this task.

Write about the following topic:

Schools concentrate far too much on traditional subjects which do not adequately prepare students for the realistic demands of the modern working world.

To what extent do you agree or disagree?

Give reasons for your answer and include any relevant examples from your own knowledge or experience.

3
The second-to-last sentence tells you what you must include in your answer. It is important to provide both reasons for your views and examples to explain them. Failing to do so will result in the loss of a significant amount of marks.

4
Before proceeding any further, think of ways you can paraphrase the statement in bold in order to introduce the subject of your composition in paragraph 1.

NOTE
In Task 1 you were given a lot of input material to write about. This is not the case in Task 2. You must come up with your own ideas and justify them; therefore, planning is very important in the context of this question.

TASK ANALYSIS : SUMMARY OF STEPS

1 READ THE FIRST BOLD SECTION OF THE QUESTION TO FIND OUT THE SUBJECT AND HIGHLIGHT KEY WORDS TO SIMPLIFY WHAT YOU ARE BEING ASKED TO WRITE ABOUT.

↓↓↓

2 READ THE SECOND BOLD SECTION TO CONFIRM THE REASON FOR WRITING I.E. TO GIVE YOUR OPINION.

↓↓↓

3 READ THE SECOND-TO-LAST SENTENCE TO CONFIRM THE INFORMATION YOU MUST INCLUDE I.E. REASONS FOR YOUR VIEWS AND EXAMPLES TO JUSTIFY THEM.

↓↓↓

4 PARAPHRASE THE QUESTION FOR YOUR INTRODUCTION.

FOCUS ON PLANNING

- The first thing you need to do is 'brainstorm'; basically think of as many points/ideas for and against the opinion expressed in the question statement as you can and write these down in note form.

- You then need to select the points you want to use in your composition and think of examples and reasons to justify them.

- Next, fit the ideas you wish to write about into your composition plan to help you focus on what points need to be discussed where in the composition.

SAMPLE BRAINSTORM

Paraphrase the question statement now - never repeat the question statement word-for-word in your introduction or you will lose marks.

Always start by looking at both sides of the argument. This will help you formulate a well-balanced discussion.

When brainstorming, write down as many ideas as you can come up with quickly. Don't worry about whether they are good or bad, or the order they come in; this can be decided when you fill in your plan.

Having considered both sides of the argument, decide where you stand. You do not have to agree or disagree with the question statement, you can choose to partially agree if you wish, though sometimes it is easier to take sides.

Topic:

the school curriculum's focus on academic subjects leads to a failure to prepare students for the challenges of the real world of work

Agree:
True ... school overly focused on academic subjects ... disadvantageous for two reasons ... many students are not academically-minded so school does not cater for them or equip them with skills to help them find a job in future ... school doesn't teach life skills - doesn't show students how to cope with life problems i.e. dealing with people, managing stress etc. ... moreover, most subjects we learn at school we never make use of in day-to-day lives

Disagree:
School doesn't have to officially 'teach' life skills ; it's where we learn them naturally ... learn how to communicate and make friends ... cope with stress (exams) ... organise our workload (study) ... teaches us value of respect, discipline and hard work ... moreover, academic subjects are vital ... broaden perspective ... history might not seem that useful, but we learn from the mistakes of the past and have a better understanding of who we are and who other people are ... besides, traditional subjects are key - English for communication and literacy, Maths for basic numerical skills ... fundamental skills needed in almost any job

My view?
School prepares us well, but does let those who are not academically minded down ... broaden curriculum ... include more practical courses ... possibly life skills courses too

---

PLANNING
Here are two of the most common paragraph plan outlines.

Option 1

Paragraph 1 - Introduction
Rephrase the question and express your opinion (in agreement or disagreement with the statement).

Paragraph 2 - Main body
Give one reason that supports your opinion. Use facts, observations and examples to support this statement.

Paragraph 3 - Main body
Give another reason that supports your opinion and justify.

Paragraph 4 - Conclusion
Summarise the reasons for your opinion and state again what you believe. Don't use the same words that you used in the introduction and main body; paraphrase.

Option 2

Paragraph 1 - Introduction
Introduce the topic by restating the question statement (in your own words) and giving your reaction to it.

Paragraph 2 - Main body
Discuss the points in favour of the question statement citing examples where relevant.

Paragraph 3 - Main body
Discuss the points against the question statement citing examples where relevant.

Paragraph 4 - Conclusion
State your opinion and give reasons why you hold this view.

SAMPLE PLAN

Intro: people often say... school doesn't adequately prepare students for real world ... is it true?

P2: True that many students aren't academic ... fail at school ... example; might be poor at maths and English, get bad grades ... skilful and good at making things ... pointless going to school ... wasted talent ... also no practical life-skills classes ... doesn't teach us how to deal with office politics, communicating with people, working in team, managing stress

P3: School offers all-round education ... teaches life skills indirectly ... discipline ... coping with stress - exams ... working with other people - sports class and projects ... communicating - making friends and school politics ... like a microcosm of real world ... also academic subjects crucial ... broaden mind ... teach us key skills like numeracy and literacy ... help us to develop analytical minds

Conclusion: true school is imperfect ... but a lot of value in getting good education ... maybe needs to cater more for those who are not academic and could give students more advice on dealing with real-life situations ... overall though, the failures are far outnumbered by successes and school is a very productive and relevant learning environment

SAMPLE ANSWER

Generalising the statement and then asking an open-ended question is a very effective way of opening the discussion / introducing the topic.

It is very important to use linking words/phrases to help your ideas flow smoothly from one to the next and improve the flow of the composition generally.

Note:
Marks will be lost if you fail to structure your composition well. Good paragraphing is essential, therefore. As a general rule, use four paragraphs; an introduction, two for the main body, and a concluding paragraph.

Paragraph 2 examines the points which support the question statement.

Use examples to illustrate points.

Paragraph 3 examines the other side of the argument.

Using examples adds credibility to the points you are making.

In the final paragraph you present your opinion. It is not necessary to take a clear stance in total agreement or disagreement with the question statement if you don't want to - here the writer agrees that school has some failings, but believes it prepares students well overall.

People often say that school's greatest failure is that it focuses too intently on academic subjects and fails to equip students with the real-life skills necessary to cope in the world of work. But is it fair to criticise the education system in this way?

Certainly, not all students have the attributes necessary to excel in an academic environment, so, if the focus of school is solely on the traditional academic subjects, then it would seem to be failing the more practically- and technically-minded children. A teenager with a talent for crafting things with his hands, for example, is letting his talent go to waste if he does not hone his skills during adolescence. School is also failing children if it does not equip them with life skills - in the real world, knowing how to deal with office politics, communicate with people, manage stress, and work in a team is far more important than being academically-minded.

On the other hand, it could be argued that school does not need to offer formal classes in life skills because it is a lesson in life skills from the start to the very end. School life indirectly teaches students self-discipline and how to motivate themselves to work hard. It also teaches them how to cope with the stress of exams and deadlines. Finally, they learn how to work with other people, such as their classmates and teachers, and even how to make friends. Basically, what happens inside the school building is a microcosm of what is happening outside in the real world. And not only that, but it is also teaching students numeracy and literacy - the two most vital skills of all.

No one would argue that school is perfect; however, a good education is still invaluable. While school could perhaps cater for the non-academic student more fairly and should work on developing programmes suited to the more technically-minded, the strengths of the school system far outnumber its failings. School is still a very productive and relevant learning environment today; one that does prepare students for the 'big bad world' of work.

Useful Language

Positive comments:	Negative comments:
The first advantage of ... is...	One of the (major) drawbacks of ... is ...
Among the many advantages of ... is/are...	A negative aspect of ... is ...
The benefits of ... include/are ...	... is disadvantageous in the sense that ...
... is (extremely) beneficial on account of the fact that...	Among the many drawbacks of ... is/are ...
Another positive result of ... is ...	One of the disadvantages of ... is ...
One of the major pros / plus points of ... is ...	The benefits of ... are far outweighed by the drawbacks.
A positive aspect of ... is ...	There is a long list of disadvantages / drawbacks including ...
One of the advantages of ... is ...	... is disadvantageous on account of the fact that ...
... is advantageous in the sense that ...	The first drawback of ... is ...
The benefits of ... far outweigh the drawbacks.	

General Notes / Summary

1 There are two tasks. **Task 1** requires you to summarise a chart/graph/diagram. **Task 2** is a discursive essay.

2 You should spend around 20 minutes on task 1. Summarise the input material by:
(i) describing what the chart/graph/diagram is about
(ii) explaining the main idea (the main trend or feature)
(iii) comparing the chart/graph/diagram data in greater detail

3 You should spend around 40 minutes on task 2. There is little input material. You must
(i) paraphrase the question statement in an introduction and state your opinion
(ii) support your opinion
(iii) re-state your view and paraphrase the reasons that support it and reach a conclusion

4 Do:
- Highlight key information in the task question.
- Plan your answer.
- Structure your answer into paragraphs.
- Use linking words to connect your ideas and points and improve the flow of the essay/ summary as a whole.
- Check your answer for minor errors at the end.

IELTS

SPEAKING SECTION

EXAM GUIDE

This section contains a detailed analysis of the Speaking section of the exam with Exam Tips, Guidance and Useful Vocabulary for the three parts of the IELTS Speaking section.

Speaking Section Format

Section	Time	Task Type
1	4-5 minutes	giving personal information and talking about everyday subjects
2	1 minute preparation, 2 minutes talking	giving a prepared talk on a subject the examiner has given to you and answering one or two follow-up questions
3	4-5 minutes	a discussion with the examiner based on the topic in Part 2, offering the opportunity to discuss more complex and abstract issues and ideas

PART 1

is...
- a short introductory conversation lasting between 4 and 5 minutes
- testing your ability to talk about personal experiences and interests

you must...
- be able to answer questions about everyday topics such as *family and friends, home life, studies / work, leisure, pastimes* etc.
- answer each question in at least one or two sentences

DEVELOPING YOUR ANSWERS

A simple question like *Where do you live?* can be replied to with a simple, yet detailed response. Always show off what you know!
For example:

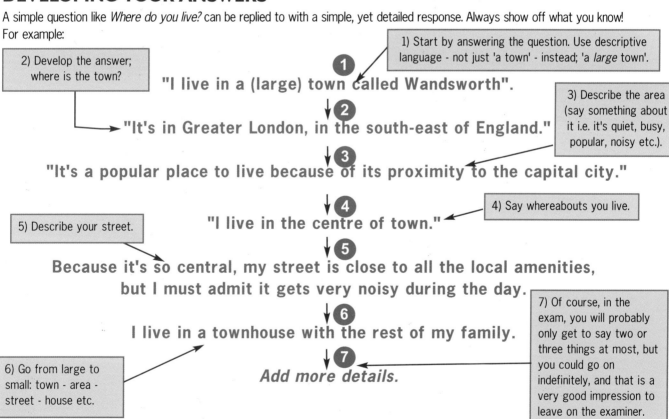

1) Start by answering the question. Use descriptive language - not just 'a town' - instead; 'a *large* town'.

2) Develop the answer; where is the town?

❶ "I live in a (large) town called Wandsworth".

3) Describe the area (say something about it i.e. it's quiet, busy, popular, noisy etc.).

❷ "It's in Greater London, in the south-east of England."

❸ "It's a popular place to live because of its proximity to the capital city."

4) Say whereabouts you live.

❹ "I live in the centre of town."

5) Describe your street.

❺ Because it's so central, my street is close to all the local amenities, but I must admit it gets very noisy during the day.

6) Go from large to small: town - area - street - house etc.

❻ I live in a townhouse with the rest of my family.

7) Of course, in the exam, you will probably only get to say two or three things at most, but you could go on indefinitely, and that is a very good impression to leave on the examiner.

❼ *Add more details.*

DO NOT be tempted to **MEMORISE** answers though, just practise often, saying as much as you can in relation to the different subjects you might get asked about.

SPEAKING PART 1 - EXAM TIPS

DO:
- avoid yes/no answers
- avoid one-word answers
- show off your English
- this is a relatively easy section, so continue expanding each answer until prompted to move on to the next question

PREPARE:
- you know the general topics that come up in this section, so prepare for them in advance
- practise talking about your family, friends, hobbies, work, pastimes, study etc. and try to say as much as you can about each topic
- Be prepared to talk about your likes and dislikes in general, too, for example:
  Where you like to travel/eat out.   What types of food/books/films/music/sports you like.
  Whether you prefer the cinema or DVDs / fast food or home-cooked food / public or private transport etc.

And finally, remember...

- **Part 1** is not graded separately; marks are awarded across all three parts (an overall mark).
- If the examiner asks you to stop before you have finished what you are saying, don't worry; he/she is constrained by time and may simply have to move on. It is not a reflection on how well you have answered the last question.
- The speaking will be recorded, but this is for administrative purposes only; don't let that distract you.
- Listen carefully to the tense in the question, and respond using the right one in your answer.

EXAMPLE QUESTIONS FOR YOU TO PRACTISE:

Home / local area / travel	Studies / work	Leisure time	Family / friends
Where are you from? What's the area where you live like? What is there to do near where you live? If you could live anywhere, where would it be? What are the advantages/disadvantages of living in your town/city/country? What would you change about the area where you live, if you could? Have you always lived in your home town? Do you like living there? Do you think your home town is likely to change much in the future? Do many tourists visit your area? What do they come to see? Have you ever been abroad? Where would you like to go on holiday? Would you prefer to live in the city, countryside or by the sea? Where did you go on holiday last year? Where are you planning to go on holiday this year?	How do you get to school/college/work every day? Are you a full-time student at the moment? Where do you study? How long have you studied there? What job would you like to have in the future? What work do you do? How long have you been working there? What job did you want to do when you were a child? What would you regard as the perfect job? How long have you been learning English? Have you studied any other languages? Why is it important to get a good education?	Do you have a lot of free time? What do you like to do to relax when you are at home? Where do you go when you go out? Do you try to keep fit? Why is it important for young people to keep fit? Do you play any sports/have any hobbies? What is the value of having hobbies? How often do you watch T.V./go to the movies/go to the theatre? What kind of music/sport/entertainment do you like? Do you ever go to concerts? Do you play or would you like to play a musical instrument? Do you enjoy reading or do you prefer watching T.V.? Given the choice, would you sooner go to the cinema or watch a DVD? Are there any hobbies/sports you would like to try?	Are your friends interested in the same kind of music as you? Do you spend more time with your family or friends? Who do you confide in when you have a problem? With whom in your family do you have the best relationship? Do you have / would you like to have any siblings? Who are more important; your family or friends? Where do you and your friends hang out at the weekend? What likes and interests do you share with your friends? Tell me about your best friend. Do you think you will stay friends for life with the friends you have now?

PART 2

is...
- a short talk
- testing your ability to speak continuously for about 2 minutes
- testing your ability to organise your ideas and speak fluently and cohesively

you must...
- prepare and talk about a topic given to you during the test by the examiner

DO:
- read the card with the task on it
- make notes on each of the separate parts of the task
- talk about the topic in the task, answering the questions on the card
- stop talking once the examiner indicates that you should
- answer the follow-up questions the examiner puts to you

EXAMPLE TASK

Describe a person you admire.
You should say:
- who the person is
- what kind of person they are
- what they have achieved in life

and explain the reasons you admire them.

Instructions:
The examiner will give you a topic on a card like this one. You will then have one minute to think about what you are going to say. You will be provided with some paper and a pencil so you can make notes if you want to.

Remember:
- you will be told when to begin your talk
- the examiner may ask you some questions during or after your talk
- don't worry if you haven't finished when the examiner tells you to stop; this is never an indication of having done well or badly.

WEB DIAGRAM
One of the most effective methods of note-making is to use what is called a *Web* or *Spider* **diagram**. The main idea goes in the middle and the items to discuss branch out on different threads.

This is only an outline of a Web Diagram. A detailed example is shown on the next page. Note-making is a very important part of this section of the speaking exam. It is highly recommended that you **DO** make notes as this will help you to focus your mind clearly and order your thoughts. It will also provide you with something on which to fall back if you get stuck as you can refer back to your notes during the talk.

TAKING NOTES

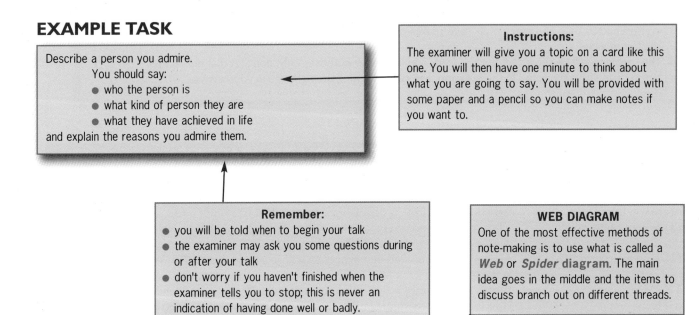

Who it is

What kind of person they are

Person I admire

Why I admire them

What they have achieved in life

Practise note-making as much as possible. You should not be writing full sentences but rather key words or ideas which you can link together in a logical way.

Use the points on the card as the themes of each of your four threads.

TAKING NOTES

Completed Web Diagram

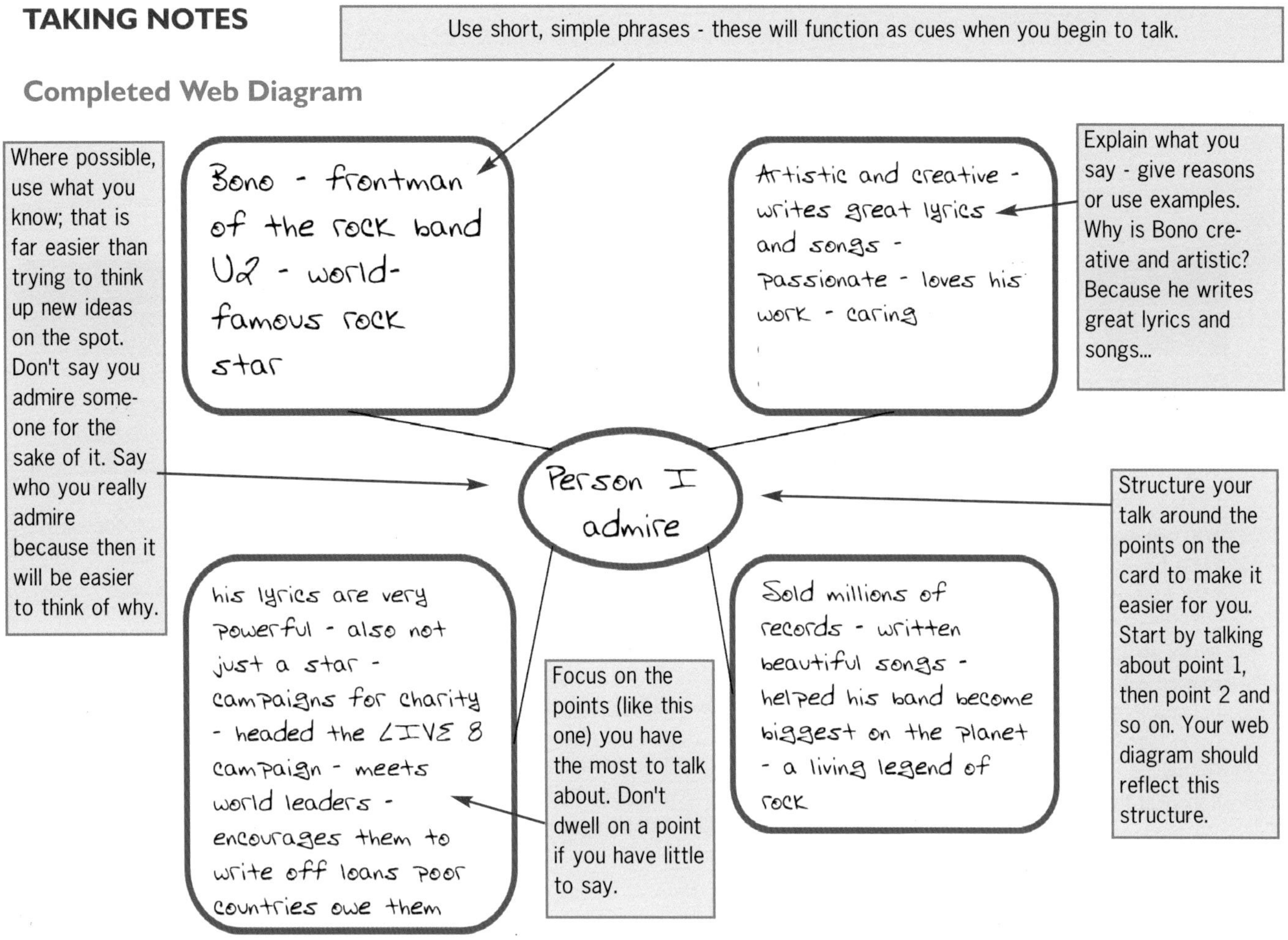

Use short, simple phrases - these will function as cues when you begin to talk.

Where possible, use what you know; that is far easier than trying to think up new ideas on the spot. Don't say you admire someone for the sake of it. Say who you really admire because then it will be easier to think of why.

Bono - frontman of the rock band U2 - world-famous rock star

Artistic and creative - writes great lyrics and songs - passionate - loves his work - caring

Explain what you say - give reasons or use examples. Why is Bono creative and artistic? Because he writes great lyrics and songs...

Person I admire

Structure your talk around the points on the card to make it easier for you. Start by talking about point 1, then point 2 and so on. Your web diagram should reflect this structure.

his lyrics are very powerful - also not just a star - campaigns for charity - headed the LIVE 8 campaign - meets world leaders - encourages them to write off loans poor countries owe them

Focus on the points (like this one) you have the most to talk about. Don't dwell on a point if you have little to say.

Sold millions of records - written beautiful songs - helped his band become biggest on the planet - a living legend of rock

---

SPEAKING PART 2 - EXAM TIPS

1 Use Stock or Opening phrases for each new point you make to give you some time to think. For example (based on the question and diagram above):

Box (i): I admire many people, but I think the person most worthy of my admiration is Bono....
Box (ii): Bono has all the qualities you would look for in a great person. He is...
Box (iii): Bono has done quite an amazing amount in his life so far; he has
Box (iv): The list of reasons why I admire him is very long; here are just a few ....

You are not giving any detail when you use these opening or stock phrases; you are talking in general terms but staying on-topic. This gives you a chance to order your thoughts and compose yourself.

2 Stock phrases can also be used to buy you thinking time when the examiner asks you a question. Examples of useful stock phrases include:

(i) That's a difficult question to answer...   (ii) Interesting question...
(iii) That's a very good question...   (iv) I need to think about this for a moment; hmm, let me see...

PART 3

is...
- a discussion of general and abstract ideas lasting 4-5 minutes
- testing your ability to analyse and discuss ideas in depth

you must...
- answer questions which are broadly related to the topic in part 2
- express your opinions and justify them

Stock phrases : Responding when someone gives their opinion.

Agree	Strongly Agree	Disagree	Strongly disagree
With a person: I see what you're saying... I see where you're coming from... What you say is true... I agree with you... We're in agreement... I feel the same way... I think so, too... **With an idea** I agree with the idea that... I support the idea that... I'm in favour of... I'm behind the idea that... I applaud the idea that...	**With a person** I completely agree... I couldn't agree more... You're absolutely right... I'm totally behind you... We're in complete agreement... I couldn't have said it better myself... **With an idea** I'm totally for the idea that... I'm completely behind the idea that... I'm totally in favour of... I'm very much in favour of the idea that... I completely agree with the notion that...	**With a person** I see what you're saying, but... We don't quite see eye to eye... I see where you're coming from, but... I know what you mean, but... I disagree because... I can't say I feel exactly the same way... I'm inclined to disagree with you... I'm not so sure about that... **With an idea** I'm against the idea of... I'm not in favour of... I don't support the idea that... I'm not behind the idea that... I don't agree that...	**With a person** I couldn't disagree more with what you're saying... I completely disagree with you... I feel the exact opposite... We're poles apart in our views... **With an idea** I'm totally against the idea that... I'm absolutely not in favour of... I am not at all behind the idea that... I'm not at all in favour of... There's no way I would agree that...

Expressing your opinion...

- If you ask me....
- In my view...
- I'm of the belief that...
- I'm of the view that...
- I'm inclined to believe...
- It's my firm belief that...
- As far as I see it...
- As far as I'm concerned...
- The way I see it...
- In my opinion...

SPEAKING PARTS 2 & 3 - EXAM TIPS

- MAKE SURE YOU INTRODUCE THE TOPIC

- COVER ALL THE POINTS ON THE CARD (*THEY DO NOT HAVE TO BE IN THE ORDER THEY APPEAR, BUT THIS IS THE SIMPLEST METHOD*)

- CONNECT YOUR SENTENCES AND IDEAS TOGETHER USING LINKING WORDS.

- TRY TO USE A RANGE OF VOCABULARY

- STAY ON-TOPIC AND ANSWER THE QUESTION DIRECTLY

- IF YOU DON'T HEAR A QUESTION THE EXAMINER CAN REPEAT IT FOR YOU.

- AVOID GIVING REHEARSED OR OFF-BY-HEART ANSWERS; THIS WILL REFLECT NEGATIVELY ON YOUR SCORE.

EXAMPLE TASK (QUESTIONS 1-11)

Describe a person you admire.
You should say:
- who the person is
- what kind of person they are
- what they have achieved in life
and explain the reasons you admire them.

Subject matter:
This is the topic card used in Part 2.
Part 3 is a series of questions related to the theme of Part Two which, in this case, is people we admire.

1 **What makes a person popular or admirable?**

2 **Do you have to be popular to be admired?**

The questions will be more difficult than in Part in 1. You might be asked for your opinion, as in this question.

3 **Do you admire a lot of famous people or look up to them?**

4 **Do you regard celebrities as good role models?**

5 **What are the qualities we should look for in someone to admire?**

6 **Would you like to be the object of other people's admiration?**

You might be asked about hypothetical situations.

7 **Are you influenced by the way people you look up to behave?**

8 **Have you ever tried to copy another person; perhaps their behaviour or style?**

9 **Why do you think so many people want to be like celebrities?**

You might be asked to speculate on the cause of something or why something is.

10 **Why are famous and rich people the object of so much admiration?**

11 **Do you think celebrities of the future will be better role models?**
[Example answer] I think it is highly unlikely that....

You might also be asked: to comment on what might happen in the future or to predict the possible consequences of something

Stock phrases : Talking about the Future	
Probable	**Improbable**
It is (highly) likely that....	I (highly) doubt that...
It seems (quite/very) probable that...	It's doubtful whether...
I would expect that...	I can't imagine that...
It seems (quite/very) likely that...	I think it is unlikely that...
I would imagine that...	It's highly unlikely that...
In all likelihood, ...	It's highly improbable that...
In all probability...	It seems unlikely that...
I'm quite sure that...	
I'm fairly certain that...	

Stock phrases: Making general statements

Before giving our own opinion, we often make a general statement. A general statement describes what most people believe, what is popularly believed or what is usually true. For example:

Q: *Do you think people today are too concerned about their appearance?*
A: *<u>Most people would say that looking good is extremely important, but, in my experience,</u> whether a person looks good or not is no indication of their character and I think people should learn to look beyond appearances. We are definitely too concerned with the way we look and not concerned enough with other more important qualities.*

The underlined section is an example of a general statement, which is followed by a personal statement.

Here are some more STOCK PHRASES to help you make GENERAL STATEMENTS:

(i) For the most part....
(ii) In general,...
(iii) Most people believe that...
(iv) It's widely acknowledged that...

(v) Most people are of the view that...
(vi) Generally speaking,...
(vii) It's widely believed that...
(viii) According to popular belief...

Example Question: *Do you think people will live longer lives in the future?*

Example Answer:
<u>I think it is highly likely</u> that life expectancy will improve over the coming years because of the <u>advances we are seeing in medical science</u>. New cures are being discovered all the time, and many diseases considered deadly today will no doubt be treatable in a few years' time. <u>Moreover,</u> as the wealth of the world increases, more people have access to clean water, good sanitation and nutrition. This will improve the average life expectancy across the developing world.

Stock phrase for expressing probability.

Reason for / justification of your opinion.

The use of linking words is very important to connect your ideas and make them flow.

Stock phrases: Where the correct answer / your opinion can change

Some questions are not easy to answer 'yes' or 'no' to; sometimes there is a situation where, in some cases, we would say yes, or agree, and, in other cases, we would say no, or disagree. For example;

Q: *Do you think television has a negative impact on children?*
A: <u>*That depends.*</u> *Certainly, watching too much television is harmful because it promotes a sedentary and anti-social lifestyle. Having said that, television in small doses can be quite educational.*

The underlined section is an example of a phrase used to indicate that the answer changes depending on the situation.

Here are some more stock phrases to help you express this notion:

(i) In some circumstances.... In others....
(ii) To some extent... but...
(iii) Some believe... while others...
(iv) Some would say... while others...
(v) In some cases... In other cases...
(vi) Sometimes... Having said that...
(vii) For some people... For others...
(viii) That can vary according to the situation.

Stock phrases: Contrasting your opinion with what most people think

Here are some more stock phrases to help you express the idea that you disagree with other people:

(i) For many people... but I believe...
(ii) To some people... but to me...
(iii) Some believe... but I...
(iv) Some would say... but I...
(v) A lot of people think... but I beg to differ.
(vi) For some people... but for me...
(vii) I differ from a lot of people in that I believe...
(viii) You might expect me to say ... but actually...

Example Question: *How do you feel about nuclear energy?*

Example Answer:
<u>*Most people believe that*</u> *nuclear energy is quite dangerous and, for that reason, they are against it, but,* <u>*if you ask me*</u>*, I think nuclear energy is a clean fuel source; therefore,* <u>*I am strongly in favour of it*</u>*. Energy sources such as oil and coal have been polluting the atmosphere for a very long time now, and scientists think* <u>*this could lead to global warming*</u>*. Perhaps clean energy sources like nuclear fuel are the answer to the problem.*

Stock phrase for making a general statement.

Stock phrase for giving your opinion.

Always give examples or evidence to support your points.

Stock phrase for expressing your agreement with an idea.

Speaking Tips

- The speaking section of the exam lasts approximately 11-13 minutes in total.

- It is common to both the General and Academic modules.

- It is a face-to-face interview and it will be recorded.

- You receive one grade for the entire speaking exam; the individual parts are not graded separately.

- You will be provided with a pen and some note paper for Section 2.

- Avoid yes/no answers and always respond as fully as possible to questions posed to you by the examiner.

- If the examiner interrupts you, this is not a sign you have done badly; he/she is working to strict guidelines on timing.

- Remember to bring your passport or I.D. card with you on the day.

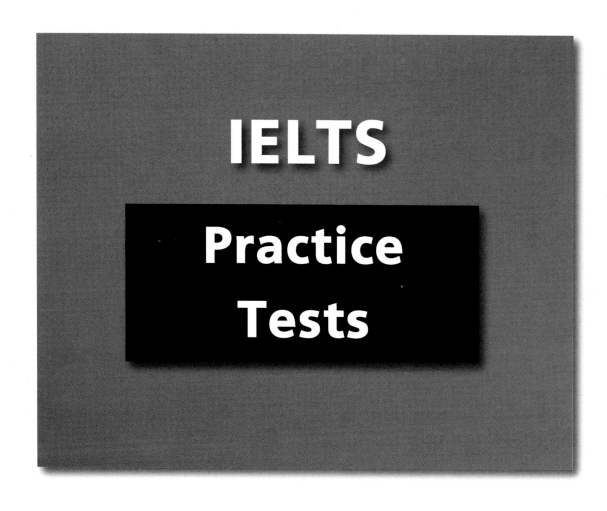

IELTS

Practice Tests

Listening

SECTION 1   *Questions 1 - 10*

Questions 1 - 10

Complete the notes below.

*Write **NO MORE THAN TWO WORDS AND/OR A NUMBER** for each answer.*

NOTES: travelling to France

Example   *Answer*
Time of travel   ....*September*..............

Advantages of travelling by train:

   1. ....

   2. ....

   3. take as much .... as you need

The Eurostar:

   ● runs on schedule **4** .... of the time

   ● can reach speeds of **5** .... miles per hour

Two options from Paris to Nice:

   1. Catch the TGV train at **6** ....

   2. Catch the TGV train at **7** .... and travel **8** ....

Single tickets cost approximately **9** .... the return fare.

Flying from London to Nice takes **10** ....

SECTION 2   *Questions 11 - 20*

Questions 11 - 15

Complete the table below.

*Write **NO MORE THAN THREE WORDS AND/OR A NUMBER** for each answer.*

PROJECT DEVELOPMENT SCHEDULE		
Project name: .....The Cube......	Length of project: 11	Current stage of project: ......halfway through......

ACTIVITY	TIME FRAME
Completion of each floor	12 ....
Installation of exterior	Beginning in 13 ....
"Topping out" of frame	Towards the end of 14 ....
Installation of fretwork screen	Coming together in 15 ....

Questions 16 - 20

Label the floor plan below.

*Write the correct letter **A - G** next to the questions below.*

16 restaurant with view	
17 hotel	
18 office space	
19 exclusive shops	
20 Waterside restaurant	

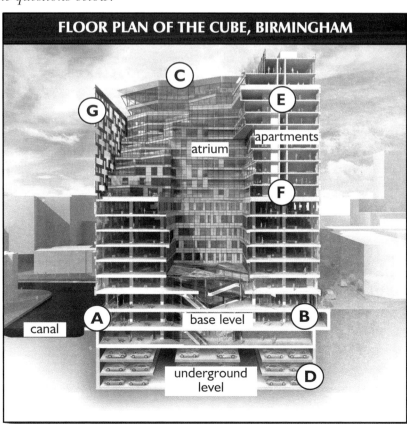

FLOOR PLAN OF THE CUBE, BIRMINGHAM

Practice Test 1

Listening

SECTION 3 *Questions 21 - 30*

Questions 21 - 25

Which student expresses each of the opinions about their tutor?

*Choose your answer from the box and write the letters **A - D** next to questions 21 - 25.*

> **A David**
>
> **B Thomas**
>
> **C Sophie**
>
> **D Lynn**

When things don't make sense I think it's my mistake at first.	**21** ....
I find the tutor's mistakes entertaining.	**22** ....
I think it's unfortunate when tutors confuse people.	**23** ....
I don't believe the situation is so serious.	**24** ....
The professor should be aware of his tutor's abilities.	**25** ....

Questions 26 - 30

Complete the sentences below.

*Write **NO MORE THAN TWO WORDS** for each answer.*

> ### RECOMMENDATIONS FOR SURVIVING THE CONFUSING LAB CLASS
>
> ◆ Remember that English is not Marlena's first language. She doesn't understand when you're joking around, so don't **26** .... her so much.
>
> ◆ If you pick on her, you will make her **27** .... that she can't think clearly.
>
> ◆ If you need help, make an appointment to meet with her **28** ....
> and you might see a **29** .... of her.
>
> ◆ Remember that tutors are not old academics; she is not yet experienced as a **30** ....

SECTION 4 *Questions 31 - 40*

Questions 31 - 40

Complete the notes below.

Write **NO MORE THAN THREE WORDS AND/OR A NUMBER** *for each answer.*

COURSE: *Epidemiology 101*   **DATE:** *23 May*

Tuberculosis (also called TB)

- *Tuberculosis is closely associated with the 31 ....*

In the UK:

- *common in the 19th century*
- *since then better living conditions, 32 ....*
  immunisation and effective treatments have made it uncommon

Globally:

- *still common in 33 .... and parts of 34 ....*
- *causes 35........................... deaths per year; more than any other infectious disease*
- *overall, 36 .... of the world's population is infected but not everyone*
  gets sick

Risk factors

- *a weakened immune system - due to HIV infection, immune-suppressing treatment, or*
  alcohol or 37 ....
- *age - babies and the elderly are more likely to become sick*
- *certain environments - more common among homeless people, among prisoners, and*
  people in 38 .... and in more impoverished areas

Treatment

- *50 years ago, a way 39 .... TB was found*
- *The most recent form of tuberculosis, XDR-TB, poses a 40 ....*
  to general TB control.

Reading

READING PASSAGE 1

You should spend about 20 minutes on **Questions 1 - 13,** *which are based on Reading Passage 1 below.*

Hello Happiness!

Ask 100 people what would make them happy, and a sizeable majority would say "winning the lottery." Yet, if they won a vast fortune, within a year they would be back to their previous level of happiness. The fact is that money has many uses, but more money does not mean more happiness. Surveys carried out in recent years by leading psychologists and sociologists all confirm that while individuals may increase their material wealth during the course of their lifetime, this has no bearing on their well-being. And what is true for individuals can be applied on a larger scale to the world population. Statistically, wealthier nations do not achieve higher scores on the happiness-ometer than developing or underdeveloped nations. Once the basic criteria of adequate shelter and nutrition are satisfied, increased wealth plays no significant role. So why the obsession with getting rich? The answer, say researchers, is simple. Call it jealousy, competitiveness, or just keeping up with the Joneses, however well we are doing, there is always someone else who is doing better. Just as we acquire a new $25,000 car, our neighbour parks his brand spanking new $40,000 set of wheels in his drive, causing us much consternation, but fuelling us with new aspirations in the process. And so the cycle continues. Money, or material wealth, may be a prime mover, but it is not the foundation of our well-being.

If money isn't the key to happiness, then, what is? In all 44 countries surveyed by a prominent research centre, family life provided the greatest source of satisfaction. Married people live on average three years longer and enjoy greater physical and psychological health than the unmarried and, surprisingly, couples in a cohabitational relationship. Having a family enhances well-being, and spending more time with one's family helps even more. Social interaction among families, neighbourhoods, workplaces, communities and religious groups correlates strongly with subjective well-being. In fact, the degree of individuals' social connections is the best benchmark of their happiness.

Friendship is another major factor. Indeed, to return to the dollar-equals-happiness equation, in one survey, having a friend converted into $50,000 worth of happiness, and confirms the well-known phenomenon that loneliness can lead to depression. Work is another area central to well-being, and certain features correlate highly with happiness. These include autonomy over how, where, and at what pace work is done, trust between employer and employee, fair treatment, and active participation in the making of decisions. Occupationally, happiness tends to be more common among professionals and managers, that is, people who are in control of the work they do, rather than subservient to their bosses. Inequality implies less control for those who are in the weaker position, although there are more risks of losing their privileges for those in the stronger position.

Control of one's life in general is also key. Happiness is clearly correlated with the presence of favourable events such as promotion or marriage, and the absence of troubles or bad luck such as accidents, being laid off or conflicts. These events on their own signal the success or failure to reach one's goals, and therefore the control one has. On a national level, the more that governments recognise individual preferences, the happier their citizens will be. Choice, and citizens' belief that they can affect the political process, increase subjective well-being. Furthermore, evidence exists for an association between unhappiness and poor health: people from the former Soviet Union are among the unhappiest in the world, and their life expectancy has been falling steadily. People are more satisfied in societies which minimally restrict their freedom of action, in other words, where they are in control rather than being controlled. Happy people are characterised by the belief that they are able to control their situation, whereas unhappy people tend to believe that they are a victim of fate. Happy people are also more psychologically resilient, assertive and open to experience.

But how good is the evidence for this alternative viewpoint then - that happiness, and not financial status, contributes to good health, and long life? A study of nuns, spanning seven decades, supports this theory. Autobiographies written by the nuns in their early 1920s were scored for positive and negative emotions. Nuns expressing the most positive emotions lived on average ten years longer than those expressing the least positive emotions. Happy people, it seems, are much less likely to fall ill and die than unhappy people.

But what must we do to be happy? Experts cite the old maxim "be happy with what you've got." Look around you, they say, and identify the positive factors in your life. Concentrating on the negative aspects of one's life is a no-no, and so is worrying. Worrying is a negative thinking habit that is nearly always about something that lies in the future. It stems, apparently, from our cave dwelling days, when we had to think on a day-to-day basis about how and where to find food and warmth, for example. But in the modern world, worrying simply undermines our ability to enjoy life in the present. More often than not, the things we worry about never come to pass anyway. Just as important is not to dwell on the past - past mistakes, bad experiences, missed opportunities and so on.

What else can we do? Well, engage in a loving relationship with another adult, and work hard to sustain it. Try to plan frequent interactions with your family, friends and neighbours (in that order). Make sure you're not working so hard that you've no time left for personal relationships and leisure. If you are, leave your job voluntarily to become self-employed, but don't get sacked — that's more damaging to well-being than the loss of a spouse, and its effects last longer. In your spare time, join a club, volunteer for community service, or take up religion.

If none of the above works, then vote for a political party with the same agenda as the King of Bhutan, who announced that his nation's objective is national happiness.

Reading

Questions 1 - 3

Choose **THREE** *letters* ***A - H***.

Circle the correct letters, ***A - H***, *below.*

NB *Your answers may be given in any order.*

Which **THREE** of the following statements are true, according to the text?

A	Money can bring misery.
B	Wealthier nations place more emphasis on happiness than poorer ones.
C	Securing a place to live is a basic human need.
D	The desire for social status is a global phenomenon.
E	An unmarried couple living together are less likely to be happy than a married couple.
F	The less responsibility one has, the happier one is.
G	Involvement in policy making can increase well-being.
H	Our prehistoric ancestors were happier than we are.

Questions 4 - 7

Complete the summary using the list of words, ***A - I***, *below.*

Write the correct letter, ***A - I***, *in the spaces below.*

> **Reading Tip:**
> When reading, remember to scan for key words and practise scanning for paraphrases of key words.

Money can buy you just about anything, but not, it seems, happiness. Whether on a personal or national **4** .... , your bank balance won't make you happier. Once the basic criteria of a roof over your head and food on the table have been met, money ceases to play a part. One of the most important factors in achieving happiness is the extent of our social **5** .... - our relationships with family, friends, colleagues and so on. Equally important is the amount of **6** .... we have, either in our personal life, working life, or even in our ability to influence the political **7** .... that our country embarks on.

A episode	**B** interaction	**C** cooperation
D control	**E** number	**F** level
G course	**H** conflict	**I** limit

Questions 8 - 13

Do the following statements agree with the information given in Reading Passage 1?

In spaces 8 - 13 below write

TRUE	*if the statement agrees with the information*
FALSE	*if the statement contradicts the information*
NOT GIVEN	*if there is no information on this*

8   People from underdeveloped nations try to attain the same standard of living as those from developed nations.   ....

9   Seeing what others have makes people want to have it too.   ....

10   The larger the family is, the happier the parents will probably be.   ....

11   One's attitude to life has no influence on one's health.   ....

12   Instinct can be a barrier to happiness.   ....

13   Family and friends rank equally as sources of happiness.   ....

Reading

READING PASSAGE 2

*You should spend about 20 minutes on **Questions 14 - 26**, which are based on Reading Passage 2 below.*

One Who Hopes

A

Language lovers, just like music lovers, enjoy variety. For the latter there's Mozart, The Rolling Stones and Beyonce. For the former there's English, French, Swahili, Urdu... the list is endless. But what about those poor overworked students who find learning difficult, confusing languages a drudge? Wouldn't it put a smile on their faces if there were just one simple, easy-to-learn tongue that would cut their study time by years? Well, of course, it exists. It's called Esperanto, and it's been around for more than 120 years. Esperanto is the most widely spoken artificially constructed international language. The name derives from Doktoro Esperanto, the pseudonym under which L. L. Zamenhof first published his *Unua Libro* in 1887. The phrase itself means 'one who hopes'. Zamenhof's goal was to create an easy and flexible language as a universal second language to promote peace and international understanding.

B

Zamenhof, after ten years of developing his brain-child from the late 1870s to the early 1880s, had the first Esperanto grammar published in Warsaw in July 1887. The number of speakers grew rapidly over the next few decades, at first primarily in the Russian empire and Eastern Europe, then in Western Europe and the Americas, China, and Japan. In the early years, speakers of Esperanto kept in contact primarily through correspondence and periodicals, but since 1905 world congresses have been held on five continents every year except during the two World Wars. Latest estimates for the numbers of Esperanto speakers are around 2 million. Put in percentage terms, that's about 0.03% of the world's population - no staggering figure, comparatively speaking. One reason is that Esperanto has no official status in any country, but it is an optional subject on the curriculum of several state education systems. It is widely estimated that it can be learned in anywhere between a quarter to a twentieth of the time required for other languages.

C

As a constructed language, Esperanto is not genealogically related to any ethnic language. Whilst it is described as 'a language lexically predominantly Romanic', the phonology, grammar, vocabulary, and semantics are based on the western Indo-European languages. For those of us who are not naturally predisposed to tucking languages under our belts, it is an easy language to learn. It has 5 vowels and 23 consonants. It has one simple way of conjugating all of its verbs. Words are often made from many other roots, making the number of words which one must memorise much smaller. The language is phonetic, and the rules of pronunciation are very simple, so that everyone knows how to pronounce a written word and vice-versa, and word order follows a standard, logical pattern. Through prefixing and suffixing, Esperanto makes it easy to identify words as nouns, verbs, adjectives, adverbs, direct objects and so on, by means of easy-to-spot endings. All this makes for easy language learning. What's more, several research studies demonstrate that studying Esperanto before another foreign language speeds up and improves the learning of the other language. This is presumably because learning subsequent foreign languages is easier than learning one's first, while the use of a grammatically simple and culturally flexible language like Esperanto softens the blow of learning one's first foreign language. In one study, a group of European high school students studied Esperanto for one year, then French for three years, and ended up with a significantly better command of French than a control group who had studied French for all four years.

D

Needless to say, the language has its critics. Some point to the Eastern European features of the language as being harsh and difficult to pronounce, and argue that Esperanto has an artificial feel to it, without the flow of a natural tongue, and that by nature of its artificiality, it is impossible to become emotionally involved with the language. Others cite its lack of cultural history, indigenous literature - "no one has ever written a novel straight into Esperanto" - together with its minimal vocabulary and its inability to express all the necessary philosophical, emotional and psychological concepts.

E

The champions of Esperanto - *Esperantists* - disagree. They claim that it is a language in which a great body of world literature has appeared in translation: in poetry, novels, literary journals, and, to rebut the accusation that it is not a 'real' language, point out that it is frequently used at international meetings which draw hundreds and thousands of participants. Moreover, on an international scale, it is most useful - and fair - for neutral communication. That means that communication through Esperanto does not give advantages to the members of any particular people or culture, but provides an ethos of equality of rights, tolerance and true internationalism.

F

Esperantists further claim that Esperanto has the potential – were it universally taught for a year or two throughout the world – to empower ordinary people to communicate effectively worldwide on a scale that far exceeds that which is attainable today by only the most linguistically brilliant among us. It offers the opportunity to improve communication in business, diplomacy, scholarship and other fields so that those who speak many different native languages will be able to participate fluently in international conferences and chat comfortably with each other after the formal presentations are made. Nowadays that privilege is often restricted to native speakers of English and those who have special talents and opportunities for learning English as a foreign language.

G

What Esperanto does offer in concrete terms is the potential of saving billions of dollars which are now being spent on translators and interpreters, billions which would be freed up to serve the purposes of governments and organisations that spend so much of their resources to change words from one language into the words of others. Take, for example, the enormously costly conferences, meetings and documentation involved in the European Union parliamentary and administrative procedures - all funded, essentially, by tax payers. And instead of the World Health Organisation, and all NGOs for that matter, devoting enormous sums to provide interpreters and translations, they would be able to devote those huge amounts of money to improving the health of stricken populations throughout the world.

Reading

Questions 14 - 19

Reading Passage 2 has seven paragraphs, **A - G**.

Choose the correct heading for paragraphs **B - G** *from the list of headings below.*

Write the correct number **i - ix** *in spaces 14 - 19 below.*

i	A non-exclusive language			
ii	Fewer languages, more results	*Example*	Paragraph **A**	*Answer* **vii**
iii	Language is personal	**14** Paragraph **B**	....
iv	What's fashionable in language	**15** Paragraph **C**	....
v	From the written word to the spoken word	**16** Paragraph **D**	....
vi	A real language	**17** Paragraph **E**	....
vii	Harmony through language	**18** Paragraph **F**	....
viii	The mechanics of a language	**19** Paragraph **G**	....
ix	Lost in translation			

Questions 20 - 22

Choose the correct letter **A, B, C** *or* **D**.

20 What advantage is there to learning Esperanto as one's first foreign language?
   A Its pronunciation rules follow those of most European languages.
   B There are no grammar rules to learn.
   C It can make the learning of other foreign languages less complicated.
   D Its verbs are not conjugated.

21 What do its critics say of Esperanto?
   A It is only used in artificial situations.
   B It requires emotional involvement.
   C It cannot translate works of literature.
   D It lacks depth of expression.

22 How could Esperanto help on a global level?
   A It would eliminate the need for conferences.
   B More aid money would reach those who need it.
   C The world population would be speaking only one language.
   D More funds could be made available for learning foreign languages.

Questions 23 - 26

Do the following statements agree with the information given in Reading Passage 2?

In spaces 23 - 26 below, write

YES	*if the statement agrees with the information*
NO	*if the statement contradicts the information*
NOT GIVEN	*if there is no information on this*

23   Supporters of Esperanto say it gives everyone an equal voice.   ....

24   Esperanto is the only artificially-constructed language.   ....

25   Esperanto can be learned as part of a self-study course.   ....

26   Esperanto can be used equally in formal and casual situations.   ....

Reading

READING PASSAGE 3

*You should spend about 20 minutes on **Questions 27 - 40**, which are based on Reading Passage 3 below.*

LONG-TERM FORECAST: HOT AND DRY

A

Melting land ice in the Arctic is set to cause a global rise in sea levels, leading to disastrous effects for both man and wildlife. Many species worldwide are threatened with extinction, and low-lying islands and land masses will disappear entirely. But the havoc wreaked by the effect of greenhouse gases won't be confined to just too much water, but the absence of it, as well. In other words, desertification. A decrease in the total amount of rainfall in arid and semi-arid areas could increase the total area of dry-lands worldwide, and thus the total amount of land potentially at risk from desertification.

B

Desertification is officially recognised as 'land degradation in arid, semi-arid and dry sub-humid areas resulting from various factors including climatic variations and human activities. This degradation of formerly productive land is a complex process. It involves multiple causes, and it proceeds at varying rates in different climates. Desertification may intensify a general climatic trend, or initiate a change in local climate, both leading towards greater aridity. The more arid conditions associated with desertification accelerate the depletion of vegetation and soils. Land degradation occurs all over the world, but it is only referred to as desertification when it takes place in drylands. This is because these areas are especially prone to more permanent damage as different areas of degraded land spread and merge together to form desert-like conditions.

C

Global warming brought about by increasing greenhouse gas levels in the atmosphere is expected to increase the variability of weather conditions and extreme events. Many dryland areas face increasingly low and erratic rainfalls, coupled with soil erosion by wind and the drying-up of water resources through increased regional temperatures. Deforestation can also reduce rainfall in certain areas, increasing the threat of desertification. It is not yet possible, despite sophisticated technology, to identify with an acceptable degree of reliability those parts of the Earth where desertification will occur. Existing drylands, which cover over 40% of the total land area of the world, most significantly in Africa and Asia, will probably be most at risk from climate change. These areas already experience low rainfall, and any that falls is usually in the form of short, erratic, high-intensity storms. In addition, such areas also suffer from land degradation due to over-cultivation, overgrazing, deforestation and poor irrigation practices.

D

It is a misconception that droughts cause desertification. Droughts are common in arid and semi-arid lands. Well-managed lands can recover from drought when the rains return. Continued land abuse during droughts, however, increases land degradation. Nor does desertification occur in linear, easily definable patterns. Deserts advance erratically, forming patches on their borders. Areas far from natural deserts can degrade quickly to barren soil, rock, or sand through poor land management. The presence of a nearby desert has no direct relationship to desertification. Unfortunately, an area undergoing desertification is brought to public attention only after the process is well underway. Often little or no data are available to indicate the previous state of the ecosystem or the rate of degradation. Scientists still question whether desertification, as a process of global change, is permanent or how and when it can be halted or reversed.

E

But desertification will not be limited to the drylands of Africa and Asia. According to the environmental organisation Greenpeace, the Mediterranean will suffer substantially, too. If current trends in emissions of greenhouse gases continue, global temperatures are expected to rise faster over the next century than over any time during the last 10,000 years. Significant uncertainties surround predictions of region-al climate changes, but it is likely that the Mediterranean region will also warm significantly, increasing the frequency and severity of droughts across the region. As the world warms, global sea levels will rise as oceans expand and glaciers melt. Around much of the Mediterranean basin, sea levels could rise by close to 1m by 2100. As a result, some low-lying coastal areas would be lost through flooding or erosion, while rivers and coastal aquifers would become more salty. The worst affected areas will be the Nile Delta, Venice in Italy and Thessaloniki in Greece, two major cities where local subsidence means that sea levels could rise by at least one-and-a-half times as much as elsewhere.

F

The consequences of all this, says Greenpeace, are far-reaching, and the picture is a gloomy one. Livestock production would suffer due to a deterioration in the quality of rangeland. Yields of grains and other crops could decrease substantially across the Mediterranean region due to increased frequency of drought. Crop production would be further threatened by increases in competition for water and the prevalence of pests and diseases and land loss through desertification and sea-level rise. The combination of heat and pollution would lead to an upsurge in respiratory illness among urban populations, while extreme weather events could increase death and injury rates. Water shortages and damaged infrastructure would increase the risk of cholera and dysentery, while higher temperatures would increase the incidence of infectious diseases, such as malaria and dengue fever. Serious social disruption could occur as millions are forced from their homelands as a result of desertification, poor harvests and sea-level rise, while international disputes over shared water resources could turn into conflict.

G

Future climate change could critically undermine efforts for sustainable development in the Mediterranean region through its impacts on the environment and social and economic well-being. While in many respects climate change exacerbates existing problems instead of creating new ones, the sheer magnitude of the potential problem means it cannot be ignored. There is some scope for adaptation, but the fact that many measures would be beneficial irrespective of climate change suggests that radical changes in our policies and practices will be needed. It is also vital that developed countries meet their obligations to assist adaptation in developing countries through access to know-how and financial assis-tance. Ultimately, however, the long-term sustainability of the Mediterranean region requires keeping cli-mate change within tolerable bounds. Current understanding of safe limits points to the need for prompt international agreement - and action - to make the drastic cuts in emissions of greenhouse gases required to stabilise atmospheric concentrations of these gases.

Reading

Questions 27 - 32
Complete the flow-chart below.

Write **NO MORE THAN THREE WORDS** for each answer.

Reading Tip:
Pay attention to how many words
are required for each answer.

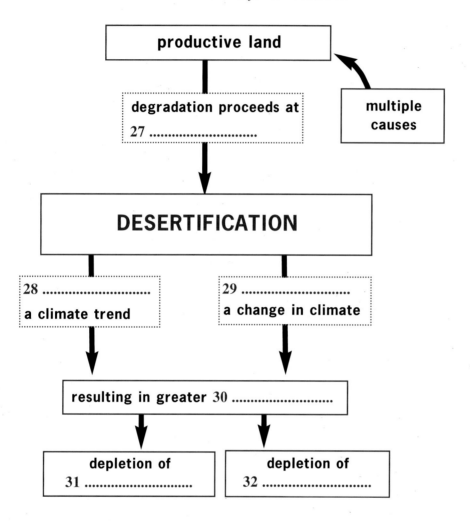

Questions 33 - 36

Reading Passage 3 has seven paragraphs, **A - G**.

Which paragraph contains the following information?

*Write the correct letter **A - G** in spaces 33 - 36 below.*

33	Human intervention is a potential solution to potential disaster.	....
34	The rate of climate change is set to accelerate dramatically.	....
35	There is seldom enough information available in some areas to track how fast the effects of climate change have happened in the past.	....
36	Desertification is attributable to a number of factors.	....

Questions 37 - 40

Complete the summary with the list of words ***A - I*** *below.*

Write the correct letter ***A - I*** *in spaces 37 - 40 below.*

Climate change may have catastrophic effects on the human and animal world. As glaciers
melt, sea levels will rise, causing extensive flooding and land **37** ....
Another consequence of global warming is **38** ...., which affects areas
known as **39** .... These areas are subject to irregular weather patterns,
but also suffer from human intervention or neglect, such as inadequate or inefficient
40 .... systems.

A irrigation	B cooling	C drylands
D cause	E loss	F abuse
G desertification	H deserts	I emission

Writing

> **Writing Tip:**
> Read the instructions carefully and pay attention to how many words you must write.

WRITING TASK 1

You should spend about 20 minutes on this task.

> *The graph below shows the weekday volume of passenger activity on the Toronto Metro system for July, 2007.*
>
> *Summarise the information by selecting and reporting the main features, and make comparisons where necessary.*

Write at least 150 words.

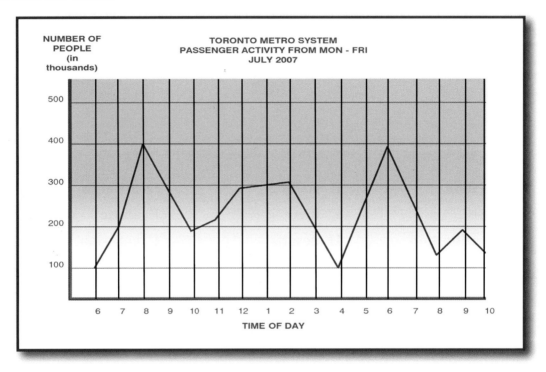

WRITING TASK 2

You should spend about 40 minutes on this task.

Write about the following topic:

> *Schools concentrate far too much on traditional subjects which do not adequately prepare students for the realistic demands of the modern working world.*
>
> *To what extent do you agree or disagree?*

Give reasons for your answer and include any relevant examples from your own knowledge or experience.

Write at least 250 words.

Speaking

PART 1   (4-5 minutes)

The examiner asks the candidate about him/herself, his/her home, work or studies and other familiar topics.

Language

- What language do you speak at home?
- Do you speak any other languages?
- What is the best way to learn a foreign language?
- What is your opinion about English as an international language?

PART 2   (2 minutes)

You will have to talk about the topic for one to two minutes. You have one minute to think about what you are going to say. You can make some notes to help you if you wish.

> **Describe a celebration that is important in your country.**
>
> **You should say:**
> - **when the celebration takes place**
> - **what people do during the celebration**
> - **what you like or dislike about it**
>
> **and explain why this celebration is important.**

PART 3   (4-5 minutes)

Discussion topics:

Customs and Traditions

- How important do you think customs and traditions are for a country?

- Do you think that a country's customs and traditions are just as important to younger people as older people? Why (not)?

- Are there any traditions in your culture that you would like to see disappear?

International Customs

- What influence have cultures from other countries had on your country?

- Should people who immigrate to a new country keep the customs of their home country?

- Are movies, TV and the internet making customs the same all over the world?

  Do you think this is a good or bad thing?

Test 2

Listening

SECTION 1   *Questions 1 - 10*

Questions 1 - 7

Complete the notes below.

Write **NO MORE THAN TWO WORDS AND/OR A NUMBER** *for each answer.*

Visiting Gaudi's Exhibition

Example   *Answer*

Day of visit: *tomorrow*
....

Laurel's schedule:
● Class at college until: **1** ....

Jason's schedule:
● He says that his lecture finishes at: **2** ....

● Gallery's name: **Tate**

● Jason suggests they meet at the **3** .... at 12.30

● Laurel suggests they meet at the gallery's **4** ....

Tickets prices:
● Jason does not get a concession so he will pay **5** ....

● Laurel will pay **6** .... because she gets a concession.

● They will get there in Jason's **7** ....

Questions 8 - 10

Complete the sentences below.

Write **NO MORE THAN THREE WORDS AND/OR A NUMBER** *for each answer.*

Address:	
8 Flat:	**9** Number: ....
10 Street: .... Avenue, West Hampstead	

SECTION 2   *Questions 11 - 20*

Questions 11 - 16
Label the diagram below.
*Choose **SIX** answers from the box and write the correct letter, **A - H**, next to questions 11 - 16.*

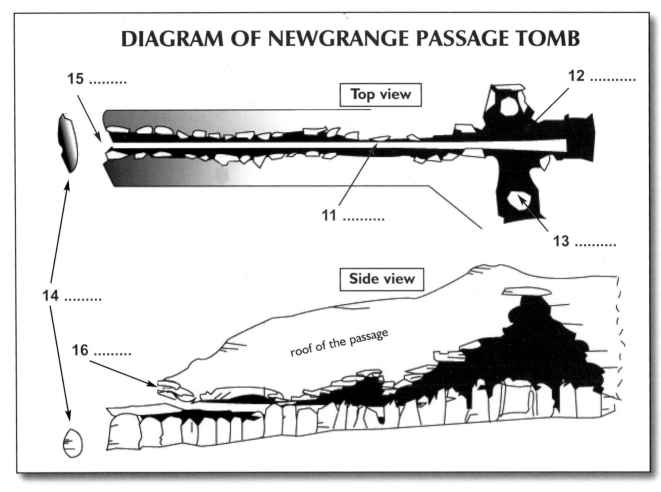

A spiral column	E light box
B passage	F entrance
C stone basin	G kerb stone
D entrance stone	H chamber rooms

Questions 17 - 20
Complete the sentences below.
*Write **ONLY ONE WORD** for each answer.*

The Winter Solstice at Newgrange
17   Anyone may join the gathering of people at Newgrange for the Solstice sunrise; however, access to the chamber itself is ....
18   Access to the chamber is decided in advance by ....
19   The winners of the draw will be notified by the middle of ....
20   Each winner may bring a ....

Listening

SECTION 3   *Questions 21 - 30*

Questions 21 - 24

Choose the best answer A, B, C, or D.

21 What is the doctor's name?

    A Dr Garrison

    B Dr Peters

    C Dr Smith

23 How often does the patient exercise?

    A about once a month

    B every five days

    C every hour

22 The patient is looking for a remedy for his

    A obesity.

    B lack of exercise.

    C stomach complaint.

24 What does the doctor think?

    A that the patient should make a list of what he likes to eat

    B that the patient should change his lifestyle

    C that there is no point in the patient going on exercising so hard

Questions 25 - 30

Complete the summary below.

*Write **NO MORE THAN THREE WORDS AND/OR A NUMBER** for each answer.*

Patient's Diet:

Breakfast is to consist of hot water with squeezed lemon juice, which should be followed 25 .... later by juice and cereal or toast. Organic honey or jam is permitted, but no 26 ...., salt, or sugar is allowed. Lunch is to be a sandwich with salad and, for dinner 27 .... of brown rice or pasta with vegetables and fish.

For dessert you can have a piece of fruit or 28 .... that can be bought from the shop opposite the 29 .... in the High Street. The patient must also absolutely abstain from 30 .... and cigarettes.

SECTION 4 *Questions 31 - 40*

Questions 31 - 40

Complete the notes below.

Write **NO MORE THAN TWO WORDS** *for each answer.*

Notes from Photography Lecture 2

✦ *Exposure = the amount of light you let strike your 31 ....*

✦ *A good photographer must know:*   *1. how much light is required*
                                                       2. how to control light reaching film

   1. how much light is required:
      Usually determined by camera's 32 .... light metre

   2. how to control light reaching film:
      Usually taken care of by aperture and shutter 33 ....

✦ *An aperture is simply a 34 .... that lets light pass through.*
   - aperture size is 35........................ in f-numbers
   - a smaller f-number allows more light in

✦ *The shutter has a 36 .... role.*
   - prevents light from reaching film until the 37 .... of exposure
   - opens for a predetermined amount of time
   - shutter 38 .... is expressed in fractions of a second

✦ *Overexposure = 39 .... than necessary to capture image*
   - pale shades and poor, washed-out colours

✦ *Underexposure = not enough light to capture image*
   - dark image, poor details and 40 ....

Reading

READING PASSAGE 1

*You should spend about 20 minutes on **Questions 1 - 13**, which are based on Reading Passage 1 below.*

DISORDERS: AN OVERVIEW

Autistic Spectrum Disorder

Children with Autistic Spectrum Disorder have difficulty understanding what other people are saying, need help to play with other children, enjoy routines and find unfamiliar situations difficult. People with Autistic Spectrum Disorder can be good at creative activities like art, music and poetry. They can concentrate on one thing for a long time so they can become very good at something that they like doing.

ADHD - Attention Deficit Hyperactivity Disorder

People with ADHD have three types of problems. Overactive behaviour (hyperactivity), impulsive behaviour and difficulty paying attention. Children with ADHD are not just very active but have a wide range of problem behaviours which can make them very difficult to care for and control. Those who have ADHD often find it difficult to fit in at school. They may also have problems getting on with other children. Some children have significant problems with concentration and attention, but are not necessarily overactive or impulsive. These children are sometimes described as having Attention Deficit Disorder (ADD) rather than ADHD. ADD can easily be missed because the child is quiet and dreamy rather than disruptive. ADHD is not related to intelligence. Children with all levels of ability can have ADHD.

Stress

Stress can be defined as the way you feel when you're under abnormal pressure. All sorts of situations can cause stress. The most common, however, involve work, money matters and relationships with partners, children or other family members. Stress may be caused either by major upheavals and life events such as divorce, unemployment, moving house and bereavement, or by a series of minor irritations such as feeling undervalued at work or dealing with difficult children. Some stress can be positive and research has suggested that a moderate level of stress makes us perform better. It also makes us more alert and can help us in challenging situations such as job interviews or public speaking. Stressful situations can also be exhilarating and some people actually thrive on the excitement that comes with dangerous sports or other 'high-risk' activities.

Schizophrenia

Schizophrenia is a diagnosis given to some people who have severely disrupted beliefs and experiences. During an episode of schizophrenia, a person's experience and interpretation of the outside world is disrupted - they may lose touch with reality, see or hear things that are not there and act in unusual ways in response to these 'hallucinations'. An episode of schizophrenia can last for several weeks and can be very frightening. The causes are unknown but episodes of schizophrenia appear to be associated with changes in some brain chemicals. Stressful experiences and some recreational drugs are sometimes thought to trigger an episode.

Depression

Depression describes a range of moods, from the low spirits that we all experience, to a severe problem that interferes with everyday life. The latter type, sometimes referred to as 'clinical depression', is defined as 'a persistent exaggeration of the everyday feelings that accompany sadness'. If you have severe depression you may experience low mood, loss of interest and pleasure as well as feelings of worthlessness and guilt. You may also experience tearfulness, poor concentration, reduced energy, reduced or increased appetite, changes in weight, sleep problems and anxiety. You may even feel that life is not worth living, and plan or attempt suicide.

Obsessive Compulsive Disorder in Adults

Imagine you are getting up in the morning. You know you will need to go to the bathroom, but the thought of accidentally touching the doorknob is frightening. There may be dangerous bacteria on it. Of course you cleaned the entire bathroom yesterday, including the usual series of spraying disinfectant, washing and rinsing. As usual it took a couple of hours to do it the right way. Even then you weren't sure whether you had missed an area, so you had to re-wash the floor. Naturally the doorknob was sprayed and rubbed three times with a bactericidal spray. Now the thought that you could have missed a spot on the doorknob makes you very nervous.

This description might give you some sense of the tormented and anxious world that people with Obsessive Compulsive Disorder (OCD) live in. It is a world filled with dangers from outside and from within. Often elaborate rituals and thoughts are used to ward off feared events, but no amount of mental or physical activity seems adequate, so doubt and anxiety are often present.

People who do not have OCD may perform behaviours in a ritualistic way, repeating, checking, or washing things out of habit or concern. Generally this is done without much, if any, worry. What distinguishes OCD as a psychiatric disorder is that the experience of obsessions, and the performance of rituals, reaches such an intensity or frequency that it causes significant psychological distress and interferes in a significant way with psychosocial functioning. The guideline of at least one hour spent on symptoms per day is often used as a measure of 'significant interference'. However, among patients who try to avoid situations that bring on anxiety and compulsions, the actual symptoms may not consume an hour. Yet the quantity of time lost from having to avoid objects or situations would clearly constitute interfering with functioning. Consider, for instance, a welfare mother who throws out more than $100 of groceries a week because of contamination fears. Although this behaviour has a major effect on her functioning, it might not consume one hour per day.

Patients with OCD describe their experience as having thoughts (obsessions) that they associate with some danger. The sufferer generally recognises that it is his or her own thoughts, rather than something imposed by someone else (as in some paranoid schizophrenic patients). However, the disturbing thoughts cannot be dismissed, and simply nag at the sufferer. Something must then be done to relieve the danger and mitigate the fear. This leads to actions and thoughts that are intended to neutralise the danger. These are the compulsions. Because these behaviours seem to give the otherwise 'helplessly anxious' person something to combat the danger, they are temporarily reassuring. However, since the 'danger' is typically irrational or imaginary, it simply returns, thereby triggering another cycle of the briefly reassuring compulsions. From the standpoint of classic conditioning, this pattern of painful obsession followed by temporarily reassuring compulsion eventually produces an intensely ingrained habit. It is rare to see obsessions without compulsions.

The two most common obsessions are fears of contamination and fear of harming oneself or others, while the two most common compulsions are checking and cleaning.

Reading

Questions 1 - 5

Look at the statements (Questions 1 - 5) and the lists of disorders (A - G) below.

Match each statement with the correct disorder A - G.

Write the correct letter A - G next to questions 1 - 5 below.

NB *There are more disorders than descriptions, so you will not use them all.*

1	can be positive in small doses but is generally associated with pressure	....
2	feeling that there is danger constantly present	....
3	has experiences that may or may not be part of the 'real' world	....
4	active to the point of losing concentration and becoming disruptive	....
5	good at art but not at communicating	....

TYPES OF DISORDERS

A   Stress

B   Autistic Spectrum Disorder

C   Attention Deficit Disorder

D   Schizophrenia

E   Attention Deficit Hyperactivity Disorder

F   Depression

G   Obsessive Compulsive Disorder

Reading Tip:

Remember that there is more than one way to read a text. It is not always necessary to read slowly and carefully. Remember that you are reading texts in order to answer questions and that should be your main focus.

Questions 6 - 9

Complete the table below.

*Write **NO MORE THAN THREE WORDS** from the passage for each answer.*

Disorder	Personality Trait Exhibited by Sufferer
Autism Spectrum Disorder	May excel in activities of a **6** ....,... nature.
Attention Deficit Disorder	May appear **7** ....
Schizophrenia	May respond to experiencing episodes of the disease by behaving in very **8** ....
Depression	May experience feelings of futility that lead to thoughts of **9** ....
Obsessive Compulsive Disorder	May frequently experience feelings of doubt and anxiety.

Questions 10 - 13

*Choose the correct letter, **A, B, C** or **D**.*

10 Which disorder could cause visible physical changes?

A   Autistic Spectrum Disorder

B   Stress

C   Schizophrenia

D   Depression

11 Episodes of which disorder may last for a limited period of time?

A   ADHD

B   Autistic Spectrum Disorder

C   schizophrenia

D   depression

12 Which disorder can be triggered by the death of a loved one?

A   Autistic Spectrum Disorder

B   ADHD

C   Stress

D   OCD

13 What characterises sufferers of OCD?

A   the fear of going outside

B   the performance of rituals

C   the desire to hurt others

D   the feeling that they are helpless to ease their distress

Reading

READING PASSAGE 2

*You should spend about 20 minutes on **Questions 14 - 26**, which are based on Reading Passage 2 below.*

THE DEVELOPING WORLD

A

THE DEVELOPING WORLD - the economically underdeveloped countries of Asia, Africa, Oceania and Latin America - is considered as an entity with common characteristics, such as poverty, high birth rates, and economic dependence on the advanced countries. Until recently, the developing world was known as 'the third world'. The French demographer Alfred Sauvy coined the expression (in French) in 1952 by analogy with the 'third estate' - the commoners of France before and during the French Revolution - as opposed to priests and nobles, comprising the first and second estates respectively. 'Like the third estate', wrote Sauvy, 'the third world is nothing, and it wants to be something'. The term therefore implies that the third world is exploited, much as the third estate was exploited and that, like the third estate, its destiny is a revolutionary one. It conveys as well a second idea, also discussed by Sauvy – that of non-alignment, for the developing world belongs neither to the industrialised capitalist world nor to the industrialised former communist bloc. The expression 'third world' was used at the 1955 conference of Afro-Asian countries held in Bandung, Indonesia. In 1956 a group of social scientists associated with Sauvy's National Institute of Demographic Studies, in Paris, published a book called 'Le Tiers-Monde'. Three years later, the French economist Francois Perroux launched a new journal, on problems of underdevelopment, with the same title. By the end of the 1950s the term was frequently employed in the French media to refer to the underdeveloped countries of Asia, Africa, Oceania and Latin America. Present-day politicians and social commentators, however, now use the term 'developing world' in a politically correct effort to dispel the negative connotations of 'third world'.

B

Countries in the developing world have a number of common traits: distorted and highly dependent economies devoted to producing primary products for the developed world; traditional, rural social structures; high population growth and widespread poverty. Nevertheless, the developing world is sharply differentiated, for it includes countries on various levels of economic development. And despite the poverty of the countryside and the urban shanty towns, the ruling elites of most third world countries are wealthy.

C

This combination of conditions in Asia, Africa, Oceania and Latin America is linked to the absorption of the developing world into the international capitalist economy, by way of conquest or indirect domination. The main economic consequence of Western domination was the creation, for the first time in history, of a world market. By setting up sub-economies linked to the West throughout the developing world, and by introducing other modern institutions, industrial capitalism disrupted traditional economies and, indeed, societies. This disruption led to underdevelopment.

D

Because the economies of underdeveloped countries have been geared to the needs of industrialised countries, they often comprise only a few modern economic activities, such as mining or the cultivation of plantation crops. Control over these activities has often remained in the hands of large foreign firms. The prices of developing world products are usually determined by large buyers in the economically dominant countries of the West, and trade with the West provides almost all the developing world's income. Throughout the colonial period, outright exploitation severely limited the accumulation of capital within the foreign-dominated countries. Even after decolonisation (in

the 1950s, 1960s, and 1970s), the economies of the developing world grew slowly, or not at all, owing largely to the deterioration of the 'terms of trade' – the relationship between the cost of the goods a nation must import from abroad and its income from the exports it sends to foreign countries. Terms of trade are said to deteriorate when the cost of imports rises faster than income from exports. Since buyers in the industrialised countries determined the prices of most products involved in international trade, the worsening position of the developing world was scarcely surprising. Only the oil-producing countries – after 1973 – succeeded in escaping the effects of Western domination of the world economy.

E

No study of the developing world could hope to assess its future prospects without taking into account population growth. While the mortality rate from poverty-related diseases continues to cause international concern, the birth rate continues to rise at unprecedented levels. This population explosion in the developing world will surely prevent any substantial improvements in living standards, as well as threaten people in stagnant economies with worsening poverty and starvation levels.

Reading

Questions 14 - 18

Reading Passage 2 has five paragraphs, **A - E**.

Choose the most suitable heading for each paragraph from the list of headings below.

Write the appropriate number i - viii in spaces 14 - 18 below.

List of Headings

i   The great divide between rich and poor.

ii   The status and destiny of the developing world follows a European precedent.

iii   Economic progress in the developing world slowed down by political unrest.

iv   More people, less food.

v   Western countries refuse to acknowledge their history of colonisation.

vi   Open trade is the main reason these countries become impoverished.

vii   Rivalry in the developing world between capitalist and former communist bloc countries.

viii Prices and conditions set by outsiders.

14	Paragraph **A**	....
15	Paragraph **B**	....
16	Paragraph **C**	....
17	Paragraph **D**	....
18	Paragraph **E**	....

Reading Tip:
If you are having a difficult time with a particular question, simply leave it and go on to the next one. If you have time you can come back and answer that question later.

Questions 19 - 22

Do the following statements agree with the information given in Reading Passage 2?

In spaces 19 - 22 below, write

YES	*if the statement agrees with the information*
NO	*if the statement contradicts the information*
NOT GIVEN	*if there is no information on this*

19   Agriculture still plays a role in the economy of developing countries.   ....

20   The population of the developing world increases at such a fast
      rate because they constantly need to renew the labour force.   ....

21   Countries that spend more on imports than they earn
      from exports can experience problems.   ....

22   Like the developing world, oil-rich countries are also
      victims of dominance by Western powers.   ....

Questions 23 - 26

*Complete each sentence with the correct ending **A - F** below.*

*Write the correct letter **A - F** in spaces 23 - 26 below.*

23   Countries in the developing world   ....
24   The term 'the third world' implies   ....
25   One factor that is prevalent in the developing world is   ....
26   One consequence of the terms of trade was   ....

A	economic dependence on developed countries.
B	that decolonisation took a long time to achieve.
C	dictate the needs of industrialised countries.
D	share common characteristics.
E	that many economies stagnated.
F	a society that wants something it does not have.

Reading

READING PASSAGE 3

*You should spend about 20 minutes on **Questions 27 - 40**, which are based on Reading Passage 3 below.*

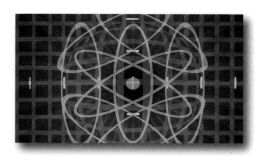

BIOMETRICS

A

The term "biometrics" is derived from the Greek words bio (life) and metric (to measure). It refers to technologies for measuring and analysing a person's physiological or behavioural characteristics, such as fingerprints, irises, voice patterns, facial patterns and hand measurements, for identification and verification purposes. One of the earliest known examples of biometrics in practice was a form of fingerprinting used in China in the 14th century. Chinese merchants stamped children's palm prints and footprints on paper with ink to distinguish the young children from one another. This method of biometrics is still being practised today.

B

Until the late 1800s, identification largely relied upon 'photographic memory.' In the 1890s, an anthropologist and police desk clerk in Paris named Alphonse Bertillon sought to fix the problem of identifying convicted criminals and turned biometrics into a distinct field of study. He developed a method of multiple body measurements which was named after him - *Bertillonage*. Bertillon based his system on the claim that measurement of adult bones does not change after the age of 20. He also introduced a cataloguing system, which enabled the filing and checking of records quite quickly. His system was used by police authorities throughout the world, until 1903, when two identical measurements were obtained for two different persons at Fort Leavenworth prison. The prison switched to fingerprinting the following day and the rest of the world soon followed, abandoning Bertillonage forever. After the failure of Bertillonage, the police started using fingerprinting, which was developed by Richard Edward Henry of Scotland Yard, essentially reverting to the same methods used by the Chinese for years.

C

In the past three decades biometrics has moved from a single method (fingerprinting) to more than ten different methods. Hundreds of companies are involved with this development and continue to improve their methods as the technology available to them advances. As the industry grows, however, so does the public concern over privacy issues. Laws and regulations continue to be drafted and standards are beginning to be developed. While no other biometric has yet reached the wide range of use of fingerprinting, some are beginning to be used in both legal and business areas.

D

Identification and verification have long been in practice by presenting a personal document, such as a licence, ID card or a passport. It may also require personal information such as passwords or PINs. For security reasons, often two, or all three, of these systems are combined but as times progress, we are in constant need for more secure and accurate measures. Authentication by biometric verification is becoming increasingly common in corporate and public security systems, consumer electronics and point-of-sale applications. In addition to security, the driving force behind biometric verification has been convenience. Already, many European countries are introducing a biometric passport which will carry a paper-thin computer chip to store the facial image and at least one additional biometric identifier. This will help to counter fraudulent efforts to obtain duplicate passports and will verify the identity of the holder against the document.

E

Identification and verification are mainly used today in the fight against crime with the methods of fingerprint and DNA analysis. It is also used in security for granting access rights by voice pattern recognition. Additionally, it is used for personal comfort by identifying a person and changing personal settings accordingly, as in setting car seats by facial recognition. Starting in early 2000, the use of biometrics in schools has become widespread, particularly in the UK and USA. A number of justifications are given for such practices, including combatting truancy, and replacing library cards or meal cards with fingerprinting systems. Opponents of school biometrics have raised privacy concerns against the creation of databases that would progressively include the entire population.

F

Biometric devices consist of a reader or scanning device, software that converts the gathered information into digital form, and a database that stores the biometric data for comparison with previous records. When converting the biometric input, the software identifies specific points of data as match points. The match points are processed using an algorithm into a value that can be compared with biometric data in the database. There are two types of biometrics: behavioural and physical. Behavioural biometrics are generally used for verification while physical biometrics can be used for either identification or verification.

G

Iris-pattern and retina-pattern authentication methods are already employed in some bank automatic teller machines. Voice waveform recognition, a method of verification that has been used for many years with tape recordings in telephone wiretaps, is now being used for access to proprietary databanks in research facilities. Facial-recognition technology has been used by law enforcement to pick out individuals in large crowds with considerable reliability. Hand geometry is being used in industry to provide physical access to buildings. Earlobe geometry has been used to disprove the identity of individuals who claim to be someone they are not (identity theft). Signature comparison is not as reliable, all by itself, as other biometric verification methods but offers an extra layer of verification when used in conjunction with one or more other methods. No matter what biometric methodology is used, the identification verification process remains the same. A record of a person's unique characteristic is captured and kept in a database. Later on, when identification verification is required, a new record is captured and compared with the previous record in the database. If the data in the new record matches that in the database record, the person's identity is confirmed.

H

As technology advances, and time goes on, more and more private companies and public utilities will use biometrics for safe, accurate identification. However, these advances will raise many concerns throughout society, where many may not be educated on the methods. Some believe this technology can cause physical harm to an individual using it, or that instruments used are unsanitary. For example, there are concerns that retina scanners might not always be clean. There are also concerns as to whether our personal information taken through biometric methods can be misused, tampered with, or sold, eg. by criminals stealing, rearranging or copying the biometric data. Also, the data obtained using biometrics can be used in unauthorised ways without the individual's consent. Much still remains to be seen in the effectiveness of biometric verification before we can identify it as the safest system for identification.

Reading

Questions 27 - 31

Reading Passage 3 has eight paragraphs, **A - H**.

Which paragraph contains the following information?

*Write the correct letter **A - H** in spaces 27 - 31 below.*

27   possible health hazards associated with the use of biometrics   ....

28   convicted criminals were not the first to be identified by the use of biometrics   ....

29   the application of mathematics in assessing biometric data   ....

30   despite its limitations, biometrics has become a commercial field of activity   ....

31   some biometric methods are useful only in conjunction with others   ....

Questions 32 - 34

Complete the sentences below.

*Choose **NO MORE THAN TWO WORDS** from the passage for each answer.*

32   Members of the public are becoming increasingly worried about the

        .... that may accompany the use of biometrics.

33   Biometrics can be used to improve the ....

        of drivers and passengers.

34   Regardless of the technology used, it has one common purpose:

        to find somebody's .... and store it on computer.

> **Reading Tip:**
> Always remain conscious of time limits.
> Never spend too much time on just one question.

Practice Test 2

Questions 35 - 40

Complete the summary with the list of words A - L below.

Write the correct letter A - L in spaces 35 - 40 below.

BIOMETRICS

As long ago as the 14th century, the Chinese made use of biometrics in order to tell young children apart, but it was only in the 1890s when it was first used by the authorities as a means of **35** .... in criminal cases. The system developed by the Frenchman Bertillon – that of measuring adult bones - was flawed, however, and so police adopted **36** .... as a more reliable way of identifying suspects. Governments, companies and even schools employ biometric technology to ensure, for example, that people do not enter a country illegally, gain access to certain buildings, or assume someone else's **37** .... Apart from security, another important **38** .... behind biometric verification has been **39** .... The use of biometrics, however, has its critics, who say that the data collected could be used for different purposes without our **40** ....

A	identification	B	security	C	convenience
D	scanning	E	fingerprinting	F	identity
G	violation	H	measuring	I	justification
J	approval	K	factor	L	apprehension

Writing

WRITING TASK 1

You should spend about 20 minutes on this task.

> *The graph below shows the working hours for men and women in the developing world between the years 1998 and 2003.*
>
> *Summarise the information by selecting and reporting the main features, and make comparisons where necessary.*

Write at least 150 words.

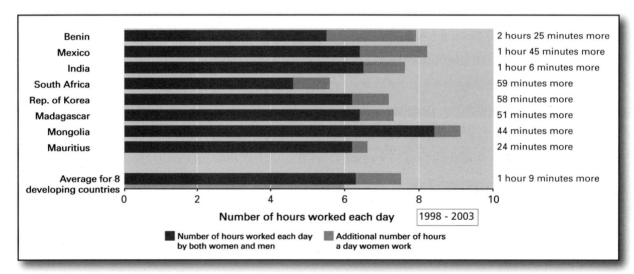

Writing Tip:
Writing Task 2 carries more marks than Writing Task 1, so leave plenty of time for it.

WRITING TASK 2

You should spend about 40 minutes on this task.

Write about the following topic:

> *Most people in the world have to work to earn a living. However, many people work only for the financial gain that it involves, and not for any other rewards that a job can offer.*
>
> *What do you think the main considerations when deciding what job to take should be?*

Give reasons for your answer and include any relevant examples from your own knowledge or experience.

Write at least 250 words.

Speaking

PART 1   (4-5 minutes)

The examiner asks the candidate about him/herself, his/her home, work or studies and other familiar topics.

Leisure Time

- What do you like to do to relax in your free time?
- What is your idea of a perfect weekend?
- Do you prefer to watch TV or go to the cinema?
- What forms of entertainment exist in the area where you live?

PART 2   (2 minutes)

You will have to talk about the topic for one to two minutes. You have one minute to think about what you are going to say. You can make some notes to help you if you wish.

> **Describe a sport you enjoy doing or watching.**
>
> **You should say**
> - **what the sport or activity is**
> - **what its main features are**
> - **when and where you first played or saw it**
>
> **and explain why you like it.**

PART 3   (4-5 minutes)

Discussion topics:

Sports

- What personal benefits may be gained by participating in sports?
- What qualities do you think are necessary in order to work as part of a team?
- Why do you think some people enjoy extreme, or dangerous, sports?

Financial Aspect of Sports

- Many sports are cost prohibitive. Can you think of any? Why are they so expensive?
- Do you think that some professional sports people earn too much money?
- Would you pay money for a T-shirt or other gear with a team logo? Why or why not?

Test 3

Listening

SECTION 1   *Questions 1 - 10*

Complete the form below.

Write **NO MORE THAN THREE WORDS AND/OR A NUMBER** *for each answer.*

TOM'S COMPUTER MAINTENANCE

Customer Information Form

Date: *Sunday, 12th May*

Example: *Answer:*

Reason for call: .... *computer problem* ....

....

What happened: the screen **1** ....

Troubleshooting checklist:

☑ restarted computer

☑ The computer is **2** .... - not running on battery

Activity when the problem occurred: **3** ....

Possible diagnosis: **a virus**

Anti-virus programme: 4 ....

Appointment

Location: 5 ....

Time scheduled for visit: 6 ....

Street address: *14* **7** .... *Crescent, 2F3*

Customer name: *Sandra* **8** ....

Name on buzzer: *the same as above*

Fee: 9 .... *for the first hour's work, then £40 per hour*

Estimated time for job: *less than* **10** ....

SECTION 2   *Questions 11 - 20*

Questions 11 - 17
Choose the correct letter, A, B or C.

11   The speaker's job requires
   A   a great deal of walking.
   B   extensive travel.
   C   clean water.

12   Why is this story being told?
   A   to promote Charity-Water
   B   for entertainment purposes
   C   to encourage Helen

13   Why do the charity workers usually surprise communities?
   A   It makes people happy.
   B   It is difficult to spread news.
   C   It makes their work easier.

14   When villagers heard of the charity workers' arrival, they
   A   had a party.
   B   were suspicious.
   C   took no notice.

15   Helen is feeling
   A   ecstatic about her new life.
   B   curious about the charity workers.
   C   nostalgic about her old life.

16   What did the speaker notice about Helen?
   A   that she had bathed recently
   B   the care she took with her appearance
   C   that she was wearing a green uniform

17   Making someone feel beautiful was
   A   part of the speaker's job description.
   B   an unexpected bonus for the speaker.
   C   of little importance to the speaker.

Questions 18 - 20

*In what **THREE** ways did the new well improve Helen's life?*
*Choose **THREE** letters A - G.*

              18 ......   **19** ......   **20** ......

A Her children enjoyed better health.	**E** She had more choices and options.
B It increased her household income.	**F** She made new friends in her village.
C It gave her more free time.	**G** It allowed her to go to school.
D She got a leadership position.	

Listening

SECTION 3   *Questions 21 - 30*

Questions 21 - 25

Complete the sentences below.

Write **NO MORE THAN TWO WORDS AND/OR A NUMBER** *for each answer.*

---

21 Jessica is interviewing Dr. Kitching for .... for the school newspaper.

22 Everyone Jessica knows is rather .... about how to ask for references.

23 Dr. Kitching gives Jessica permission to .... their conversation.

24 Dr. Kitching writes more than .... a year.

25 The majority of .... are in the spring or early summer when students start thinking about their future.

Questions 26 - 30

Complete the flow-chart below.
*Choose **FIVE** answers from the box and write the correct letter **A - G** next to questions 26 - 30.*

A. message

B. meeting

C. information

D. exam

E. telephone call

F. course

G. email

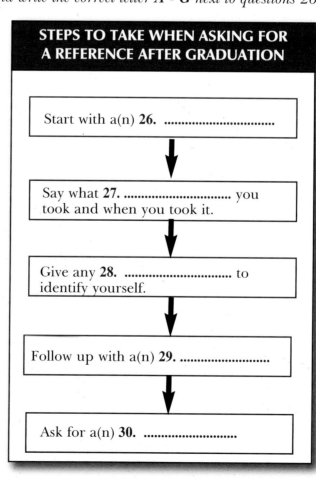

STEPS TO TAKE WHEN ASKING FOR A REFERENCE AFTER GRADUATION

Start with a(n) **26.** ....

⬇

Say what **27.** .... you took and when you took it.

⬇

Give any **28.** .... to identify yourself.

⬇

Follow up with a(n) **29.** ....

⬇

Ask for a(n) **30.** ....

SECTION 4   Questions 31 - 40

Questions 31 - 40

Complete the notes below.

Write **NO MORE THAN THREE WORDS** for each answer.

Date: *6th November*

Lecture Topic: **Primate Behaviour**

Review - Last lecture we talked about how physical features apply to:

- *living primates*
- *classification*
- *31 ....*

- *Human evolution is not just about how people have 32 ....,
  but also about how our behaviour evolved.*
- *The most notable thing about humans is not just that they walk on two legs
  but that they can 33 ....*

◄ • ►

Primate Cognitive Abilities

Cognition = the amount of 34.......................... that goes into a behaviour.

It's difficult to come up with 35 .... to measure cognition.

How sentient are the 36 .... ?

Sentient = there is 37 .... conscious thought

Behaviours that support the presence of conscious thought in primates:

- *Various sorts of 38.............................. (helping others without benefit)*
- *"Machiavellian Intelligence" or deliberate 39 ....*
- *Chimps can be language trained - highly intelligent*

- *Cognition and intelligence in primates has deep 40 ....
  ramifications.*

Reading

READING PASSAGE 1

*You should spend about 20 minutes on **Questions 1 - 13**, which are based on Reading Passage 1 below.*

PROJECT: Reform Of The Prison System In The UK

Penal progress:

The UK's large prison population is fuelled by a high level of recidivism - when criminals repeatedly relapse into crime. This project for a model prison tackles issues of architecture, management and funding in an enlightened attempt to achieve lasting rehabilitation.

Project:

The penal system is one of the most direct manifestations of the power of the state, but is often also a revealing reflection of the national psyche and the public's attitude to punishment and rehabilitation. Surprisingly, for a prosperous, progressive Western democracy, the UK has a lamentable penal record. Britain's prison population is currently in excess of 60,000 (up 50 per cent from a decade ago) making it the second largest in Europe. The average cost of keeping an individual prisoner incarcerated for a year is £27,000 (ten times the average expenditure on a secondary school pupil in the state sector). Despite such substantial investment, over half of British prisoners re-offend within two years of release.

Such high rates of recidivism is a serious problem. It means that the prison population is continuing to grow at an alarming rate (recently by as many as 700 a week), so overcrowding is endemic, hampering opportunities for education and rehabilitation and lowering staff and prisoner morale. To ease this pressure, the UK government is investing in the prison estate at historic levels, with 12,000 new prison places proposed within the next few years. Yet, like their nineteenth-century predecessors, Britain's 'new Victorian' prisons are designed for security and control rather than for the rehabilitation and education which is increasingly recognised as what prisoners need. Most are poorly

educated young men under 30 (at least 60 per cent of whom are functionally illiterate and innumerate), so without education and skills few will be able to build meaningful lives away from crime, no matter how often they go to prison, or how long they spend there.

Any transformation of the penal system must start with the redesign of prison buildings. Prison architecture has a clearly discernible effect on behaviour, operational efficiency, interaction and morale. Last year, architects Buschow Henley were commissioned by a think tank organisation working with the Home Office Prison Service to research and develop an alternative prison model that focuses more intensely on rehabilitation through a concentrated programme of intellectual, physical and social education. The model is not intended as a blueprint but rather a series of principles that might be adapted to support the wider concept of the 'Learning Prison' in which other aspects such as organisation, management and funding would obviously play a part. Key to this is the introduction of a system that groups together prisoners in small communities or 'houses' of between 30 and 40 inmates. This has two important consequences. First, the more compact spatial organisation of the house reduces staff time spent on supervising and escorting prisoners. Second, the system places educational and other facilities at the heart of the building, within easy reach at all times of day, reinforced by a supportive social environment. This model also enables resources to be dramatically redeployed, from a current estimated ratio of 80:20 (costs of security versus rehabilitation) to a predicted reversed figure of 20:80, freeing up much-needed funds to invest in educational programmes, thereby helping to promote rehabilitation, reduce recidivism and initiate a virtuous cycle.

In Buschow Henley's scheme, the proposed group size of 30-40 has the potential for social accountability - each prisoner being known within the community and personally accountable for his behaviour. Houses are semi-autonomous, not just dormitories, with communal, as opposed to centralised, facilities. Circulation is simplified and reduced. Buildings are arranged in a chess-board formation, as opposed to pavilions marooned in space, each with a discrete external area that can be productively used for sport, games or gardening with a minimum of supervision.

Individual cells are replanned to make them less like domestic lavatories and more conducive to learning. In an inversion of the conventional layout, the bed is placed lengthways along the external wall at high level, freeing up space below. Storage is built in and each inmate is provided with a moveable table equipped with electronic tools for study. Washing facilities are contained in a small adjoining space (included in the basic 8 sqm allowance) so reducing pressure on prison staff to manage inmate hygiene and ablution. Each cell is paired with a neighbouring 'buddy' cell linked by sliding doors controlled by individual prisoners to mitigate the risk of self-harm.

While this new type of prison appears to be somewhat liberal, the arrangement of spaces and functions both inside and out is actually tightly controlled. Paradoxically, however, this proscription enables a greater range of activities to take place, and makes general supervision easier. In this environment the prisoners are judged not by their

degree of conformity, but by the scope of their activities and achievements, so laying the foundations for genuine rehabilitation. As Martin Narey, Director General of the UK Prison Services observes, 'We have got to accept that prison must be a humane and constructive place, not least because all but 23 of my population are going home some day.'

Reading

Questions 1 - 5

Complete each sentence with the correct ending, A - H, below.
*Write the correct letter **A - H** in spaces 1 - 5 below.*

1	The agenda of current British prison systems is primarily	1. ....
2	The primary role of prisons should be	2. ....
3	The new prison scheme will create	3. ....
4	Existing prison architecture causes	4. ....
5	The positive results of reducing the number of prisoners in one space include	5. ....

A   improved security, supervision and education.

B   rehabilitation and education.

C   reduced efficiency, morale and interaction.

D   reduced risk of self harm.

E   security and control.

F   an alternative prison model

G   a learning environment rather than a punitive compound.

H   organisation, management and funding.

Questions 6 - 9

Choose the correct letter A, B, C or D.

6   The project to reform the penal system in the UK

      A   is progressive.
      B   is inexpensive.
      C   will eliminate the need for supervision.
      D   is, primarily, to make prisoners more comfortable.

7   The proposal to create 12,000 new prison places, within the next few years, indicates that

      A   prison cells are too small.
      B   a lot of money is invested into educating offenders.
      C   there is an increasing population of offenders in the UK.
      D   the government is getting tougher on offenders.

8   The proposed changes to prison architecture are designed primarily to

      A   improve the aesthetic value of the building.
      B   boost self-esteem and social behaviour.
      C   allow prisoners more living space.
      D   increase running costs within prisons.

9   Why is the bed placed lengthways along the external wall at high level?

      A   to make room below for washing facilities
      B   for the improvement of the inmates' hygiene
      C   to allow room below for storage and shelves
      D   to make room for sliding doors

Questions 10 - 13

Label the diagram below.

*Write **NO MORE THAN THREE WORDS** from the passage for each answer.*

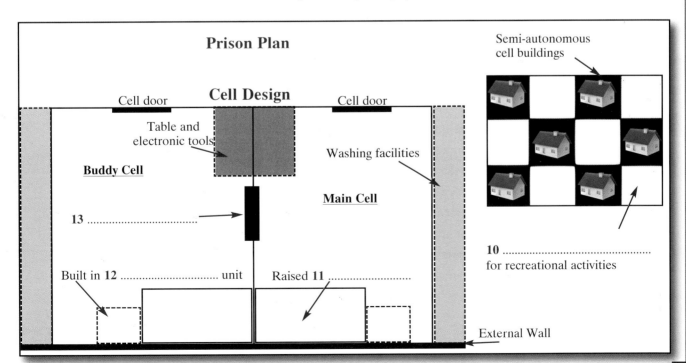

Prison Plan

Semi-autonomous cell buildings

Cell Design

Cell door   Cell door

Table and electronic tools

Washing facilities

Buddy Cell

Main Cell

13 ....

10 ....
for recreational activities

Built in 12 .... unit   Raised 11 ....

External Wall

Reading

READING PASSAGE 2

*You should spend about 20 minutes on **Questions 14 - 26**, which are based on Reading Passage 2 below.*

SPECIAL OLYMPICS

CONDITIONS OF PARTICIPATION

To be eligible for participation in the Special Olympics an individual with an intellectual disability must agree to observe and abide by the SOC Sports Rules. 'Mental Retardation' refers to substantial limitations in present functioning. It is characterised by significantly sub-average intellectual functioning, existing concurrently with related limitations in two or more of the following applicable adaptive skill areas: communication, self-care, home living, social skills, community use, self-direction, health and safety, functional academics, leisure and work. Mental retardation manifests itself before the age of 18. The following four assumptions are essential to the application of the definition:

1.   Valid assessment considers cultural and linguistic diversity as well as differences in communication and behavioural factors.
2.   The existence of limitations in adaptive skills occurs within the context of community environments typical of the individual's age-peers and is indexed to the person's individualised needs for support.
3.   Specific adaptive limitations often co-exist with strengths in other adaptive skills or other personal capabilities.
4.   With appropriate support over a sustained period, the life functioning of the person with mental retardation will generally improve.

The term 'mental retardation' is a diagnostic term used to describe the condition defined above. In keeping with the current language practised within the field, the term 'mental retardation' is no longer commonly used. In its place, if it is absolutely necessary to use a label, i.e. in an educational setting or in a SOC/NCCP Technical Programme, then the term that is in keeping with the current practices is *a person with an intellectual disability*. Special Olympics was created and developed to give individuals with an intellectual disability the opportunity to train and compete in sport activities. No person shall, on the grounds of gender, race, religion, colour, national origin or financial constraint be excluded from participation in, or be denied the benefits of, or otherwise be subjected to discrimination under any programme or activity of Special Olympics. Flexibility is left to the Local, Region/Zone, Chapter and National Special Olympics organisations for determining the eligibility of the participants because of the variety of situations and needs that exist in the many localities where Special Olympics programmes have been and will be instituted. Inclusion is preferred to exclusion when eligibility is in question. Individuals who have both an intellectual disability and multiple disabilities may participate in Special Olympics programmes and competitions.

A. *Participation by individuals with Down Syndrome who have Atlantoaxial Instability.*

There is evidence from medical research that up to 15 percent of individuals with Down Syndrome have a defect in the cervical vertebrae C-1 and C-2 in the neck. This condition exposes Down Syndrome individuals to the heightened possibility of a neck injury if they participate in activities that hyperextend or radically flex the neck or upper spine.

B. *SOC requires temporary restriction of individuals with Down Syndrome from participation in certain activities.*

1) Accredited Programmes may allow all individuals with Down Syndrome to continue in most Special Olympics sports training and competition activities. However, such individuals shall not be permitted to participate in sport training and competitions which, by their nature, result in hyperextension, radical flexion or direct pressure on the neck or upper spine. Such sports training and competition activities include: the butterfly stroke and diving starts in swimming, diving, pentathlon, high jump, equestrian sports, artistic gymnastics, soccer, alpine skiing and any warm-up exercise placing undue stress on the head and neck.

2) Restriction from participation in the above-listed activities shall continue until an individual with Down Syndrome has been examined (including X-ray views of full extension and flexion of the neck) by a physician who has been briefed on the nature of the Atlantoaxial Instability condition, and the results of such an examination demonstrate that the individual does not have the Atlantoaxial Instability condition.

3) For any individual diagnosed as having Atlantoaxial Instability condition, the examining physician shall notify the athlete's parents or guardians of the nature and extent of the individual's condition and such athlete shall be allowed to participate in the activities listed in 1) above only if the athlete submits written certification from two physicians combined with an acknowledgment of the risks signed by the adult athlete or his/her parent or guardian if the athlete is a minor.

4) It is the responsibility of parents/guardians to monitor the individual and take appropriate action if neurological symptoms appear.

Terminology note: the term intellectual disability is used to replace the clinical term of Mental Retardation. Intellectual disability is not a disease, nor should it be confused with mental illness. People with mental disabilities have both a slower rate of learning and a limited capacity to learn. They may also have difficulty managing the ordinary activities of daily living, understanding the behaviour of others, and determining their own appropriate social responses (adaptive behaviour). Children with intellectual disabilities grow into adults with intellectual disabilities; they do not remain 'eternal children'.

People with intellectual disabilities constitute one of the largest groups of citizens with disabilities. There are an estimated 156 million individuals in the world who have intellectual disabilities. Intellectual disability cuts across lines of race, education, and social and economic background. It can occur in anyone. Hereditary components are known to account for only a fraction of the cases of intellectual disability. There are well over 350 causes of intellectual disability and in three-quarters of the cases the specific cause is unknown. About 87 percent of all people with intellectual disabilities are mildly afflicted and in many respects are indistinguishable from people who do not have intellectual disabilities.

Reading

Questions 14 - 20

Do the following statements agree with the information given in Reading Passage 2?

In spaces 14 - 20 below, write

TRUE	*if the statement agrees with the information*
FALSE	*if the statement contradicts the information*
NOT GIVEN	*if there is no information on this*

14   To be eligible to take part in the Special Olympics, the athlete has to be not only less than intellectually capable, but must also be lacking in a number of other functions.   ....

15   People with intellectual disabilities never improve their lives.   ....

16   All people with intellectual disabilities need the written permission of a parent or guardian in order to participate.   ....

17   Down Syndrome participants often excel in their chosen field of athletic activity.   ....

18   People with Down Syndrome cannot participate in any swimming events.   ....

19   If you have Down Syndrome, your neck may be at risk of damage in certain sports.   ....

20   Participation in sports helps people with intellectual disabilities to improve their communication and social skills.   ....

Questions 21 - 23

Choose the correct letter A, B, C or D.

21   What were the objectives of the Special Olympics document?
    A   to inform the public about what they are to expect from the Special Olympics
    B   to provide information for future candidates
    C   to promote awareness in the general population of the plight of disabled people
    D   to list the problems intellectually disabled people have

22   What does the passage say about intellectual disability?
    A   The majority of cases are inherited.
    B   Sufferers of the condition outnumber those with physical disabilities.
    C   In most cases, the cause of the condition cannot be determined.
    D   It may be determined by race, education, or social and economic background.

23   What word best describes the Special Olympics participation policy?
    A   inconsistent
    B   ambiguous
    C   controversial
    D   non-discriminatory

Questions 24 - 26

Which **THREE** of the following facts relating to Down Syndrome are mentioned ?
Choose three letter A - F

24. ___   25. ___   26. ___

A	It is thought that about one Down Syndrome person in every seven has Atlantoaxial Instability.
B	A person with Down Syndrome cannot participate in any winter competitions.
C	Down Syndrome sufferers with Atlantoaxial Instability who are minors need permission from a guardian to play soccer.
D	Down Syndrome sufferers are unable to flex the upper spine.
E	Down Syndrome athletes need to wear a neck brace to participate in the Special Olympics.
F	Down Syndrome athletes can take part in sports that do not directly affect the neck or spine without any preconditions being fulfilled.

Reading

READING PASSAGE 3

*You should spend about 20 minutes on **Questions 27 - 40**, which are based on Reading Passage 3 below.*

Migrants and Refugees:
Racial Discrimination and Xenophobia

Today, one in every 50 human beings is a migrant worker, a refugee or asylum seeker, or an immigrant living in a foreign country. Current estimates by the United Nations and the International Organisation for Migration indicate that some 150 million people live temporarily or permanently outside their countries of origin (2.5% of the world population). Many of these, 80-97 million, are estimated to be migrant workers with members of their families.

Another 12 million are refugees outside their country of origin. These figures do not include the estimated 20 million Internally Displaced Persons forcibly displaced within their own country, nor the tens of millions more of internal migrants, mainly rural to urban, in countries around the world.

Increasing ethnic and racial diversity of societies is the inevitable consequence of migration. Increasing migration means that a growing number of states have become or are becoming more multi-ethnic, and are confronted with the challenge of accommodating peoples of different cultures, races, religions and languages. Addressing the reality of increased diversity means finding political, legal, social and economic mechanisms to ensure mutual respect and to mediate relations across differences. But xenophobia and racism have become manifest in some societies which have received substantial numbers of immigrants, as workers or as asylum-seekers. In those countries the migrants have become the targets in internal disputes about national identity. In the last few decades, the emergence of new nation states has often been accompanied by ethnic exclusion.

As governments grapple with the new realities of their multi-ethnic societies, there has been a marked increase in discrimination and violence directed against migrants, refugees and other non-nationals by extremist groups in many parts of the world. The lack of any systematic documentation or research over time makes it unclear whether there is a real increase in the level of abuse or in the level of exposure and reporting. Unfortunately, there is more than enough anecdotal evidence to show that violations of the human rights of migrants, refugees and other non-nationals are so generalised, widespread and commonplace that they are a defining feature of international migration today.

The extent of racial discrimination and xenophobia is often played down and sometimes denied by authorities. Racial discrimination is defined in international law as being: *any distinction, exclusion, restriction or preference based on race, colour, descent or national or ethnic origin which has the purpose or effect of nullifying or impairing the recognition, enjoyment or exercise, on an equal footing, of human rights and fundamental freedoms in the political, economic, social, cultural or any other field of public life.*

Racism and xenophobia are distinct phenomena, although they often overlap. While racism generally implies distinction based on difference in physical characteristics, such as skin colour, hair type, facial features, etc, xenophobia denotes behaviour specifically based on the perception that 'the other' is foreign to or originates from outside the community or nation. By the standard dictionary definition, xenophobia is the intense dislike or fear of strangers or people from other countries. As a sociologist puts it, 'xenophobia is an attitudinal orientation of hostility against non-natives in a given population.'

The definition of xenophobia, and its differentiation from racism and racial discrimination, is a still-evolving concept. One of the regional Preparatory Meetings for a recent World Conference suggested that:

- Racism is an ideological construct that assigns a certain race and/or ethnic group to a position of power over others on the basis of physical and cultural attributes, as well as economic wealth, involving hierarchical relations where the superior race exercises domination and control over others.
- Xenophobia describes attitudes, prejudices and behaviour that reject, exclude and often vilify persons, based on the perception that they are outsiders or foreigners in the community, society or with respect to national identity.

In many cases, it is difficult to distinguish between racism and xenophobia as motivations for behaviour, since differences in physical characteristics are often assumed to distinguish a person from the common identity. However, manifestations of xenophobia occur against people of identical physical characteristics, even of shared ancestry, when such people arrive, return or migrate to states or areas where occupants consider them outsiders.

Reading

Questions 27 - 30

Complete each sentence with the correct ending, A - F, below.

Write the correct letter, A - F, in the spaces below.

27 An upward trend in violence perpetrated against non-national minority groups by radical nationals

27. ....

28 Where racism occurs, the dominant group promotes a hierarchical system in which it

28. ....

29 Persons not considered to be culturally or physically distinct from the majority

29. ....

30 Racism differs from xenophobia in that victims of the former

30. ....

A are always culturally or physically distinct from the perpetrators of the acts of wrongdoing.

B tend to share a likeness with the perpetrators of the crime.

C may still find themselves the victims of xenophobic behaviour.

D has been observed in many different parts of the world.

E will eventually reach a position of total submission.

F has a controlling hand in the affairs of one or more of the other sections of society.

Questions 31 - 34

Choose the correct letter A, B, C or D.

31 Which of the following migrants are there more of?
  A internally displaced persons
  B refugees
  C internal migrants
  D immigrant workers

32 The author of the text believes that
  A racism is inevitable when people emigrate.
  B governments are finding it difficult to stop racism and xenophobia.
  C the exploitation of minority groups deters others from migrating.
  D xenophobia does not exist within minority groups.

33 There is no real way of knowing how many migrants are discriminated against because
  A not all racial abuse cases are documented or looked into.
  B the number of migrants is increasing at an alarming rate.
  C migrants don't complain about being abused.
  D only serious cases are documented.

34 People in authority sometimes
  A exaggerate the seriousness of the problem.
  B create the problem.
  C deny there is a problem.
  D are eager to solve the problem.

Questions 35 - 40

Do the following statements agree with the information given in Reading Passage 3?

In spaces 35 - 40 below, write

TRUE	*if the statement agrees with the information*
FALSE	*if the statement contradicts the information*
NOT GIVEN	*if there is no information on this*

35 Most migrants flee their country of origin because of political or social disorder.   ....

36 Most internal migrants leave the countryside for the cities.   ....

37 Governments are often reluctant to acknowledge that racial discrimination and xenophobia exist.   ....

38 Migrants are exploited and abused because they create a sense of insecurity for extremist groups.   ....

39 People who are racist or xenophobic are uneducated and hostile.   ....

40 People returning to their country of ancestry do not face xenophobia.   ....

Writing

> **Writing Tip:**
> Remember to use the data
> in Writing Task 1 correctly.

WRITING TASK 1

You should spend about 20 minutes on this task.

> *The graph below shows the rate of attendance for primary and
> secondary schools for boys and girls across the world.*
>
> *Summarise the information by selecting and reporting the main
> features, and make comparisons where necessary.*

Write at least 150 words.

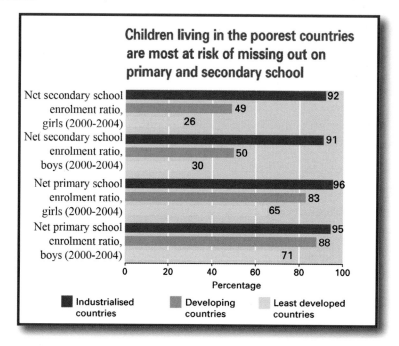

**Children living in the poorest countries
are most at risk of missing out on
primary and secondary school**

Net secondary school enrolment ratio, girls (2000-2004): 92 / 49 / 26

Net secondary school enrolment ratio, boys (2000-2004): 91 / 50 / 30

Net primary school enrolment ratio, girls (2000-2004): 96 / 83 / 65

Net primary school enrolment ratio, boys (2000-2004): 95 / 88 / 71

Percentage: 0 20 40 60 80 100

■ Industrialised countries   ■ Developing countries   ▢ Least developed countries

WRITING TASK 2

You should spend about 40 minutes on this task.

Write about the following topic:

> *In many places, prisons are overcrowded and expensive for governments to maintain.
> Yet, when offenders are released, they end up back in prison a short while later.
> Does prison work? Should lawbreakers be rehabilitated or punished?*

Give reasons for your answer and include any relevant examples from your own knowledge
or experience.

Write at least 250 words.

Speaking

> **Speaking Tip:**
> Don't memorise your answers.

PART 1   (4-5 minutes)

The examiner asks the candidate about him/herself, his/her home, work or studies and other familiar topics.

Jobs

- What would the ideal job for you be, and why?
- How easy is it to get a job in your country?
- What are the typical working hours in your country?
- How do people in your country like to relax when they're not working?

PART 2   (2 minutes)

You will have to talk about the topic for one to two minutes. You have one minute to think about what you are going to say. You can make some notes to help you if you wish.

> **Describe a time when you got into trouble, either at school or at home.**
>
> **You should say:**
> - **why you got into trouble**
> - **if you were punished for what you did**
> - **how getting into trouble affected you**

PART 3   (4-5 minutes)

Discussion topics:

Crime

- What sort of crimes are common where you live?
- What do you think makes people commit serious crimes?
- Do you think that some forms of entertainment, such as video games, promote violence?

Punishing law breakers

- Do people who break the law in your country receive the correct punishment?
- Is the death penalty ever acceptable?
- Are there any alternatives to putting someone in jail?

Test 4

Listening

Example:
Where did Julie leave her car?
(A) in the underground parking lot
  B in the outdoor parking lot
  C opposite the university building
  D near the Student Services office

SECTION 1 *Questions 1 - 10*

Questions 1 - 4

Choose the correct letter A, B, C or D.

1 What are the regulations for the underground parking area, level 1?
  A Undergraduate parking is allowed.
  B Postgraduate parking only is allowed.
  C Staff parking only is allowed.

2 If you don't have a parking permit, what action will be taken?
  A Your car will have a wheel clamped.
  B You will pay a fine only.
  C Your car will be towed away and you will pay a fine.

3 How does Julie usually travel to university?
  A by car
  B by rail
  C by bus

4 Where is Student Services located?
  A in the Science Department
  B next to the football field
  C between the cafeteria and the Science Department

Questions 5 - 10

Complete the release form below.
*Write **NO MORE THAN THREE WORDS AND/OR A NUMBER** for each answer.*

Application for the release of a vehicle in compound.
Name: **5** ....
Address: **6** ....
District: **7** ....
Faculty: **8** ....
Registration number: **9** ....
Make of car: **10** ....

Listening Tip:
Remember that rephrasing what you hear is NOT necessary. Just write down the words you hear.

SECTION 2 *Questions 11 - 20*

Questions 11 - 14
What facilities are available at each campsite?
Write the correct letter A, B or C next to questions 11 - 14.

11	Biddlecombe Cascades	
12	Crystal Falls	
13	17 Mile Falls	
14	Edith River Crossing	

A a checkpoint but no toilets
B toilets but no checkpoint
C a checkpoint and toilets

Questions 15 - 20
Label the map below.
Write the correct letter, A - H, next to the questions 15 - 20.

15	Biddlecombe Cascades	
16	Crystal Fall viewpoint	
17	The Amphitheatre	
18	17 Mile Falls Creek	
19	Sandy Camp Pool	
20	Sweetwater Pool	

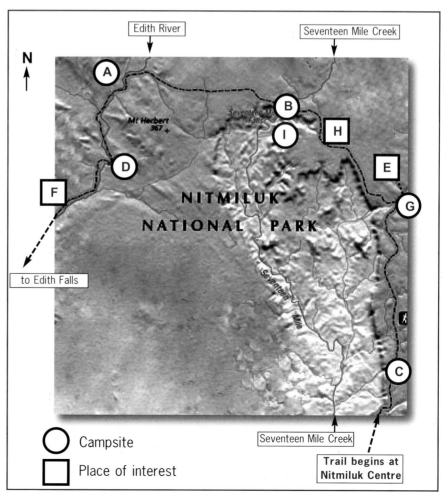

Listening

SECTION 3 *Questions 21 - 30*

Questions 21 - 25

Which person has the following opinion about the incident in 2008?

Write the correct letter, A, B or C next to questions 21 - 25.

21 It was very funny.

22 Some people must have faced serious consequences.

23 It caused embarrassment.

24 It was a very immature thing to do.

25 We are being punished for it.

A Laura
B Jamie
C Denise

Questions 26 - 30

Complete the flow-chart below.

*Choose **SIX** answers from the box and write the correct letter, **A - G**, next to questions 26 - 30.*

Experimental Design Procedure For Final Year Projects in Chemistry

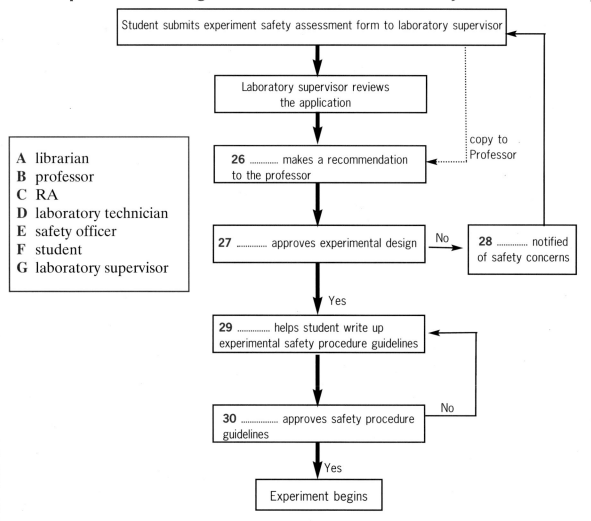

A librarian
B professor
C RA
D laboratory technician
E safety officer
F student
G laboratory supervisor

SECTION 4 *Questions 31 - 40*

Questions 31-36
Label the map below.
Write the correct letter, A-H, next to questions 31-36.

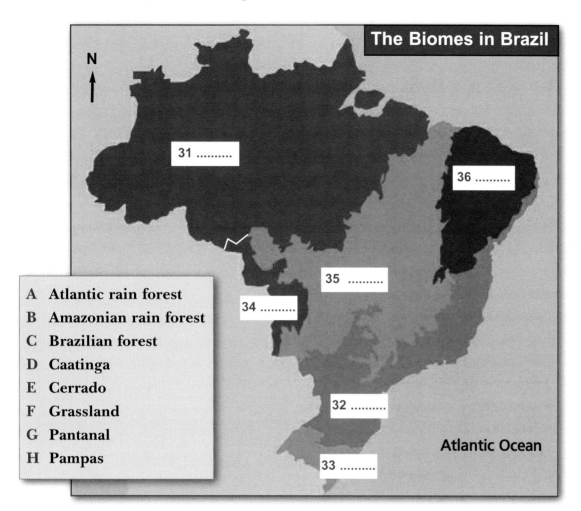

The Biomes in Brazil

N

31 ....

36 ....

35 ....

34 ....

32 ....

33 ....

A **Atlantic rain forest**
B **Amazonian rain forest**
C **Brazilian forest**
D **Caatinga**
E **Cerrado**
F **Grassland**
G **Pantanal**
H **Pampas**

Atlantic Ocean

Questions 37 - 40
Complete the table below.
*Write **NO MORE THAN ONE WORD AND/OR A NUMBER** for each answer.*

ANIMAL PRODUCTION (in millions) in the Biomes of Brazil			
AREA	Cattle	Goats	Sheep
Cerrado	37.................	none	none
Caatinga	23.9	8.8	38................
Pantanal	39.................	none	none
Pampas	26	40................	6

Reading

READING PASSAGE 1

*You should spend about 20 minutes on **Questions 1 - 13**, which are based on Reading Passage 1 below.*

ALTERNATIVE ENERGY SOURCES

A

There are many reasons why we are looking towards alternative energy sources. With many countries signing the Kyoto Treaty, efforts to reduce pollutants and greenhouse gases are a primary focus in today's culture. Alternative, or renewable, energy sources show significant promise in helping to reduce the amount of toxins that are by-products of energy use. Not only do they protect against harmful by-products, but using alternative energy helps to preserve many of the natural resources that we currently use as sources of energy. To understand how alternative energy use can help preserve the delicate ecological balance of the planet, and help us conserve the non-renewable energy sources like fossil fuels, it is important to know what types of alternative energy are out there.

B

Alternative energy sources are resources that are constantly replaced and are usually less polluting. They are not the result of the burning of fossil fuels or splitting of atoms. The use of renewable energy is contributing to our energy supply. Some alternative energy sources are: biomass energy, geothermal energy, hydroelectric power, solar power, wind power, fuel cells, ocean thermal energy conversion, tidal energy, and wave energy.

C

Biomass is renewable energy that is produced from organic matter. Biomass fuels include wood, forest and mill residues, animal waste, grains, agricultural crops, and aquatic plants. These materials are used as fuel to heat water for steam or processed into liquids and gases, which can be burned to do the same thing. With more use of biomass at lower production costs and better technology, the United States could generate as much as four-and-a-half times more biopower by 2020. It is estimated that biomass will have the largest increase among renewable energy sources, rising by 80 percent and reaching 65.7 billion KW in 2020.

D

Geothermal energy uses heat from within the earth. Wells are drilled into geothermal reservoirs to bring the hot water or steam to the surface. The steam then drives a turbine-generator to generate electricity in geothermal plants. In some places this heat is used directly to heat homes and greenhouses, or to provide process heat for businesses or industries. Reykjavik, Iceland, is heated by geothermal energy. Most geothermal resources are concentrated in the western part of the United States. Geothermal heat pumps use shallow ground energy to heat and cool homes, and this technique can be employed almost anywhere. With technological improvements much more power could be generated from hydrothermal resources. Scientists have been experimenting by pumping water into the hot dry rock that is 3-6 miles below the earth's surface for use in geothermal power plants.

E

Hydroelectric (hydropower) energy employs the force of falling water to drive turbine-generators to produce electricity. Hydropower produces more electricity than any other alternative energy source. It has been estimated that hydroelectric power will decline from 389 billion KW in the US in 1999 to 298 billion KW in 2020. This decline is expected because most of the best sites for hydropower have already been developed and because of concerns about the adverse impact that large-scale hydro-electric facilities may have on the environment.

F

Solar energy is generated without a turbine or elec-tromagnet. Special panels of photovoltaic cells cap-ture light from the sun and convert it directly into electricity. The electricity is stored in a battery. Solar energy can also be used to directly heat water for domestic use (solar thermal technology). The domestic photovoltaic (PV) industry could provide up to 15% of new US peak electricity capacity that is expected to be required in 2020.

G

Wind energy can be used to produce electricity. As wind passes through the blades of a windmill, the blades spin. The shaft that is attached to the blades turns and powers a pump or turns a generator to produce electricity. Electricity is then stored in bat-teries. The speed of the wind and the size of the blades determine how much energy can be pro-duced. Wind energy is more efficient in windier parts of the country. Most wind power is produced from wind farms — large groups of turbines locat-ed in consistently windy locations. Wind, used as a fuel, is free and non-polluting and produces no emissions or chemical wastes. Wind-powered elec-tricity is gaining in popularity.

H

Fuel cells are electrochemical devices that produce electricity through a chemical reaction. Fuel cells are rechargeable, contain no moving parts, are clean, and produce no noise. Scientists are explor-ing ways that they could be used as a power source for nearly exhaust-free automobiles and how they can be used as electricity-generating plants. The high cost of manufacturing fuel cells has prevented the mass use of this valuable energy source.

I

Ocean sources; Oceans, which cover more than 70% of the earth, contain both thermal energy from the sun's heat and mechanical energy from the tides and waves. Ocean thermal energy conver-sion (OTEC) converts solar radiation to electric power. OTEC power plants use the difference in temperature between warm surface waters heated by the sun and colder waters found at ocean depths to generate electricity. The power of tides can also be harnessed to produce electricity. Tidal energy works by harnessing the power of changing tides but it needs large tidal differences. The tidal process utilises the natural motion of the tides to fill reservoirs, which are then slowly discharged through electricity-producing turbines. Wave ener-gy conversion extracts energy from surface waves, from pressure fluctuations below the water surface, or from the full wave. Wave energy also uses the interaction of winds with the ocean surface. This technology is still in the exploratory phase in the United States.

Reading

Questions 1 - 2

The writer mentions a number of facts relating to alternative power sources.

Which **TWO** of the following facts are mentioned?

A	International co-operation has yet to result in the largescale implementation and effective use of alternative power sources.
B	One alternative energy source in particular will have a great impact in the years to come.
C	A side-effect of one of these forms of energy is the production of chemical waste.
D	Expense is the main factor that is an obstacle to developing one of these forms of energy.
E	Approximately one in five US homes will be using one of these forms of energy within twenty years.
F	One attraction of these forms of energy in general is the relatively low production costs.

Questions 3 and 4

Choose the correct letter A, B, C or D.

3   Geothermal energy is produced by

        A   heating the air below the surface of the ground.
        B   employing the force of falling water.
        C   extracting water or steam from beneath the earth's surface.
        D   using the earth's natural electricity.

4   Which form of alternative energy does not involve the use of turbines?

        A   wind energy
        B   geothermal energy
        C   tidal energy
        D   fuel cell energy

Questions 5 - 8

Do the following statements agree with the information given in Reading Passage 1?

In spaces 5 - 8 below, write

TRUE	*if the statement agrees with the information*
FALSE	*if the statement contradicts the information*
NOT GIVEN	*if there is no information on this*

5   Wind power is the most efficient form of alternative energy.   ....

6   Wave energy can be derived from a number of sources.   ....

7   Alternative energy sources serve several purposes.   ....

8   Fossil fuels are needed in at least one of these alternative
energy sources.   ....

Questions 9 - 13

Complete the sentences.
*Choose **NO MORE THAN THREE WORDS** from the passage for each answer.*

9   By using alternative energy sources, we can cut the .... that
are produced by current power sources.

10   In addition to fossil fuels and atom splitting, we presently use ....
as part of our power source.

11   Renewable energy called biomass is produced from ....

12   The renewable energy that comes from within the earth is called ....

13   One of the reasons that fuel cells are not widely used is the .... of
manufacturing.

Reading

READING PASSAGE 2

You should spend about 20 minutes on **Questions 14 - 26**, *which are based on Reading Passage 2 below.*

Colour Blindness

Colour blindness results from an absence or malfunction of certain colour-sensitive cells in the retina. The retina is a neuro-membrane lining the inside back of the eye, behind the lens. The retina contains both rod cells (active in low light or night vision but which cannot distinguish colour) and cone cells (active in normal daylight, sensitive to colour). Cone cells, also called photoreceptors, are concentrated mostly in the central part of the retina, in an area called the macula. Cone cells provide clear, sharp colour vision. The cones contain light-sensitive pigments that are sensitive to the range of wavelengths. There are three different types of cones with one sensitive to short wavelengths, or the colour blue, one sensitive to medium wavelengths, or the colour green, and the other sensitive to higher wavelengths, or the colour red. All of these cells send information about colour to the brain via the optic nerve which connects to the retina at a point very close to the macula. Normal persons, referred to as trichromats, are able to match all colours of the spectrum by using a combination of these three fundamental colour sensitivities. Hence, the huge variety of colours we perceive stems from the cone cells' response to different compositions of wavelengths of light.

There are many types of colour blindness. When there are deficiencies in the cones, either at birth or acquired in other ways, the cones are not able to distinguish the particular wavelengths and thus, that colour range is seen differently. Those with defective colour vision have a deficiency or absence in one or more of the pigments. People with a deficiency in one of the pigments (the most common type of colour vision problem) are called anomalous trichromats. When one of the cone pigments is absent and colour is reduced to two dimensions, dichromacy occurs. These individuals normally know they have a colour vision problem and it can affect their lives on a daily basis. They see no perceptible difference between red, orange, yellow, and green. All these colours that seem so different to the normal viewer appear to them to be the same colour. Missing the cones responsible for green and red hues can also affect the sensitivity to brightness.

Most cases of colour blindness, about 99%, are inherited, resulting from partial or complete loss of function in one or more of the different cone systems and affect both eyes without worsening over time. The most common are red-green hereditary (genetic) photoreceptor disorders collectively referred to as "red-green colour blindness". It affects 8% of all males of European origin and 0.4% of all females. The gene for this is carried in the X chromosome. Since males have an X-Y pairing and females have X-X, colour blindness can occur much more easily in males and is typically passed to them by their mothers. In other words, females may be carriers of colour blindness, but males are more commonly affected. People with this disorder cannot identify red or green by itself but can if among a coloured group. Other forms of colour blindness are much more rare. They include problems in discriminating blues from yellows. Both colours are seen as white or grey. This disorder occurs with equal frequency in men and women and usually accompanies certain other physical disorders, such as liver disease or diabetes.

The rarest forms of all is total colour blindness, monochromacy, where one can only see grey or shades of black, grey and white as in a black-and-white film or photograph. Monochromacy occurs when two or all three of the cone pigments are missing and colour and lightness vision is reduced to one dimension. Another term for total colour blindness is *achromatopsia*, the inability to see colour.

Inherited colour vision problems cannot be treated or corrected. Some acquired colour vision problems can be treated with surgery, such as the removal of a cataract, depending on the cause. Certain types of tinted filters and contact lenses may also help an individual to distinguish different colours better. Additionally, computer software has been developed to assist those with visual colour difficulties and those with mild colour deficiencies to learn to associate colours with certain objects and are usually able to identify colour in the same way as everyone else. One frequent problem encountered is with traffic lights, and worst of all, warning lights: colour-blind people always know the position of the colours on the traffic light - in most situations; red on top, yellow in the centre, green on the bottom. But warning lights present an entirely different problem. In this situation there is only one light; no top or bottom, no right or left, just one light that is either red or yellow.

Colour vision problems can have a significant impact on a person's life, learning abilities and career choices. On an everyday basis, there are some annoyances and frustrations: not being able to differentiate between green or ripe tomatoes when preparing food, for example, or buying clothes that to the 'normal' eye seem positively garish. However, people with colour vision problems usually learn to compensate for their inability to see colours. Although there is little or no treatment for colour blindness, most colour deficient persons compensate well for their defect and may even discover instances in which they can discern details and images that would escape normal-sighted persons. At one time the US Army found that colour blind persons can spot camouflage colours in cases where those with normal colour vision are typically fooled.

Reading

Questions 14 - 20

*Complete each sentence with the correct ending **A - K** from the box below.*

*Write the correct letter **A - K** in spaces 14 - 20 below.*

14   Colour blindness can be caused by a birth defect, or   ....

15   Surprisingly, some people who are colour blind   ....

16   People with hereditary colour blindness   ....

17   Because of our genetic make-up, colour blindness   ....

18   Red-green genetic photoreceptor disorders mean that people   ....

19   People with monochromacy   ....

20   The inability to see certain lights   ....

A   can see better at night than during the day.

B   cannot be treated by surgery.

C   can affect men much more easily than women.

D   can affect their sensitivity to bright lights.

E   can see no colour at all, other than shades of black, grey and white.

F   can see things that people with normal vision cannot.

G   can have very dangerous consequences for colour blind people.

H   can be acquired or inherited.

I   can mean having to wear contact lenses.

J   cannot distinguish certain colours if they stand alone.

K   can match all colours of the spectrum.

Questions 21 - 23

Choose the correct letter A, B, C or D.

21   What causes colour blindness?
    A   the absence of rod cells
    B   the malfunction of rod cells
    C   the malfunction of cone cells
    D   the retina's inability to detect light

22   Which group of people are the least common?
    A   people who cannot detect blues from yellows
    B   anachromous trichromats
    C   people with dichromacy
    D   people with achromatopsia

23   What would colour blind people consider an everyday nuisance?
    A   not being able to identify the colour of warning lights
    B   not being able to tell an apple from a tomato
    C   not being able to cook
    D   not being able to buy matching clothes

Questions 24 - 26

Complete the diagram below.

*Choose **NO MORE THAN TWO WORDS** from the passage for each answer.*

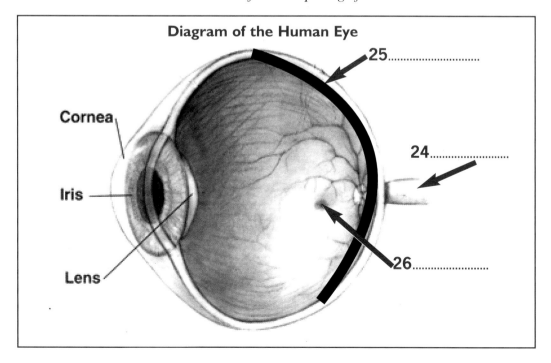

Diagram of the Human Eye

Reading

READING PASSAGE 3

*You should spend about 20 minutes on **Questions 27 - 40**, which are based on Reading Passage 3 below.*

Population growth sentencing millions to hydrological poverty

A

At a time when drought in the United States, Ethiopia, and Afghanistan is in the news, it is easy to forget that far more serious water shortages are emerging as the demand for water in many countries simply outruns the supply. Water tables are now falling on every continent; literally scores of countries are facing water shortages as the tables fall and wells go dry. We live in a water-challenged world, one that is becoming more so each year as 80 million additional people stake their claims to the Earth's water resources. Unfortunately, nearly all the projected 3 billion people to be added over the next half century will be born in countries that are already experiencing water shortages. Even now, many in these countries lack enough water to drink, to satisfy cleanliness needs, and to produce food.

B

By 2050, India is projected to have added 519 million people and China 211 million. Pakistan is projected to have added nearly 200 million, going from 151 million at present to 348 million. Egypt, Iran, and Mexico are slated to increase their populations by more than half by 2050. In these and other water-short countries, population growth is sentencing millions of people to hydrological poverty, a local form of poverty that is difficult to escape.

C

Even with today's 6 billion people, the world has a huge water deficit. Using data on over-pumping for China, India, Saudi Arabia, North Africa, and the United States, Sandra Postel, author of *Pillar of Sand: Can the Irrigation Miracle Last?* reports the annual depletion of aquifer to be at 160 billion cubic meters or 160 billion tons. Using the rule of thumb that it takes 1,000 tons of water to produce 1 ton of grain, this 160-billion-ton water deficit is equal to 160 million tons of grain or one-half the US grain harvest.

D

Average world grain consumption is just over 300 kilograms per person per annum - one third of a ton per person per year - and grain reserves directly or indirectly feed 480 million people globally. Stated otherwise, 480 million of the world's 6 billion people are being fed with grain produced with the unsustainable use of water.

E

Over-pumping is a new phenomenon, one largely confined to the last half century. Only since the development of powerful diesel- and electrically-driven pumps have we had the capacity to pull water out of aquifer faster than it is replaced by precipitation. Some 70 percent of the water consumed worldwide, including both that diverted from rivers and that pumped from underground, is used for irrigation, while some 20 percent is used by industry, and 10 percent for residential purposes. In the increasingly intense competition for water among sectors, agriculture almost always loses. The 1,000 tons of water used in India to produce 1 ton of wheat worth perhaps $200 can also be used to expand industrial output by easily $10,000, or 50 times as much. This ratio helps explain why, in the American West, the sale of irrigation water rights by farmers to cities is an almost daily occurrence.

F

In addition to population growth, urbanisation and industrialisation also expand the demand for water. As developing country villagers, traditionally reliant on the village well, move to urban high-rise apartment buildings with indoor plumbing, their residential water use can easily triple. Industrialisation takes even more water than urbanisation. Rising affluence in itself generates additional demand for water. As people move up the food chain, consuming more beef, pork, poultry, eggs, and dairy products, they use more grain. A US diet rich in livestock products requires 800 kilograms of grain per person a year, whereas diets in India, dominated by a starchy food staple such as rice, typically need only 200 kilograms. Using four times as much grain per person means using four times as much water.

G

Once a localised phenomenon, water scarcity is now crossing national borders via the international grain trade. The world's fastest growing grain import market is North Africa and the Middle East; an area that includes Morocco, Algeria, Tunisia, Libya, Egypt, and Iran. Virtually every country in this region is simultaneously experiencing water shortages and rapid population growth.

H

As the demand for water in the region's cities and industries increases, it is typically satisfied by diverting water from irrigation. The loss in food production capacity is then offset by importing grain from abroad. Since 1 ton of grain represents 1,000 tons of water, this becomes the most efficient way to import water.

I

Last year, Iran imported 7 million tons of wheat, eclipsing Japan to become the world's leading wheat importer. This year, Egypt is also projected to move ahead of Japan. Iran and Egypt have nearly 70 million people each. Both populations are increasing by more than a million a year and both are pressing the limits of their water supplies.

J

The water required to produce the grain and other foodstuffs imported into North Africa and the Middle East last year was roughly equal to the annual flow of the Nile River. Stated otherwise, the fast-growing water deficit of this region is equal to another Nile flowing into the region in the form of imported grain.

K

It is now often said that future wars in the region will more likely be fought over water than oil. Perhaps, but given the difficulty in winning a water war, the competition for water seems more likely to take place in world grain markets. The countries that will "win" in this competition will be those that are financially strongest, not those that are militarily strongest. The world water deficit grows larger with each year, making it potentially more difficult to manage. If we decided abruptly to stabilise water tables everywhere by simply pumping less water, the world grain harvest would fall by some 160 million tons, or 8 percent, and grain prices would go off the chart. If the deficit continues to widen, the eventual adjustment will be even greater.

L

Unless governments in water-short countries act quickly to stabilise their populations and to raise water productivity, their water shortages may soon become food shortages. The risk is that the growing number of water-short countries, including population giants China and India, with rising grain-import needs will overwhelm the exportable supply in food surplus countries, such as the United States, Canada, and Australia. This in turn could destabilise world grain markets. Another risk of delay in dealing with the deficit is that some low-income, water-short countries will not be able to afford to import needed grain, trapping millions of their people in hydrological poverty; thirsty and hungry, unable to escape.

M

Although there are still some opportunities for developing new water resources, restoring the balance between water use and developing a sustainable supply will depend primarily on demand-side initiatives, such as stabilising population and raising water productivity. Governments can no longer separate population policy from the supply of water. And just as the world turned to raising land productivity a half century ago when the frontiers of agricultural settlement disappeared, so it must now turn to raising water productivity. The first step toward this goal is to eliminate the water subsidies that foster inefficiency. The second step is to raise the price of water to reflect its cost. Shifting to more water-efficient technologies, more water-efficient crops, and more water-efficient forms of animal protein offers a huge potential for raising water productivity. These shifts will move faster if the price of water more closely reflects its real value.

Reading

Reading Tip:
Make sure you are aware of the different types of texts that may be on the test and how to approach each one.

Questions 27 - 32

Do the following statements agree with the information given in Reading Passage 3?

In spaces 27 - 32 below, write

TRUE	*if the statement agrees with the writer's claims*
FALSE	*if the statement contradicts the writer's claims*
NOT GIVEN	*if it is impossible to say what the writer thinks about this*

27   Vegetarians drink less water than meat eaters.   ....

28   A typical Indian diet requires less grain than a typical USA diet.   ....

29   Growing grain uses more water than raising beef.   ....

30   People that move from the country to the city may increase their water consumption considerably.   ....

31   Future conflicts will be fought as much over food as they will over oil.   ....

32   Egypt and Japan also import 7 million tons of oil annually.   ....

Questions 33 - 36

Reading passage 3 has 13 paragraphs A - M.

Which paragraph contains information about the following threats to water supplies?

Write the correct letter A - M in spaces 33 - 36 below.

33 The volume of water that is needed for irrigation in grain production.	Paragraph	....
34 Over-pumping our underground water supplies.	Paragraph	....
35 Population growth will be responsible for a new type of water-related poverty.	Paragraph	....
36 Industrialisation demands greater water supplies.	Paragraph	....

Questions 37 - 40

Choose the correct letter A, B, C or D.

37   Our water supply is running low because

    A   grain is now exported globally.

    B   the world's population is increasing rapidly.

    C   more people are moving to cities.

    D   people waste water foolishly.

38   People who have a high-meat diet cause more water to be used because

    A   it takes more grain to feed livestock than it does a human.

    B   the industrial processes to produce meat require a lot of water.

    C   livestock drink a lot of water.

    D   packaging of meat products goes through an intensive washing process.

39   What would reduce the use of water without adversely affecting the food supply?

    A   growing fewer crops

    B   increasing water subsidies

    C   diverting water from irrigation

    D   falling population levels

40   If there is a water war, who will win?

    A   the driest countries

    B   the richest countries

    C   the countries that are more forceful

    D   the countries that have the biggest population

Writing

> **Writing Tip:**
> Make sure your ideas are relevant.

WRITING TASK 1

You should spend about 20 minutes on this task.

> *The graph below shows the daily water consumption for Americans in their homes.*
>
> *Summarise the information by selecting and reporting the main features, and make comparisons where necessary.*

Write at least 150 words.

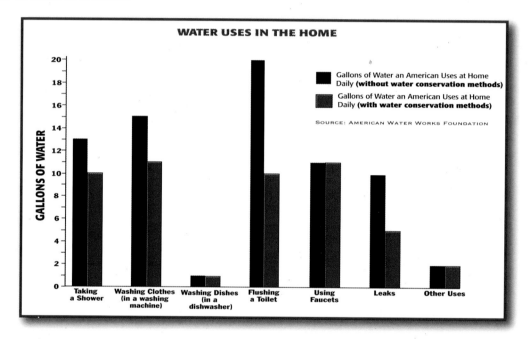

WRITING TASK 2

You should spend about 40 minutes on this task.

Write about the following topic:

> *If racism and xenophobia are attitudes that we are taught, not born with, then the problems that come from them can be resolved.*
>
> *Discuss this view and give your own opinion.*

Give reasons for your answer and include any relevant examples from your own knowledge or experience.

Write at least 250 words.

Speaking

> **Speaking Tip:**
> Don't worry if, in Part 2, the examiner stops you. This means you have said enough.

PART 1   (4-5 minutes)

The examiner asks the candidate about him/herself, his/her home, work or studies and other familiar topics.

Studies

- What do you think is the most useful subject you have studied?
- What are you currently studying / planning to study at university?
- Why have you chosen this field?
- What do you hope to do after you graduate?

PART 2   (2 minutes)

You will have to talk about the topic for one to two minutes. You have one minute to think about what you are going to say. You can make some notes to help you if you wish.

> **Describe someone you know who comes from a different country or who has a different origin from you.**
>
> **You should say:**
> - **what you like about this person**
> - **what you have learned about their culture from the friendship you have formed**
> - **if knowing this person has encouraged you to experience other cultures**

PART 3   (4-5 minutes)

Discussion topics:

Other cultures
- How important is it to learn about other people's cultures?
- What difficulties can people living in a foreign country experience?
- What benefits can there be for people living in a foreign country?

A global culture
- Do you believe in stereotypes about different nationalities?
- Are you in favour of adopting a universal language?
- What negative effects might come from a country losing its traditional culture?

Test 5

Listening

SECTION 1   *Questions 1 - 10*

Questions 1 - 5

Complete the notes below.

Write **NO MORE THAN THREE WORDS AND/OR A NUMBER** *for each answer.*

Ratner Athletics Centre

Example: Current students get membership for ....**no charge / free**..............

- a yearly membership costs 1 .... for alumni

- Features offered include:
    - the Emily Pankhurst 2 ....
    - the Dalton 3 ....
    - personal 4 .... at an extra charge

- Hours: 6 a.m. to 5 .... on weekdays and 6 a.m. to 9 p.m. on weekends

---

Questions 6 - 10

Complete the form below.

Write **NO MORE THAN THREE WORDS AND/OR A NUMBER** *for each answer.*

NEW CUSTOMER MEMBERSHIP FORM

- **Customer name:** Shannon 6 ....
- **Street Address:**   7 ....
- **City:**   Newcastle
- **Postcode:**   8 ....
- **Telephone number:** 9 ....
- **Payment method:** cash
- **Proof of address:** 10 ....

SECTION 2   *Questions 11 - 20*

> **Listening Tip:**
> Make sure your answers make sense within
> the context of what you're listening to.

Complete the notes below.

*Write **NO MORE THAN TWO WORDS** for each answer.*

Orientation Meeting for students
studying abroad in South America

Remember to sign the attendance lists on the way out!

To get a student visa you must make a folder of health information including:

- vaccination **11** ....

- proof you don't have a serious **12** ....

Have a consultation with a doctor specialised in **13** .... to get information on:

- what vaccines you will need to get

- **14** .... for malaria

- what to expect if you have any existing **15** ....

Health issues in South America

Malaria is a concern for most people going to South America.

- In each country, it is **16** .... in some areas but not others.

- You must **17** .... and not travel to high risk areas if you

  are not protected.

To prevent insect bites:

- wear long-sleeved shirts and **18** ....

- use insect repellent on **19** .... and flying-insect spray in rooms

- stay indoors in the peak biting periods of **20** .... and ....

Listening

SECTION 3   *Questions 21 - 30*

Questions 21 - 23

Which opinion does each person express about filling out the evaluation forms?
*Choose your answer from the box and write the letters **A - F** next to questions 21 - 23.*

A They encourage students to work hard.	
B Important changes have been made because of the forms.	
C We could be judged because of what we write.	Joshua **21** ....
D It is alright to say that you don't have an opinion.	Ethan **22** ....
E Probably no one reads them anyway.	Lily **23** ....
F They are required; if we don't do them we will get bad marks.	

Questions 24 - 30

Complete the table below.

Write **NO MORE THAN THREE WORDS AND/OR A NUMBER** *for each answer.*

Opinions about project:	Lily	Joshua	Ethan
Initial Suggested Rating	**24**	**25**	**26** ....
Good Points	nothing specific	**27**	choice between **28** ....
Bad Points	no practical point / choices were both **29**	should have given us **30**	no opinion

SECTION 4 *Questions 31 - 40*

Questions 31 - 40

Complete the flow-chart below.

*Write **NO MORE THAN THREE WORDS** for each answer.*

Product Life Cycle
Marketing Aims by Stage

Stage 1: Market Introduction

Features:

- Costs **31** ....
- Sales volumes **32** ....

Marketing Strategy:

<u>Step 1</u>
Get the brand noticed by the

33 ....

<u>Step 2</u>
Encourage potential customers to

34 ....

Stage 2: Growth

Features:

- Economies **35** ....
  lead to reduced costs and rise in sales.

Marketing Strategy:

Step 1
Find a way to **36** ....
return customers.

Step 2
Differentiate the **37** ....
from rival products.

Stage 3: Maturity

Features:

- Sales will **38** ....
- Competition will be **39** ....

Marketing Strategy:

Step 1
Continue to point out the differences
between your product and rival brands.

Step 2
Find new **40** .... for
the product.

Reading

READING PASSAGE 1

You should spend about 20 minutes on **Questions 1 - 13**, *which are based on Reading Passage 1 below.*

CONTROLLING DEATHWATCH BEETLES

All of the organisms that damage timber in buildings are part of the natural process that takes dead wood to the forest floor, decomposes it into humus, and recycles the nutrients released back into trees. Each stage in this process requires the correct environment and if we replicate this in our buildings then the organisms belonging to that part of the cycle will invade. A poorly maintained roof is, after all, just an extension of the forest floor to a fungus.

The first fact to remember about deathwatch beetles in your building is that they have probably been there for centuries and will continue long after you have gone. Beetle damage in oak timbers is a slow process and if we make it slower by good maintenance then the beetle population may eventually decline to extinction. The second fact is that natural predation will help you. Spiders are a significant predator and will help to keep the beetle population under control. They will speed up the decline of a beetle population in a well-maintained building.

The beetles fly to light and some form of light trap may help to deplete a population. The place in which it is used must be dark, so that there is no competing light source, and the air temperature must rise above about 17°C during the emergence season (April to June) so that the beetles will fly. Beetle holes do not disappear when the beetles have gone so it is sometimes necessary to confirm active infestation if remedial works are planned. This is generally easy with beetle damage in sapwood because the holes will look clean and have sharp edges, usually with bore dust trickling from them. Infestation deep within modified heartwood is more difficult to detect, particularly because the beetles will not necessarily bite their own emergence holes if plenty of other holes are available. This problem may be overcome by clogging the suspected holes with furniture polish or by covering a group of holes tightly with paper or card. Any emerging beetles will make a hole that should be visible, so that the extent and magnitude of the problem can be assessed. Unnecessary pesticide treatments must be avoided.

Sometimes a building cannot be dried enough to eradicate the beetles or a localised population will have built up unnoticed. A few scattered beetles in a building need not cause much concern, but dozens of beetles below a beam-end might indicate the need for some form of treatment if the infested timber is accessible. Insecticides formulated as a paste can be effective – either applied to the surface or caulked into pre-drilled holes – but the formulations may only be obtainable by a remedial company.

Surface spray treatments are generally ineffective because they barely penetrate the surface of the timber and the beetles' natural behaviour does not bring it into much contact with the insecticide. Contact insecticides might also kill the natural predators.

Heat treatments for entire buildings are available and the continental experience is that they are effective. They are also likely to be expensive but they may be the only way to eradicate a heavy and widespread infestation without causing considerable structural degradation of the building.

Two other beetles are worth a mention.

The first is the House Longhorn Beetle (*Hylotrupes bajulus*). This is a large insect that produces oval emergence holes that are packed with little cylindrical pellets. The beetles restrict their activities to the sapwood of 20th century softwood, although there is now some evidence that they will attack older softwood. The beetle larvae can cause considerable damage but infestation has generally been restricted to the south-west of London, possibly because they need a high temperature before the beetles will fly. Old damage is, however, frequently found elsewhere, thus indicating a wider distribution in the past, and infested timber is sometimes imported. This is an insect that might become more widespread because of climate change.

The second is the Lyctus or powderpost beetle. There are several species that are rather difficult to tell apart. These beetles live in the sapwood of oak. The beetles breed rapidly so that many cylindrical beetles may be present and the round emergence holes resemble those of the furniture beetle. This is, and has always been, a pest of newly-installed oak. Timbers with an exploded sapwood surface are frequently found in old buildings and the damage will have occurred during the first few decades after the timbers were installed. Our main interest with these beetles is that they seem to have become more common of late. Beetle infestation within a few months of a new oak construction will be Lyctus beetles in the sapwood and not furniture beetles. The problem can be avoided by using oak with minimal sapwood content. The beetle infestation will cease after a few years but spray treatment may be necessary if an infestation is heavy.

Reading

Reading Tip:
Make sure you answer as many questions as you can in the time allotted.

Questions 1 - 4

Complete each sentence with the correct ending ***A - H*** *below.*

Write the correct ending ***A - H*** *in spaces 1 - 4 below.*

1   One species of the beetle population may spread   ....

2   You can detect the presence of beetles   ....

3   You may kill household spiders   ....

4   Beetles will disappear at a faster rate   ....

A   if the building is kept in good condition.

B   if you clog the suspected holes with furniture polish, paper or card.

C   if the temperature rises to above about 17° C during the emergence season.

D   if you use a contact insecticide.

E   if it was installed a few decades earlier.

F   if changes in weather patterns continue.

G   if the use of surface treatments is avoided.

H   if the wood has a low sapwood concentration.

Questions 5 - 9

Do the following statements agree with the information given in Reading Passage 1?

In spaces 5 - 9 below, write

TRUE	*if the statement agrees with the writer's claims*
FALSE	*if the statement contradicts the writer's claims*
NOT GIVEN	*if it is impossible to say what the writer thinks about this*

5 Infestation by beetles deep within modified heartwood can be identified by the type of hole visible.   ....

6 Clogging a hole with furniture polish or paper will trap the beetle inside permanently.   ....

7 Paste insecticides are less effective than any other kind.   ....

8 Surface spray treatments are sometimes effective for the House Longhorn Beetle   ....

9 Heat treatments tend to cause less damage than other treatments.   ....

Questions 10 - 13

*Choose the correct letter **A**, **B**, **C** or **D**.*

10   The point the writer makes about deathwatch beetles is that

      A   they must be eliminated quickly.
      B   only natural predation will keep them under control.
      C   with good maintenance it may be possible to eliminate them.
      D   they are here to stay and do great damage.

11   One way to trap deathwatch beetles is to attract them to

      A   daylight.
      B   a totally dark environment.
      C   a constantly warm environment.
      D   a light trap in a dark place.

12   Surface spray treatments are not effective because

      A   the beetles are immune to them.
      B   they do not reach the beetles.
      C   they react poorly to wooden surfaces.
      D   they attract other harmful creatures.

13   Damage by the House Longhorn Beetle is sometimes found further afield than London because

      A   temperatures have increased.
      B   the timber was not local timber.
      C   there was no effective treatment previously.
      D   the type of timber has changed.

Reading

READING PASSAGE 2

You should spend about 20 minutes on **Questions 14 - 26**, *which are based on Reading Passage 2 below.*

Therapeutic Jurisprudence:

An Overview

Therapeutic jurisprudence is the study of the role of the law as a therapeutic agent. It examines the law's impact on emotional life and on psychological well-being, and the therapeutic and antitherapeutic consequences of the law. It is most applicable to the fields of mental health law, criminal law, juvenile law and family law.

The general aim of therapeutic jurisprudence is the humanising of the law and addressing the human, emotional and psychological side of the legal process. It promotes the perspective that the law is a social force that produces behaviours and consequences. Therapeutic jurisprudence strives to have laws made or applied in a more therapeutic way so long as other values, such as justice and due process, can be fully respected. It is important to recognise that therapeutic jurisprudence does not itself suggest that therapeutic goals should trump other goals. It does not support paternalism or coercion by any means. It is simply a way of looking at the law in a richer way, and then bringing to the table some areas and issues that previously have gone unnoticed. Therapeutic jurisprudence simply suggests that we think about the therapeutic consequences of law and see if they can be factored into the processes of law-making, lawyering, and judging.

The law can be divided into the following categories: (1) legal rules, (2) legal procedures, such as hearings and trials and (3) the roles of legal actors - the behaviour of judges, lawyers, and of therapists acting in a legal context. Much of what legal actors do has an impact on the psychological well-being or emotional life of persons affected by the law, for example, in the dialogues that judges have with defendants or that lawyers have with clients. Therefore, therapeutic jurisprudence is especially applicable to this third category.

Therapeutic jurisprudence is a relatively new phenomenon. In the early days of law, attitudes were very different and efforts were focused primarily on what was wrong with various sorts of testimony. While there were good reasons for that early emphasis, an exclusive focus on what is wrong, rather than also looking at what is right and how these aspects could be further developed, is seriously short-sighted. Therapeutic jurisprudence focuses attention on this previously under-appreciated aspect, encouraging us to look very hard for promising developments, and to borrow from the behavioural science literature, even when this literature has nothing obviously to do with the law. It encourages people to think creatively about how promising developments from other fields might be brought into the legal system.

Recently, as a result of this multidisciplinary approach, certain kinds of rehabilitative programmes have begun to emerge that look rather promising. One type of cognitive behavioural treatment encourages offenders to prepare relapse prevention plans which require them to think through the chain of events that lead to criminality. These reasoning and rehabilitation type programmes teach offenders cognitive self-change, to stop and think and figure out consequences, to anticipate high-risk situations, and to learn to avoid or cope with them. These programmes, so far, seem to be reasonably successful.

From a therapeutic jurisprudence standpoint, the question is how these programmes might be brought into the law. In one obvious sense, these problem-solving, reasoning and rehabilitation-type programmes can be made widely available in correctional and community settings. A way of linking them even more to the law, of course, would be to make them part of the legal process itself. The suggestion here is that if a judge or parole board becomes familiar with these techniques and is about to consider someone for probation, the judge might say, `I'm going to consider you but I want you to come up with a preliminary relapse prevention plan that we will use as a basis for discussion. I want you to figure out why I should grant you probation and why I should be comfortable that you're going to succeed. In order for me to feel comfortable, I need to know what you regard to be high-risk situations and how you're going to avoid them or cope with them.'

If that approach is followed, courts will be promoting cognitive self-change as part and parcel of the sentencing process itself. The process may operate this way; an offender would make a statement like `I realise I mess up on Friday nights; therefore, I propose that I will stay at home on Friday nights.' Suddenly, it is not a judge imposing something on the offender. It's something that the offender has come up with him or herself, so he or she should think it is fair. If a person has a voice in his rehabilitation, then he is more likely to feel a commitment to it, and with that commitment, presumably, compliance will increase dramatically.

Reading

Questions 14 - 20

Complete the notes below.

*Choose **NO MORE THAN ONE WORD** from the passage for each answer.*

NOTES: Therapeutic Jurisprudence

Therapeutic Jurisprudence: study of the law as a therapeutic **14** ....

and the therapeutic and **15** .... consequences

of the law.

Goal:

the **16** .... of the law,

but NOT at the expense of **17** .... and due process

Applicable to:

especially applicable to the role of legal **18** .... such as judges and lawyers

Therapeutic jurisprudence = new attitude

1.   It asks people to seek out **19** .... developments, not problems.

2.   It urges people to think **20** .... and borrow from other fields.

Questions 21 - 23

Complete the sentences.

Choose **NO MORE THAN THREE WORDS** *from the passage for each answer.*

---

21   One aspect of cognitive behavioural treatment includes the preparation of

.... by offenders.

22   The treatment requires offenders to consider the ....

that lead to a crime being committed.

23   Treatment programmes encourage offenders to recognise ....

before they happen, and know what to do in case they do happen.

Questions 24 - 26

Do the following statements agree with the information given in Reading Passage 2?
In spaces 24 - 26 below, write

TRUE	*if the statement agrees with the information*
FALSE	*if the statement contradicts the information*
NOT GIVEN	*if there is no information on this*

---

24   The use of rehabilitative programs has been proved to greatly
reduce the chance of a criminal re-offending.   ....

25   Therapeutic jurisprudence aims to make cognitive behavioural
treatment a part of the legal process itself.   ....

26   Offenders might be encouraged by judges to take part in deciding
what their punishment should be.   ....

Reading

READING PASSAGE 3

*You should spend about 20 minutes on **Questions 27 - 40**, which are based on Reading Passage 3 below.*

SLEEP

WHY WE SLEEP

As the field of sleep research is still relatively new, scientists have yet to determine exactly why people sleep. However, they do know that humans must sleep and, in fact, people can survive longer without food than without sleep. And people are not alone in this need. All mammals, reptiles and birds sleep.

Scientists have proposed the following theories on why humans require sleep:

- Sleep may be a way of recharging the brain. The brain has a chance to shut down and repair neurons and to exercise important neuronal connections that might otherwise deteriorate due to lack of activity.

- Sleep gives the brain an opportunity to reorganise data to help find a solution to problems, process newly-learned information and organise and archive memories.

- Sleep lowers a person's metabolic rate and energy consumption.

- The cardiovascular system also gets a break during sleep. Researchers have found that people with normal or high blood pressure experience a 20 to 30% reduction in blood pressure and 10 to 20% reduction in heart rate.

- During sleep, the body has a chance to replace chemicals and repair muscles, other tissues and aging or dead cells.

- In children and teenagers, growth hormones are released during deep sleep.

When a person falls asleep and wakes up is largely determined by his or her circadian rhythm, a day-night cycle of about 24 hours. Circadian rhythms greatly influence the timing, amount and quality of sleep.

For many small mammals such as rodents, sleep has other particular benefits, as it provides the only real opportunity for physical rest, and confines the animal to the thermal insulation of a nest. In these respects, sleep conserves much energy in such mammals, particularly as sleep can also develop into a torpor, whereby the metabolic rate drops significantly for a few hours during the sleep period. On the other hand, humans can usually rest and relax quite adequately during wakefulness, and there is only a modest further energy saving to be gained by sleeping. We do not enter torpor, and the fall in metabolic rate for a human adult sleeping compared to lying resting but awake is only about 5-10%.

A sizeable portion of the workforce are shift workers who work and sleep against their bodies' natural sleep-wake cycle. While a person's circadian rhythm cannot be ignored or reprogrammed, the cycle can be altered by the timing of things such as naps, exercise, bedtime, travel to a different time zone and exposure to light. The more stable and consistent the cycle is, the better the person sleeps. Disruption of circadian rhythms has even been found to cause mania in people with bipolar disorder.

The 'seven deadly sins' formulated by the medieval monks included Sloth. The Bible in Proverbs 6:9 includes the line: 'How long will you sleep, O sluggard? When will you arise out of your sleep?' But a more nuanced understanding of sloth sees it as a disinclination to labour or work. This isn't the same as the desire for healthy sleep. On the contrary, a person can't do work without rest periods and no one can operate at top performance without adequate sleep. The puritan work ethic can be adhered to and respect still paid to the sleep needs of healthy humans. It is wrong to see sleep as a shameful activity.

Usually sleepers pass through five stages: 1, 2, 3, 4 and REM (rapid eye movement) sleep. These stages progress cyclically from 1 through REM then begin again. A complete sleep cycle takes an average of 90 to 110 minutes. The first sleep cycles each night have relatively short REM sleeps and long periods of deep sleep but later in the night, REM periods lengthen and deep sleep time decreases. Stage 1 is light sleep where you drift in and out of sleep and can be awakened easily. In this stage, the eyes move slowly and muscle activity slows. During this stage, many people experience sudden muscle contractions preceded by a sensation of falling. In stage 2, eye movement stops and brain waves become slower with only an occasional burst of rapid brain waves. When a person enters stage 3, extremely slow brain waves called delta waves are interspersed with smaller, faster waves. In stage 4, the brain produces delta waves almost exclusively. Stages 3 and 4 are referred to as deep sleep, and it is very difficult to wake someone from them. In deep sleep, there is no eye movement or muscle activity. This is when some children experience bedwetting, sleepwalking or night terrors.

In the REM period, breathing becomes more rapid, irregular and shallow, eyes jerk rapidly and limb muscles are temporarily paralysed. Brain waves during this stage increase to levels experienced when a person is awake. Also, heart rate increases, blood pressure rises and the body loses some of the ability to regulate its temperature. This is the time when most dreams occur, and, if awoken during REM sleep, a person can remember their dreams. Most people experience three to five intervals of REM sleep each night. Infants spend almost 50% of their time in REM sleep. Adults spend nearly half of sleep time in stage 2, about 20% in REM and the other 30% is divided between the other three stages. Older adults spend progressively less time in REM sleep.

As sleep research is still a relatively young field, scientists did not discover REM sleep until 1953, when new machines were developed to monitor brain activity. Before this discovery it was believed that most brain activity ceased during sleep. Since then, scientists have also disproved the idea that deprivation of REM sleep can lead to insanity and have found that lack of REM sleep can alleviate clinical depression although they do not know why. Recent theories link REM sleep to learning and memory.

Reading

Reading Tip:
Often it is helpful to skim the questions
before reading the text.

Questions 27 - 30

Choose the correct letter, **A**, **B**, **C** *or* **D**.

27 Among other functions, sleep serves to

    A   help the adult body develop physically.

    B   push daily problems from our minds.

    C   accelerate the learning process significantly.

    D   re-energise parts of the brain.

28 'Torpor' can be described as

    A   a very deep sleep.

    B   a long state of hibernation.

    C   the sleep all non-human mammals experience.

    D   a light sleep.

29 Unlike small mammals, humans

    A   don't sleep to conserve energy.

    B   don't sleep properly.

    C   save only a small amount of energy by sleeping.

    D   show no decrease in their metabolic rate when they sleep.

30 In stage 3 deep sleep

    A   the eyes move slowly and there's little muscle activity.

    B   there is an alternation of delta waves and small fast waves.

    C   there is an occasional burst of rapid brain waves.

    D   there are no small fast waves.

Questions 31 - 35

Complete the flow-chart below.

Write **NO MORE THAN THREE WORDS** *for each answer.*

The Stages of Sleep

The individual drifts in and out of consciousness and can be woken up easily as they are only in a **31** .... Eye movement is slow and there is reduced muscle activity.

The speed of **32** .... activity slows and all movement of the eyes tends to stop.

Brain activity is dominated by delta waves, with a scattering of **33** .... also in evidence.

In a state of **34** .... , the brain emits delta waves almost exclusively. It is hard to wake the individual.

A period of rapid eye movement follows, during which **35** .... patterns are not consistent and limb muscles enter a temporary state of paralysis.

Questions 36 - 40

Complete the summary.
Choose **NO MORE THAN TWO WORDS** *from the passage for each answer.*

Sleep is so essential to a person that he can actually go longer without food than without sleep. During sleep, the brain has the chance to close down and do some repair work on neuronal connections which could otherwise **36** .... in a state of inactivity. Sleep also gives the brain the opportunity to organise data, especially newly-learned information.

During this rest period, the **37** .... drops and energy consumption goes down. At the same time, the cardiovascular system has a much-needed rest. While they go into a deep sleep, humans don't fall into **38** .... , unlike some small animals such as rodents. A **39** .... of 24 hours is described as a person's **40** .... , and this greatly influences a person's amount of sleep, and the type of sleep he gets.

Writing

WRITING TASK 1

You should spend about 20 minutes on this task.

> *The charts below show the average annual spending for Canadian households in the year 1972 and the year 2002.*
>
> *Summarise the information by selecting and reporting the main features, and make comparisons where necessary.*

Write at least 150 words.

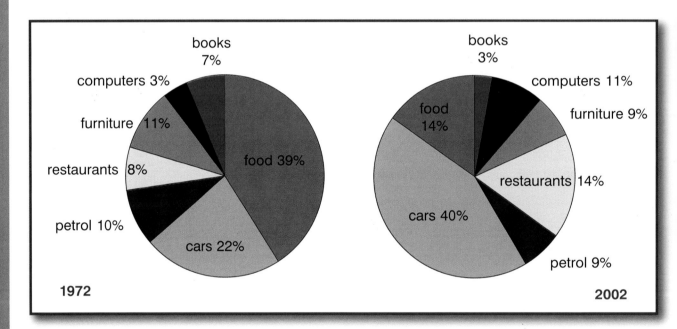

Writing Tip:
Be sure to write clearly and concisely.
Focus on organisation as much as content.

WRITING TASK 2

You should spend about 40 minutes on this task.

Write about the following topic:

> *The state of the environment is now a cause for concern in all countries across the world. Apart from government measures and policies, what can individuals do on a personal level to combat the negative effects that our lifestyles have on the environment?*

Give reasons for your answer and include any relevant examples from your own knowledge or experience.

Write at least 250 words.

Speaking

Speaking Tip:
Remember that you are allowed to correct
yourself if you realise you've made a mistake.

PART 1   (4-5 minutes)

The examiner asks the candidate about him/herself, his/her home, work or studies and other familiar topics.

Pets

- Is it common in your country for families to have pets?
- Which pets are most popular?
- Did you have a pet when you were a child?
- What is the attraction of having a pet, in your opinion?

PART 2   (2 minutes)

You will have to talk about the topic for one to two minutes. You have one minute to think about what you are going to say. You can make some notes to help you if you wish.

Describe the types of things you have in your house. You should say:

- **if your home is big or small**
- **what type of furniture you have**
- **if you have modern appliances like a DVD player, computer, mobile phone, etc.**
- **what else you would like to have in your home that you do not have already.**

PART 3   (4-5 minutes)

Discussion topics:

Lifestyle

- How important is it for you to have all the latest modern gadgets?
- Is having a luxurious home important to you?
- If you have extra money, do you prefer to spend it on a physical thing, or on an experience?

Technology and Lifestyle

- What advances in technology do you consider to be the most important, and why?
- How have mobile phones affected the way we communicate on an everyday basis?
- Computers have had a great effect on the way we live and work. What do you think will influence the way we lead our lives in the future?

Listening

SECTION 1   *Questions 1 - 10*

Questions 1 - 8

Complete the notes below.

Write **NO MORE THAN TWO WORDS AND/OR A NUMBER** *for each answer.*

Fairview Lake Camping Centre

The three functions of the centre are:
- conference centre
- *Example:* <u>educational institution</u>
- place for fun-filled weekends

The customer wants to bring children who have **1** ....
SPORTS: Sailing, windsurfing, volleyball, rowing, and a sport most children have never tried which is **2** ....

Accommodation Facilities

- The Birch Unit - sleeps **3** ....
- Greenback Row - sleeps the same number of people
- Cabins 1 - 3: sleep 10 people
- Cabins **4** .... : sleep 12 people each

Mr Bryson's booking arrangements

- The customer would bring **5** .... students for the course.

- He would like to book the course starting Sunday **6** ....

- The cost for one week would be **7** .... per child.

- The school's telephone number is **8** ....

Questions 9 and 10

Choose the correct letter *A*, *B* or *C*.

9 The receptionist suggests Mr Bryson's group eat with the other groups because

  A it works out cheaper that way.

  B it's more sociable.

  C you can do your own cooking.

10 Before he decides whether to accept the course or not, Mike Bryson will

  A check with a higher authority.

  B ask for lower prices.

  C see what the children have to say.

SECTION 2   Questions 11 - 20

Questions 11 - 15
Label the map below. Write the correct letter, A – G, next to questions 11 – 15.

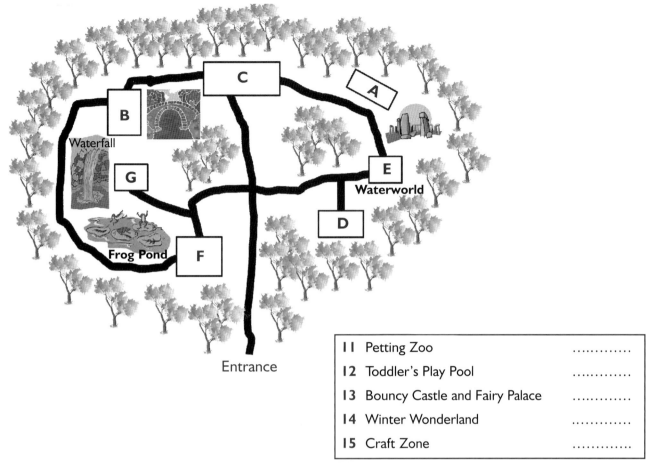

11	Petting Zoo	....
12	Toddler's Play Pool	....
13	Bouncy Castle and Fairy Palace	....
14	Winter Wonderland	....
15	Craft Zone	....

Questions 16 - 20

Label the diagram below. Write **NO MORE THAN TWO WORDS** for each answer.

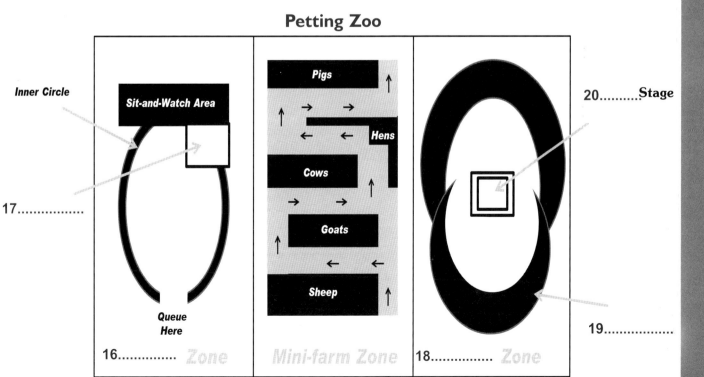

Petting Zoo

Listening

SECTION 3   Questions 21 - 30

Questions 21 - 22

*Choose **TWO** letters A - E.*

Which **TWO** courses does the summer school offer?

A preparation courses for graduate studies	**D** graduate studies
B teacher training	**E** management training course
C future employment	

Questions 23 - 27

Choose the correct letter A, B or C.

23 Paddy is interested in the sports
    programme because
    A he needs a qualification to teach PE.
    B he wants to improve his general teach-
    ing skills.
    C he has been told to attend it.

24 The swimming course concentrates on
    A competitive swimming.
    B teaching beginners.
    C technical aspects of swimming.

25 Paddy is interested in the equestrian
    course because
    A he thinks it will help him get better
    employment.
    B there is great interest in this sport in
    his present school.
    C he has always been interested in riding.

26 The beginners on the equestrian course
    will be taught
    A basic horsemanship.
    B only dressage and show jumping.
    C only flat work and show jumping.

27 When is the deadline for enrolment?
    A mid-April
    B late April
    C early May

Questions 28 - 30

Complete the summary below.

*Write **NO MORE THAN TWO WORDS** for each answer.*

Paddy is also interested in a course on 28 .... , but he knows nothing about it. Conveniently, it is a 29 .... so it doesn't matter that he is back at school. Apart from that, he is advised to take a 30 .... , which will teach him body awareness, and an appreciation of music.

SECTION 4   *Questions 31 - 40*
Questions 31 - 40

Complete the notes below.

Write **NO MORE THAN TWO WORDS AND/OR A NUMBER** *for each answer.*

Sending your child to University

- Someone with a higher education earns **31**.......................... more than someone without.
- In 1997 maintenance grants abolished and **32** .... introduced.
- University fees increasing - up to **33** .... a year.
- Average undergraduate needs **34** .... for 3 years.
- Almost 80% of students' cost are **35** ....

PAYING FOR YOUR CHILD'S EDUCATION

- Students' tuition can be paid for, in part, if they join the **36** ....

- The RAF will sponsor, but students must take up at least **37** .... service commitment.

- Students good at sport might secure a **38** ....
- The University of Kent gives a **39** .... cricket bursary to promising players.

Student Loans:
- Maximum **40** .... is 5,000 pounds.
- Needn't be paid back until after graduation.

Reading

READING PASSAGE 1

*You should spend about 20 minutes on **Questions 1 - 13**, which are based on Reading Passage 1 below.*

GRAFFITI

A

The word 'graffiti' derives from the Greek word *graphein,* meaning *to write*. This evolved into the Latin word *graffito*. Graffiti is the plural form of *graffito*. Simply put, graffiti is a drawing, scribbling or writing on a flat surface. Today, we equate graffiti with the 'New York' or 'Hip Hop' style which emerged from New York City in the 1970s. Hip Hop was originally an inner city concept. It evolved from the rap music made in Brooklyn and Harlem in the late 1960s and early 1970s. Donald Clarke, a music historian, has written that rap music was a reaction to the disco music of the period. Disco was centred in the rich, elitist clubs of Manhattan and rap emerged on street corners as an alternative. Using lyrical rhythms and 'beat boxing', the music was a way to express feelings about inner-city life. Hip Hop emerged as turntables began to be used to form part of the rhythm by 'scratching' (the sound created by running the stylus over the grooves of an LP). As Hip Hop music emerged so did a new outlet for artistic visibility. Keith Haring began using posters to place his uniquely drawn figures and characters in public places. Soon he began to draw directly on subway walls and transit posters. The uniqueness of his drawings eventually led to their being shown in galleries and published in books and his art became 'legitimate'.

B

At about the same time as Keith Haring, a delivery messenger began writing 'Taki 183' whenever he delivered documents. Soon his name was all over the city. Newspapers and magazines wrote articles about him and Keith Haring, and soon both became celebrities. This claim to fame attracted many young people, especially those involved with rapping, and they began to imitate 'Taki 183', as a means to indicate the writer's presence, i.e. the age old statement of *I was here*. Graffiti was soon incorporated into the Hip Hop culture and became a sort of triad with rapping and breakdancing. Breakdancing has since lost much of its initial popularity, while rapping has emerged as a major style in American music. New York City was inundated with graffiti during the late seventies and early eighties, but as media coverage faded so did the graffiti. Then, in the mid-eighties a national TV programme did a graffiti story and set off a graffiti wildfire which has since gone global.

C

In the past, graffiti artists usually worked alone, but the size and complexity of pieces as well as safety concerns motivated artists to work together in crews, which are groups of graffitists that vary in membership from 3 to 10 or more persons. A member of a crew can be 'down with' (affiliated with) more than one crew. To join a crew, one must have produced stylish pieces and show potential for developing one's own, unique style. A crew is headed by a king or queen who is usually that person recognised as having the best artistic ability among the members of the crew. One early crew wrote TAG as their crew name, an acronym for Tuff Artists Group. Tag has since come to mean both graffiti writing, 'tagging' and graffiti, a 'tag'. Crews often tag together, writing both the crew tag and their own personal tags. Graffiti has its own language with terms such as: piece, toy, wild-style, and racking.

D

At first pens and markers were used, but these were limited as to what types of surfaces they worked on, so very quickly everyone started using spray paint. Spray paint could mark all types of surfaces and was quick and easy to use. However, the spray nozzles on the spray cans proved inadequate to create the more colourful pieces. Caps from deodorant, insecticide, and other aerosol cans were substituted to allow for a finer or thicker stream of paint. As municipalities began passing graffiti ordinances outlawing graffiti implements, clever ways of disguising paint implements were devised. Shoe polish, deodorant roll-ons and other seemingly innocent containers were emptied and filled with paint. Markers, art pens and grease pens obtained from art supply stores were also used. In fact, nearly any object which can leave a mark on most surfaces is used by taggers, though the spray can is the medium of choice for most taggers.

E

As graffiti has grown, so too has its character. What began as an urban lower-income protest, graffiti now spans all racial and economic groups. While many inner-city kids are still heavily involved in the graffiti culture, taggers range from the ultra-rich to the ultra-poor. There is no general classification of graffitists. They range in age from 12-30 years old, and there are male and female artists. One tagger recently caught in Philadelphia was a 27-year-old stockbroker who drove to tagging sites in his BMW. Styles have dramatically evolved from the simple cursory style, which is still the most prevalent, to intricate interlocking letter graphic designs with multiple colours called 'pieces' (from masterpieces). Gang markings of territory also fit the definition of graffiti, and they mainly consist of tags and messages that provide 'news' of happenings in the neighbourhood.

F

Graffiti shops, both retail and on-line, sell a wide variety of items to taggers. Caps, markers, magazines, T-shirts, backpacks, shorts with hidden pockets, even drawing books with templates of different railroad cars can be purchased. Over 25,000 graffiti sites exist on the world wide web; the majority of these are pro-graffiti. Graffiti vandalism is a problem in nearly every urban area in the world. Pro-graffiti web sites post photos of graffiti from Europe, South America, the Philippines, Australia, South Africa, China and Japan. Billions of dollars worldwide are spent each year in an effort to curb graffiti.

G

While most taggers are simply interested in seeing their name in as many places as possible and as visibly as possible, some taggers are more content to find secluded warehouse walls where they can practise their pieces. Some of these taggers are able to sell twelve-foot canvases of their work for upwards of $10 - $12,000. As graffiti was introduced to the art world, two trends happened. One, the art world of collectors, dealers, curators, artists and the like helped graffitists evolve in style, presumably by sharing their artistic knowledge with the newcomers. Two, the exposure helped to expand graffiti into all parts of the world. Furthermore, more progressive cities have recognised the talent of graffitists by providing a means for them to do legal graffiti art, which has helped to foster the art form and lessen the amount of graffiti art that appears in the city as vandalism. Likewise, organisations who support graffiti artists seek out places to do legal graffiti such as abandoned buildings, businesses, or community walls in parks. What this shows is that some graffiti, particularly in the form of spraycan art, is recognised as art by the conventional art world.

Reading

Questions 1 - 7

Reading Passage 1 has seven paragraphs, **A - G.**

Choose the correct heading for each paragraph from the list of headings below.

*Write the correct number **i - x** in spaces 1 - 7 below.*

i	Becoming mainstream art
ii	The Culture Of Graffiti
iii	Tools Of The Trade
iv	Internet Art Styles
v	Crossing Boundaries
vi	Cashing In On The Craze
vii	Trends In Street Music
viii	Gradually gaining popularity
ix	A Solitary Existence
x	From Ancient To Modern

1 Paragraph **A** ....

2 Paragraph **B** ....

3 Paragraph **C** ....

4 Paragraph **D** ....

5 Paragraph **E** ....

6 Paragraph **F** ....

7 Paragraph **G** ....

Questions 8 - 10

Do the following statements agree with the information given in Reading Passage 1?

In spaces 8 - 10 below, write

> **TRUE**   *if the statement agrees with the writer's claims*
> **FALSE**   *if the statement contradicts the writer's claims*
> **NOT GIVEN**   *if it is impossible to say what the writer thinks about this*

8   The introduction of anti-graffiti laws managed to curb its spread in some cities.   ....

9   Along with Hip Hop music came a new way of visual expression.   ....

10 There was hostility towards graffiti artists among the established art community.   ....

Questions 11 - 13

Complete each sentence with the correct ending A - F below.

Write the correct letter A - F in spaces 11 - 13 below.

11   Graffiti is flourishing in the 21st century as
     people from all backgrounds have begun to   ....

12   As graffiti has developed, it has come to   ....

13   Graffiti artists used many ingenious methods to   ....

> **A**   use it as a means of expression of rebellion against law enforcement.
>
> **B**   become increasingly more difficult to succeed in the art world.
>
> **C**   transcend race, status and gender.
>
> **D**   realise that inner-urban areas where poverty is the norm are decreasing.
>
> **E**   conceal their intentions from law enforcement officers.
>
> **F**   embrace it as a means of expression.

Reading

READING PASSAGE 2

You should spend about 20 minutes on
Questions 14 - 26, *which are based on*
Reading Passage 2 below.

DISTANCE LEARNING

A   Distance learning is not a recent innovation in education, correspondence courses having been used for over 150 years, but new interactive technologies are providing new opportunities and strategies for teaching at a distance. Several studies have compared face-to-face classrooms to distance classrooms in order to evaluate differences in student performance and quality of instruction. A meta-analysis of these studies showed that distance-learning students performed equally well and some distance courses outperformed their classroom counterparts.

This result has been consistent over many studies across many disciplines; advances in communication technology and innovative methods of delivery of instruction at a distance have challenged the idea that laboratory courses can only be delivered in a face-to-face laboratory setting. In engineering, for example, virtual laboratories have been used to teach thermodynamics, electronic circuits, and other experimental courses as well. Programmes in nursing, engineering, technology and other sciences are beginning to use different technologies and innovative methods to deliver courses via distance-learning methodology in order to reach students in different locations and boost enrolment. A survey of online distance-learning programmes revealed a large increase in student enrolment. The availability of distance courses has made it possible for some people to attend college because courses are accessible within their locality or the time of course delivery is convenient for them.

This opportunity for learning has not been without its critics who keep a close eye on the quality of instruction, and rightly so as with any form of instructional delivery. Quality issues are a major concern for those who intend to pursue degree programmes via distance learning, especially with the proliferation of distance learning programmes. Although it is difficult for academics to agree on specific standards that constitute quality in distance learning, nonetheless, attributes such as accreditation standards for programmes, evaluating students' experiences, teacher-student interaction, student-to-student interaction, learning resources for the learner, learner assessment and performance, instructional resources for faculty, faculty training, and learner satisfaction are valid criteria. These and many other factors can determine the quality of delivery of instruction in both distance and face-to-face classrooms.

B   ***Distance Learning Technologies and Innovation in Laboratory Course Delivery***
In a selected UK university, five departments that offered laboratory courses in Technology and Engineering via distance learning used combinations of a variety of instructional technologies. The technologies most used were Interactive Microwave TV, (two-way audio and video), compressed video, Internet, CDs, computer software (virtual software), and video tapes. At the selected university in the UK, interviews were conducted on-site with faculty and staff. A wide range of teaching materials, student portfolios, and a secure website were observed. In addition to the Internet, CDs, and video, the university used the following innovative ways to deliver laboratory courses.

Residential and Summer Schools

Residential and summer schools serve a similar purpose; the difference is the duration.

The summer school is one week long and combines labs, lectures, and problem sessions. In general, these schools provide four key features, providing the opportunity for students to:

1. undertake experimental work considered too hazardous for a student working at home.
2. undertake lab work using more sophisticated equipment, or equipment too expensive to provide at home.
3. undertake assessed lab-work.
4. work together with fellow students.

Some courses even arranged to take students on a study trip, perhaps to a company with special processes, or to a geographic site of interest.

C　Demonstration Laboratory

The demonstration laboratory introduces students to the work they are going to undertake, illustrating how to proceed, how to make particular types of measurements, etc. It also covers topics considered too dangerous for students or situations in which the equipment is not available at the residential school. Many of these demonstrations are recorded on video to control both the process taught and the quality of the teaching across numerous groups of students at different levels.

D　Support Services Provided to Faculty and Students Engaged in Distance Learning

All the departments that offer distance learning courses offer support services to students and faculty. The support services include e-mail systems, graduate assistants, course websites, proctors, telephone conferencing, electronic library materials, and instructional designers to work with faculty to design and develop courses. At the selected university in the UK, interviews with instructional designers and faculty revealed the significant role played by instructional designers. Although they are not the content experts, they advise faculty, for example, on how information is presented on a website or the format in which the

information is presented. The purpose is to maintain a standard format and quality in print materials, including electronic resources. The selected university in the UK also provides a support service to faculty that is unique from other institutions in this study: staff tutors who are regionally based to provide the link between the university faculty and students within the regions. The staff tutors have a key role in quality assurance, especially in facilitating effective teaching of the university faculty's courses, and are responsible for the selection, monitoring, and development of part-time Associate Lecturers. They contribute to faculty research and the development and presentation of courses. The staff tutors are highly qualified in their fields, and as such, bridge the distance gap between the university faculty and students at different locations.

E

The UK university, by using innovative strategies such as the Residential and Summer Schools, Field Trips and Demonstration Laboratories in combination with new technologies, is able to teach all its laboratory courses via distance learning to its nearly 200,000 students within and outside the UK. Distance learning is not meant to replace a face-to-face classroom, but it is one major way to make education more accessible to society. As advances in communication and digital technology continue, residential or demonstration labs may someday be replaced with comparable experiences provided through distance education.

Reading

Reading Tip:
Practise distinguishing supporting details from the main idea.

Questions 14 - 18

Reading Passage 2 has five sections **A - E**.

Which section contains the following information?

*Write the correct letter **A - E** in spaces 14 - 18 below.*
NB Some sections may be used more than once.

---

14   One aspect of the course is that students can gain first-hand experience in a working environment and on educational excursions.   ....

15   Where the instruction takes place is not a critical factor in students' achievements.   ....

16   This method of instruction is not designed to replace traditional teaching techniques.   ....

17   In the future, the use of technology may mean students will not have to attend practical instruction sessions.   ....

18   Attending laboratory courses allows students to benefit from the use of expensive equipment not otherwise available to them.   ....

Questions 19 - 22

Choose the correct letter A, B, C or D.

19   One purpose of the summer school is to

   A   encourage students to work individually.
   B   enable students to be assessed directly.
   C   allow students to undertake simple experiments.
   D   familiarise students with laboratory equipment.

20   Instructional designers advise faculty on the

   A   course content.
   B   support services for students.
   C   suitability of library material.
   D   visual display of coursework.

21   Staff tutors are responsible for the

   A   monitoring of students' progress.
   B   suitability of courses for students' needs.
   C   appointment of certain teaching staff.
   D   training of all teaching staff.

22   With the increasing number of distance-learning courses,

   A   it has been difficult to find suitable tutors.
   B   problems arise with the timing of course delivery.
   C   the standard of teaching has become an issue.
   D   student-to-teacher interaction is no longer relevant.

Questions 23 - 26

Do the following statements agree with the information given in Reading Passage 2?

In spaces 23 - 26 below, write

YES	*if the statement agrees with the writer's claims*
NO	*if the statement contradicts the writer's claims*
NOT GIVEN	*if it is impossible to say what the writer thinks about this*

23	Many students may find the lack of student-to-student interaction a disadvantage to this method of study.	....
24	The main difference between residential and summer courses is the length of the courses they offer.	....
25	At the UK university, difficulties exist where the teaching of science subjects involves laboratory experiments.	....
26	Instructional designers receive very high salaries.	....

Reading

READING PASSAGE 3

*You should spend about 20 minutes on **Questions 27 - 40**, which are based on Reading Passage 3 below.*

LATCHKEY CHILDREN

Latchkey child was a term coined to describe children who wore or carried house keys to school so that they could let themselves into their home when they returned from school. The term came into use during the Second World War, when fathers had gone off to war, and mothers had gone into industry, making the tanks, planes, uniforms and bullets the soldiers needed. The children went home with keys on chains, ribbons or a piece of string tied around their necks. Some mothers chose to work the night shift, called the "swing shift", and tucked their children into bed, locked the door and went to the factory. The country's response was prompt and comprehensive. Programmes were set up in factories, in schools and community centres, to gather in all the children whose parents were busy with the war effort. These programmes closed promptly when the war ended, and women resumed their roles as housewives. More than sixty years on, there are large numbers of working mothers, but unlike in wartime, the country isn't organised to care for their children.

Sadly, finding young children at home without adult supervision has become much too commonplace. Latchkey children were once found only among the lower classes, but the situation has gradually spread to the middle and upper classes. The same is true of adolescent violence. In the past, shootings and stabbings were associated primarily with inner city, or poverty stricken areas permeated with abusive families and neglectful schools. However, in recent times, the "teen violence" epidemic has penetrated society at every economic level. An increase in the number of working mothers, as well as single-parent families, combined with a decrease in extended families that once helped with childcare, has contributed to the growing ranks of latchkey kids.

According to one census, one third of all school-age children in the United States are, for some part of the week, latchkey kids, that is, they go home to an empty house or apartment. The total number may be between five and seven million children between five and thirteen years old. Marian Wright Edelman, the director of the Children's Defence Fund, thinks it's close to 16 million children. The Census Bureau found that 15% were home alone before school, 76% after school and 9% at night. Presumably, the 9% have parents who work night shifts.

One-half of all children in the country aged 12 to 14 are home alone for an average of seven hours a week. The very poor in America are less likely to leave their children alone at home, or allow them to go home alone, than families who earn twice their level of income. This is probably because the very poor live in less safe neighbourhoods, and have fewer friends or family who can step in, in case of emergency. In spite of the hours spent on the job, working mothers spend an average of five-and-a-half hours a day with their children.

When latchkey children are functioning well, we don't hear about them. But we do hear about the one-third of all complaints to child welfare agencies which involve latchkey children. We know about the 51% who are doing poorly in school. Most teachers believe that being alone at home is the number one cause of school failure. The afternoon hours are the peak time for juvenile crime. In the last 11 years, juvenile crime has increased 48%. The Carnegie Council on Adolescent Development found that 8th graders who are alone 11 hours a week are twice as likely to abuse drugs as adolescents who are busy after school.

Unsupervised children are more likely to become depressed, smoke cigarettes and marijuana and drink alcohol. They are also more likely to be the victims of crimes. When home alone, latchkey children generally watch television, eat snacks, play with pets and fight with siblings.

Adolescents who fall under the classification of latchkey children are more likely than others of the same age group to experience feelings of rage and isolation and to express those emotions in a physically aggressive manner. While there are certainly genetic and biological factors involved in the development of an adolescent's propensity towards acting out their feelings of rage and isolation, environment also plays a key role in this arena. Sociologists have found that many latchkey children, because they are frequently raised in dysfunctional families, are taught by example to be manipulative, secretive and unpredictable. They often instinctively develop a sense of timing and management of their emotions. These are skills that can be easily and directly used to portray a false picture of themselves and their living situation.

Making the decision: When is a child ready to be home alone? Personality characteristics, skills, and maturity are useful criteria for determining a child's readiness to be home alone. Personality doesn't generally change much with age, although children can learn to modify some of their reactions as they learn what is expected of them. There are some children who find it very difficult to be alone, some who need time and gradual exposure to become accustomed to being by themselves, and some who adapt easily.

The personality characteristics of the child who is ready to be home alone is a child who
– is not fearful, feels at ease in the world and is self-confident
– is calm, and is not excitable when something unexpected happens
– is outgoing and talks about his or her feelings and thoughts readily with parents and others
– admits wrongdoing, even when expecting disapproval
– has courage enough to resist pressure from friends and others.

In many communities there are activities for school-age children whose parents work and cannot be at home in the afternoon. The importance of looking into these is stressed by child development professionals. According to James Comer of Yale University, "the period between 10 and 15 years is a time when young people re-examine their attitudes and values. They are being pressured by peers. They need to be protected by responsible adults who will help them examine and counter some of these attitudes."

The activities available vary as does the cost. Some are more popular with children than others, and some are more rewarding, but all are preferable to sitting at home in front of the television. These programmes can vary in cost or are free, depending upon the particular activity and the age of the child. All of them offer the opportunity to acquire skills and knowledge that are useful throughout life. Children who are not learning anything for hours every week are at a distinct disadvantage compared to children who are engaged in enriching activities. In the words of T. Berry Brazelton, of Harvard University: "During these all important bridge years between childhood and adulthood, kids really do need something constructive to do, and they also still need to have their activities supervised. Most of all, they need to know that their parents care about them, are involved in their lives, and have their best interests at heart."

Reading

Reading Tip:
Read all the instructions carefully. They will tell you important information such as where to find the answers and what type of answer is required.

Questions 27 - 29

Choose **THREE** *letters A - H.*

NB *Your answers may be given in any order.*

Which **THREE** of the following statements are mentioned in the text?

A	Youth crime is no longer attributable to economic background.
B	The greatest cause for concern is the children whose parents work the night shift.
C	Latchkey children whose parents have alcohol-abuse problems are more likely to drink alcohol when unsupervised at home.
D	The safer the neighbourhood, the lower the crime rate amongst adolescents.
E	Because of financial considerations, children from middle-class or upper-class backgrounds have more access to community activities.
F	Latchkey children are not only drawn to crime; they are victims of crime, too.
G	Expense should not be a factor in allowing children to get involved in out-of-school activities.
H	Knowing how to say no to one's peers is a sign of an adolescent's maturity.

Questions 30 - 31

Choose the correct letter A, B, C or D.

30   The writer says that during the war,

    A   children whose parents were absent from the home were better looked after than present-day children in the same situation are.

    B   the country was slow to react to the problem of latchkey children.

    C   the role of the housewife changed forever.

    D   all wives whose husbands had gone off to fight were expected to work in industry.

31   According to the Census Bureau, most children were left alone

    A   at night.

    B   in the morning.

    C   in the afternoon.

    D   all day.

Questions 32 - 35

Do the following statements agree with the information given in Reading Passage 3?

In spaces 32 - 35 below, write

TRUE	*if the statement agrees with the information*
FALSE	*if the statement contradicts the information*
NOT GIVEN	*if there is no information on this*

32   Latchkey children can be experts at hiding

the truth about their situation.   ....

33   Latchkey children leave home at a very early age.   ....

34   Latchkey children's aggressive emotional responses

are due principally to their biological make-up.   ....

35   Good communication skills are a measure of a child's

ability to be left unsupervised.   ....

Questions 36 - 40

Complete the summary.

*Choose **NO MORE THAN TWO WORDS** from the passage for each answer.*

The Second World War gave rise to the phenomenon of the latchkey child, as mothers had to abandon their traditional duties and fill the places of men in 36 ....
Fortunately, there was a quick 37 .... to this by the authorities to help mothers so that their children would not be left at home unsupervised. However, now, so many years after the war, this type of support has disappeared and the problem of having children alone at home without 38 .... is very common . These children generally perform poorly at school, display 39 .... behaviour and may take up smoking and drinking alcohol. While 40 .... and level of maturity plays a part in how a child copes with being a latchkey child, experts say that the remedy for this situation is more parental involvement and interest in their children's lives.

Writing

Writing Tip:
Do **NOT** write either Writing Task in note form or using bullet points.

WRITING TASK 1

You should spend about 20 minutes on this task.

> *The chart below shows the payment methods used most often by US consumers over a four-year period.*
>
> *Summarise the information by selecting and reporting the main features, and make comparisons where relevant.*

Write at least 150 words.

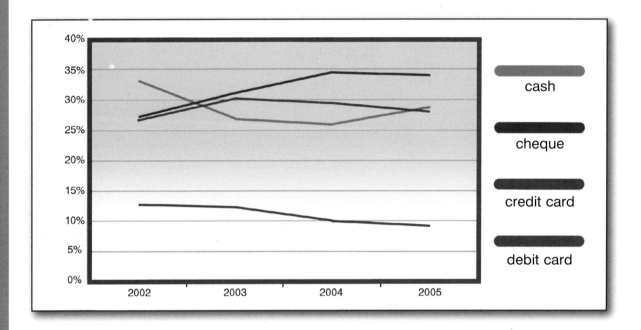

WRITING TASK 2

You should spend about 40 minutes on this task.

Write about the following topic:

> *We live in a world in which we are constantly exposed to advertising. To what extent does advertising influence our choices as consumers, and what effect does it have on our lifestyles?*
>
> *Discuss this issue and give your opinion.*

Give reasons for your answers and include any relevant examples from your own knowledge or experience.

Write at least 250 words.

Speaking

PART 1   (4-5 minutes)

The examiner asks the candidate about him/herself, his/her home, work or studies and other familiar topics.

Holidays

• What is your definition of the perfect holiday?
• What do you do to prepare for a holiday?
• Which areas of your country do you find the most appealing?
• What do tourists like to do when they come to visit your country?

PART 2   (2 minutes)

You will have to talk about the topic for one to two minutes. You have one minute to think about what you are going to say. You can make some notes to help you if you wish.

Describe a country that you would enjoy visiting.

You should say:
• where the country is
• what the country is known for
• which famous landmarks or tourist sites are associated with it
• why you would enjoy visiting it

PART 3   (4-5 minutes)

Discussion topics:

Tourism

• What do young people in your country like to do when they go on holiday?
• What do you think are the benefits of young people visiting foreign countries?
• Has tourism had a significant effect on your country?

Environmental impact of tourism

• How can tourism affect the environment?
• Do you think ecotourism is something we should take more seriously?
• What is your opinion of space tourism?

Test 7

Listening

SECTION 1   *Questions 1 - 10*

Questions 1 - 3

Choose the correct letter A, B or C.

Example: When does the special offer finish?
- A late March
- B early April
- Ⓒ at the end of May

1   What total discount is Jonathon's school being offered?
- A 25%
- B 50%
- C 65%

2   Where did Jonathon first want to take his students?
- A Madrid
- B Barcelona
- C Sainsbury

3   What is the normal price of this tour?
- A £679
- B £1261
- C £1940

Questions 4 - 10

Complete the notes below.

Write **NO MORE THAN THREE WORDS** for each answer.

Mcfadden's Travel

Two main things the all-inclusive price covers:

4 ....

5 ....

Extras also covered by the all-inclusive offer:

airport taxis, 6 ....

a city tour, 7 ....

CLIENT DETAILS:

E-mail address of contact person: 8 ....@...................com

Number of travellers: *49*	Credit Card Number: 9 ....
Date of travel: *7th of April*	Expiry Date: *01-Jan-2015*
Departure time: *7:00 a.m.*	Total cost of booking: 10 £...........................
Arrival time: *10:30 a.m. (local time)*	

SECTION 2   *Questions 11 - 20*

Questions 11 - 12

Choose the correct letter A, B or C.

11 What does the word 'formula' stand for?

   A the rules drivers must respect

   B the type of roads used for the races

   C the way they drive

12 When did the first championship race take place?

   A in 1920

   B in 1955

   C in 1950

Questions 13 - 20

Complete the table below.

*Write **NO MORE THAN TWO WORDS AND/OR A NUMBER** for each answer.*

Driver	First Title	Last Title	Notable Record/s	Interesting Fact
Juan Manuel Fangio	1951	**13**	won 5 world championships, a record which remained for **14** .... years	was the first **15** .... winner
Ayrton Senna	1988	1991	won the most races ever at the **16** .... Grand Prix	is regarded as the most **17** .... driver ever
Alain Prost	1985	1993	won the third **18** .... number of championships	was a **19** .... of Senna
Michael Schumacher	1994	2004	holds many records including most drivers' championships, pole positions, race victories and fastest laps	is the **20** .... on paper

Listening

SECTION 3   *Questions 21 - 30*

Questions 21 - 27

Complete the table below.

Write **NO MORE THAN THREE WORDS AND/OR A NUMBER** *for each answer.*

Bizz-Educators Inc.	
Upsides	**Downsides**
has a proven track record	wants to remain an independent entity, so this would be a hostile 25 ....
is an industry 21	is a production-based company
is well-respected and has a great name	is a 26 .... venture
has generated a lot of goodwill	is in a different market so there will be no synergy, and no cost savings
consistently has an annual gross profit of 22	
has a clear and ambitious 23	
has very high 24 .... for 2012 and 2013	

The official decision on whether to buy Bizz-Educators will be taken

at tomorrow's 27 ....

Questions 28 - 30

Choose **THREE** letters, *A - G.*

What **THREE** requirements are there for the takeover of Bizz-Educators to go ahead?

A	Assurances that the management of Bizz-Educators won't oppose the deal.
B	An independent mediator be used to broker the deal.
C	An audit of the company's books.
D	That a study of the company's projected profit margin be conducted.
E	That the deal be kept secret until it is finalised.
F	That an analysis of the company's goodwill assets be carried out.
G	That the asking price be lowered.

Practice Test 7

SECTION 4   *Questions 31 - 40*

Complete the notes below.

Write **NO MORE THAN TWO WORDS** *for each answer.*

Conserving Energy at Home

- Carbon footprint is:
  the **31** .... of greenhouse gas emitted into the atmosphere by an individual as a result of his day-to-day activities.

- More than **32** .... of all homes are not insulated.

Reasons to better insulate your home:
- Fitting adequate insulation in the **33** .... and outer walls of your home can reduce heating costs by as much as 25%.

- The government offers **34** .... to people who want to reinsulate their homes.

- You will recoup your investment over a short period of time.

Painting **35** .... walls in dark colours is a bad idea because dark colours **36** .... heat.
Replacing a normal light bulb with an energy-saving one could save you **37** .... over the lifetime of the bulb.

If you have large windows in your home, you should close the **38** ....

Erect **39** .... to heat your water supply.
People should continue recycling and composting their **40** .... to help protect the environment.

Reading

READING PASSAGE 1

*You should spend about 20 minutes on **Questions 1 - 13**, which are based on Reading Passage 1 below.*

The Final Frontier for Tourism

A

For some reason humankind has always looked towards the stars and dreamt of one day making the voyage into the unknown and exploring outer space. Perhaps it is our innate curiosity, perhaps the challenge presented by the seemingly impossible; whatever the lure, the quest to venture into space has become an obsession for many.

B

On a memorable July day in 1969 one man made a giant leap for his kind. Neil Armstrong touched down on the moon as the world watched with bated breath. Was this a beginning or the culmination of years of endeavour that pushed science to its very limits? Well, it has been a long time indeed since the last moon landing, more than 40 years, but science has not stood still in the interim, nor have our dreams become any less ambitious. According to NASA, plans are afoot for a manned mission to Mars at some point after 2020. A return to the moon has been scheduled sooner - perhaps 2018 if NASA's new Crew Exploration Vehicle (CEV) is rolled out on time. It may not be Hollywood razzle-dazzle-style progress; it may even be painstakingly slow, but rest assured that plans are afoot for something very ambitious and special indeed, and NASA may be back in the headlines making waves and history again, just as it did on that faithful day in 1969, in the not-too-distant future.

C

That said, it is the prospect of space tourism for the masses that has captured the headlines recently, and this may not be such a distant dream as people would expect. In 2001, an American multimillionaire, Denis Tito, became the first space tourist, spending ten days on the International Space Station along with his crew of Russian cosmonauts, and fulfilling a lifelong ambition in the process. He described the experience rather paradoxically as 'indescribable'; everything that he thought it would be and more. A year later, South African millionaire Mark Shuttleworth followed in his footsteps. On his return to Earth he said, 'every second will be with me for the rest of my life'. Clearly these men had a once-in-a-lifetime experience, but this came at a hefty price, both paying $20 million for the pleasure of their space adventures.

D

At present, space tourism is undoubtedly reserved for an elite and wealthy few, but what of the future? If Eric Anderson, president of Space Adventures, the company that organised Tito and Shuttleworth's trips, is to be believed, it will be the next big thing. 'Everyone's looking for a new experience', he says. Indeed, Space Adventures is planning to offer rocket trips to the public for $100,000 within the next few years, so perhaps space tourism is closer than we think. Another company, The Space Island Group, is planning to build a space hotel inspired by the spaceship in the film *2001: A Space Odyssey*. Gene Meyers, the company's president, predicts that in 2020 a five-day holiday at the hotel will cost less than $25,000. Imagine, he says, a five-star hotel with all the usual luxuries, except that each morning you'll be greeted by mind-blowing views of outer space. This is certainly food for thought for adventure-seeking holiday planners. That said, unless there is a serious spike in inflation between now and 2020, $25,000 will still remain a considerable sum of money to have to part with for a recreational activity, once-in-a-lifetime or not. But that is perhaps missing the point – the prospect of affordable space travel is getting closer and closer and it is only a matter of time before it becomes a reality.

E

Other companies have even more ambitious plans. Bigelow Aerospace is spending close to $500 million on a project to build a 700-metre spaceship to fly tourists to the moon. The spaceship will be able to hold 100 guests, each with a private room offering truly unique views of the Earth's sunset. Even the Hilton Hotel Group wants to get in on the act with talk of plans to build a Hilton on the moon. For the present, only millionaires can enjoy the privilege of a space journey, but in the words of one Bob Dylan, 'The times they are a changing.' And sooner than you'd think.

Questions 1 - 5

Reading passage 1 has five paragraphs A - E.
Choose the correct heading for each paragraph A - E from the list of headings below.
Write the correct number i - viii in the spaces 1 - 5 below.

List of Headings

i	Not worth the cost
ii	Space travel; past, present and future
iii	Russian innovations
iv	A profitable investment
v	The future of tourism
vi	Insatiable desire for adventure
vii	The first space tourists
viii	Moon hotels

1	
2	
3	
4	
5	

1 Paragraph **A**
2 Paragraph **B**
3 Paragraph **C**
4 Paragraph **D**
5 Paragraph **E**

Questions 6 - 9

Look at the following people (Questions 6 - 9) and the list of statements below.
Match each person with the correct statement, A - D.
Write the correct letter, A - D, in spaces 6 - 9.

6 Denis Tito

7 Mark Shuttleworth

8 Eric Anderson

9 Gene Meyers

A touched down on the moon in 1969

B believes space tourism will be popular in the near future

C spent ten days on the International Space Station

D was the second tourist to travel into space

E predicts space holidays will be more affordable by 2020

F will build a hotel inspired by a film

Questions 10 - 13

Do the following statements agree with the information given in Reading Passage 1?

In spaces 10 - 13 below, write:

TRUE	*if the statement agrees with the information*
FALSE	*if the statement contradicts the information*
NOT GIVEN	*if there is no information on this*

10 Bigelow Aerospace's spaceship will offer unique views of the Moon's sunset. ....

11 The Hilton Hotel Group has ambitious plans to organise cheap space journeys. ....

12 NASA plans to launch a mission to Mars, but first it is hoping to return to
the moon. ....

13 At the moment, space tourism is too expensive for ordinary people,
only the very rich can travel to space. ....

Reading

READING PASSAGE 2

You should spend about 20 minutes on Questions 14 - 26, which are based on Reading Passage 2 below.

Arctic Survivors

The Arctic is an area located at the northernmost part of the Earth and includes the Arctic Ocean, Canada, Russia, Greenland, the United States, Norway, Sweden, Finland and Iceland. It consists of an ice-covered ocean, surrounded by treeless permafrost. The area can be defined as north of the Arctic Circle, the approximate limit of the midnight sun and the polar night. The average temperature in July, which is the warmest month, is below 10 °C. Colder summer temperatures cause the size, abundance, productivity and variety of plants to decrease. Trees cannot grow in the Arctic, but in its warmest parts, shrubs are common and can reach 2 metres in height.

A thick blanket of snow lies several feet deep all over the ground. The sun appears for only a few brief hours each day before sinking below the horizon as blackness cloaks the land. As it vanishes, a bitter chill tightens its grip. The Arctic is not a place to be in the throes of winter, it is hostile to almost all animal life. Amphibians would freeze solid here. Nor can reptiles withstand the extreme cold. And yet there are animals here, animals that exhibit a remarkable tolerance of the most inhospitable conditions on the planet. Less than half a metre beneath the surface of the snow, a furry white creature, no bigger than a hamster, scurries along a tunnel. It is a collared lemming. It and other members of its family have excavated a complex home within the snow field, but it costs the lemmings a great deal to survive here. They pay by using some of their precious and scarce food supply to generate heat within their bodies so that their biochemical processes can continue to function efficiently. But in order to keep fuel costs to a minimum, they must conserve as much energy as they can. A thick insulating coat of fine fur covering all but the lemmings' eyes achieves this. Fur is the life preserver of the Arctic.

Only one class of animals has fur - the mammals. Fur is comprised of dense layers of hair follicles. Hair is composed of a substance called keratin. It grows constantly, its roots embedded in the skin and surrounded by nerve fibres so that its owner can sense any movement of the hair. It is this precious fur that gives land mammals the edge necessary to survive the harsh Arctic winter. Without it, wolves, lemmings and arctic foxes alike would surely perish.

The insulation provided by fur comes not from the fur itself, but largely from the layer of air trapped within the fur. Air is an extremely effective insulator, which is the same as saying it is a poor conductor, i.e. it has a very limited ability to conduct heat away from a warm surface. Studies reveal that if a layer of air of about five centimetres could be held in place close to the skin, it would provide the same insulation as does the impressively dense winter coat of the arctic fox. If an arctic fox or wolf is exposed to an air temperature of about minus ten degrees, the temperature near the tips of the fur will match the air temperature, but at the surface of the skin it will be closer to thirty degrees. This represents a temperature difference of around forty degrees. Such effective insulation is only made possible by the layer of trapped air contained within the long, fine and densely packed fur.

But Arctic mammals have more in their arsenal than just fur to protect them from the elements. Unlike amphibians, reptiles and other classes of animals, they are endotherms, meaning they can generate their own body heat. This is another of the defining characteristics of mammals. It is the mammalian ability to generate heat internally that enables the arctic fox or the lemming to remain warm and active in very cold conditions. Generating heat internally, arctic mammals can regulate their body temperature independent of external conditions; this is known as thermoregulation. When arctic mammals are cold, they raise their metabolic rate and produce more heat. When they are warm, the reverse happens. Together, thermoregulation and fur make arctic mammals perfectly equipped to face the toughest conditions the arctic can throw at them.

Reading

Questions 14 - 20

Choose the correct answer A, B, C or D.

14 Animals that live in the Arctic

   A can withstand extremely difficult living conditions.

   B often freeze solid during winter.

   C are mainly reptilian.

   D are mostly frogs or toads.

15 Where do lemmings live?

   A on the surface of the snow

   B in tunnels built under the frozen ocean

   C in wide tunnels deep underground

   D about 50 cm below the surface of the snow

16 Fur is

   A thick layers of hair.

   B common to all animal classes.

   C unhelpful to Arctic animals.

   D the life preserver only for small Arctic mammals.

17 Why is trapped air a good insulator?

   A It is a good conductor of heat.

   B Air helps us to breathe.

   C It is a bad conductor of heat.

   D It absorbs heat and cold very well.

18 If the temperature at the tip of the fur of an arctic fox is minus ten degrees, the temperature at the surface of the skin will be closer to

   A forty degrees.

   B ten degrees.

   C thirty degrees.

   D thirty five degrees.

19 What is an endotherm?

   A an animal that can generate heat inside its body

   B an animal that cannot generate heat inside its body

   C an animal that never gets cold

   D an animal that has special insulation

20 Thermoregulation and fur help arctic mammals

   A cope with hot temperatures.

   B protect themselves from the elements.

   C regulate the temperature of their surroundings.

   D create a layer of trapped air within their fur.

Questions 21 - 26

Complete the summary below.

*Choose **ONE WORD ONLY** from the passage for each answer.*

The Arctic winter is something few animals can survive, but there are a select few that show an amazing **21** .... of the severe winter conditions. These animals have to use their food resources to keep their body temperature high so that the biochemical **22** .... inside them continue to run. One thing that helps them keep their bodies warm is their **23** .... which consists of thick layers of hair that provide insulation for their bodies; it is their life **24** .... The layer of trapped air that they also have provides very effective insulation from cold because it is not a good **25** .... of heat. In the case of an arctic mammal getting cold, it deals with it by increasing its **26** .... rate to generate more heat.

Reading

READING PASSAGE 3

*You should spend about 20 minutes on **Questions 27 - 40**, which are based on Reading Passage 3 below.*

Bismarck: A Master of Political and Diplomatic Juggling?

A

Otto Von Bismarck's rise up the political ladder was swift and relentless. Having entered parliament in 1847, he always harboured lofty ambitions, chief among them perhaps being the reunification of Germany into one strong, centrally controlled state, though his own personal thirst for power was arguably even stronger. On becoming Prussian Chancellor, he set about fulfilling his ambitions and in doing so proved himself to be a diplomat of some considerable skill. Victory in the Austro-Prussian war effectively ended Austria as a factor in German affairs. His political and military juggling was taken a step further when he orchestrated a situation where France declared war on Germany in 1870, making the French seem responsible for a conflict he had always intended to create. And following another swift military triumph, this time over the French, the German empire was proclaimed in January 1871.

B

In little more than nine years, Bismarck realised his lifelong ambition, steering Germany to reunification. And by defeating Austria and France in quick succession, he also created a power vacuum on mainland Europe which he was determined to fill himself. This was another opportunity for Bismarck to demonstrate his political and diplomatic cunning. He set about creating a dictatorial

Germany in which he, as head of the Prussian parliament, would automatically become chancellor of the German empire. He drafted a new German constitution to suit his own purposes and, despite maintaining a veneer of democracy, the German parliament was effectively powerless to oppose him. Provinces that were slow to support him were enticed with bribes and before long the German empire was his to command.

C

It is testament to his political skill that Bismarck achieved so much so quickly. At this point in his colourful political career he did appear, for all intents and purposes, a master of political and diplomatic juggling. But challenges lay ahead and Bismarck's next target was the Catholic church, which he deemed too powerful and a threat to his political dominance. He proceeded to enact a series of laws which seriously eroded the power of the church. However his plans backfired and Bismarck was forced to make a political U-turn. Though here again, he somehow managed to save face. The damage to his reputation was limited and indeed by the late 1870s he had even managed to win over the church whose support he now needed.

D

Bismarck viewed the growing popularity of the Socialist Democratic Party as a serious threat. He bided his time and used the attempted assassination of the Kaiser as an excuse to attack the socialists in 1878, blaming them for the attempt on the Kaiser's life. He immediately arrested the leaders, banned party meetings and suppressed socialist newspapers. But despite his efforts to destroy the socialist movement, its popularity had trebled by 1890. Just as his interventions with the church had not gone as planned, Bismarck once again failed to achieve his objective; though, to his credit, he held on to power.

E

His domestic position was relatively secure after 1871 and Bismarck devoted a lot of his time to foreign policy. Having used war to unite Germany and make her great, Bismarck now believed that his ambitions were best served by peace. His plan to isolate a hostile France would require all his considerable diplomatic skills. The Dreikaiserbund agreement of 1873 between Germany, Austria-Hungary and Russia was a first step towards doing just that. The Balkan crisis, a conflict involving Russia and Austria-Hungary, severely tested his diplomatic credentials, but his answer was to offer himself as an 'honest broker' to help resolve the dispute. The subsequent Congress of Berlin which he hosted was an outstanding success and only served to reinforce Bismarck's reputation as a shrewd diplomat. Bismarck's foreign policy would continue in this vein throughout his reign as Chancellor. He built up strategic alliances with the big powers, Russia, Italy and Austria-Hungary, in the hope that he could keep his main threats, France and Britain, isolated.

F

In truth, Bismarck's reign as chancellor of the German empire does seem to confirm him as a shrewd and wily diplomat and politician, one whose objectives were broadly achieved. Does this mean his so-called juggling was a success? Perhaps, but Bismarck left a less than perfect legacy. He created a Germany in which the Kaiser had the ultimate say in domestic affairs and enjoyed far too much power should he choose to wield it. This meant that the future of the empire largely depended on the strength and character of just one man, the Kaiser. A weak Kaiser would be disastrous for the country's welfare, and so it would soon prove. In the final analysis, Bismarck put Germany back on the map again as a great power during his reign, but we should not forget that he created the political situation that would be the downfall of his country in the end. His political and diplomatic juggling, therefore, simply cannot be considered a total success.

Reading

Questions 27 - 31

Choose the correct answer A, B, C or D.

Write the correct letter in the boxes 14-20 on your answer sheet.

27 In little more than nine years as Prussian Chancellor Bismarck had

    A succeeded in reuniting Germany and defeating Austria and France.

    B divided his country and lost two wars.

    C succeeded in suppressing the Socialist party.

    D abolished the parliament.

28 What happened after Bismarck enacted laws to weaken the Catholic church?

    A He changed his policy and made the church an ally.

    B The church's influence weakened.

    C France declared war on Germany.

    D He didn't succeed and his influence was severely weakened.

29 What had happened to the Socialist party by 1890?

    A It had taken power from Bismarck.

    B It had lost its influence.

    C Its popularity had risen three-fold.

    D It became very powerful in the parliament.

30 After reuniting Germany what was Bismarck's belief on foreign policy?

    A He needed to wage war with all countries that posed a military threat.

    B Preserving the peace and isolating France would benefit him.

    C Germany needed to befriend France to form a powerful alliance.

    D He wanted to form an alliance with Britain and France.

31 The article concludes that Bismark

    A made few mistakes and left a positive legacy.

    B was not at all successful.

    C was always tolerant of those who had different opinions.

    D was not actually a master of political juggling.

Questions 32 - 34

Do the following statements agree with the information given in Reading Passage 3?

In spaces 32 - 34 below, write

TRUE	*if the statement agrees with the information*
FALSE	*if the statement contradicts the information*
NOT GIVEN	*if there is no information on this*

32   The Congress of Berlin was a great personal success for Bismarck.   ....

33   Bismarck refused to build alliances with Russia or Austria.   ....

34   Bismarck considered his reign as German chancellor a failure.   ....

Questions 35 - 40

Reading passage 3 has six paragraphs, **A - F**.

Choose the correct heading, A - F, from the list of headings below.

Write the correct number, i - ix, in spaces 35 - 40 below.

35	Paragraph A	....
36	Paragraph B	....
37	Paragraph C	....
38	Paragraph D	....
39	Paragraph E	....
40	Paragraph F	....

List of Headings

i	A critical analysis
ii	Early career and rise to power
iii	Foreign policy
iv	Powerful friends
v	Separating church and state
vi	Socialist threat
vii	Political decline
viii	Creating a virtual dictatorship
ix	A change of mind

Practice Test 7

Writing

WRITING TASK 1

You should spend about 20 minutes on this task.

The chart shows the end of year value for four major international money market indices in 2005, 2006, 2007 and 2008. [FTSE 100 = UK Market Index,   Dow Jones = US Market Index, KOSPI = Korean Market Index,   CAC 40 = French Market Index]

Summarise the information by selecting and reporting the main features, and make comparisons where relevant.

Write at least 150 words.

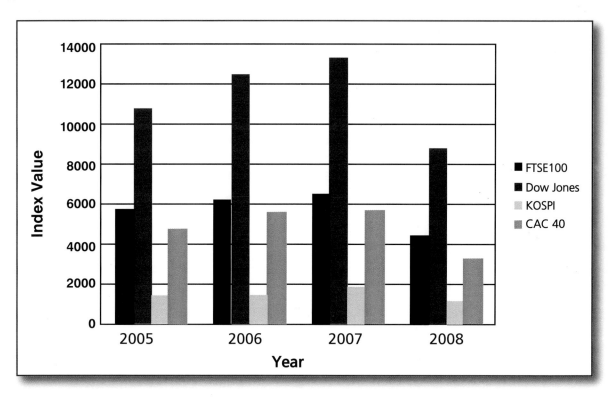

WRITING TASK 2

You should spend about 40 minutes on this task.

Write about the following topic:

Society is becoming obsessed with material goods like fast cars, designer clothes and flashy jewellery. We have stopped caring about the important things and that is why divorce rates are so high and family bonds are not as strong anymore; our value system is disintegrating.
To what extent do you agree or disagree?

Give reasons for your answer and include any relevant examples from your own knowledge or experience.

Write at least 250 words.

Speaking

PART 1   (4-5 minutes)

The examiner asks the candidate about him/herself, his/her home, work or studies and other familiar topics.

Living Arrangements
* Would you prefer to live in a traditional house or in a modern apartment building? Why?
* Can you tell me something about the area you live in?
* If you could make changes to your area or home town, what would you change?
* Would you prefer to live in a big city or in the countryside? Why?

PART 2   (2 minutes)

You will have to talk about the topic for one to two minutes. You have one minute to think about what you are going to say. You can make some notes to help you if you wish.

> Describe an individual who you regard as a role model.
> You should say:
> * why you look up to him/her
> * which of his/her characteristics you admire
> and explain what, in your opinion, makes a good role model, especially for young people today.

PART 3   (4-5 minutes)

Discussion topics:

Role Models
* Are parents ever role models? Why/Why not?
* Do you think today's celebrities are good role models?
* Should famous people think about how their actions might influence young people?

Celebrities
* Many people say there is one rule for celebrities and another for ordinary people. Do you believe this?
* Do celebrities have a right to their privacy or should they accept that their lives will always be played out in the public eye?
* Many people believe that celebrities and public figures like politicians make the worst role models. Do you agree?

Listening

SECTION 1   Questions 1 - 10

Questions 1 - 3

Choose the correct letter A, B or C.

Example: When is there a 50% discount on Lasagna?

    A On the weekends and on weekdays

    B On weekdays only

    C On weekends only

1 How many bottles of wine do you have to buy to get one free?

    A one

    B three

    C four

2 Which type of wine do David's friends prefer?

    A French

    B Italian

    C Spanish

3 What is the price of the champagne?

    A £20

    B £35

    C £25

Questions 4 - 10

Answer the questions below.

Write **NO MORE THAN THREE WORDS AND/OR A NUMBER** *for each answer.*

Belluci's Restaurant

Sam's suggestions
Would go best with the Lasagna:

4 ....

5 ....

Other side dishes that Sam mentions:

6 .... with ....

7 .... with ....

CUSTOMER DETAILS

Booking made on: *5th August*   Date when customers will be at the restaurant: **8** ....

Time: *7:00 pm*   Number of people: **9** ....

Email address: **10** ....@........................ .com

Customer phone number: *01445 333 6451*   Customer willing to have emails sent to them: *Yes*

SECTION 2   *Questions 11 - 20*

Questions 11 - 12

Choose the correct letter A, B or C.

11 How did the players hit the ball when the game first launched in the 12th century?

   A with a bat

   B with a racquet

   C with their bare hand

12 In the 16th century what kind of people found tennis most appealing?

   A royal families

   B wealthy merchants

   C everyday people

Questions 13 - 20

Complete the table below.

*Write **NO MORE THAN THREE WORDS AND/OR A NUMBER** for each answer.*

Tennis Player	Year Born	Nationality	Number of Major Titles Won	Interesting Fact
Bjorn Borg	**13**	Swedish	**14**	won both Wimbledon and the French open in **15** .... more than once
Boris Becker	1967	German	**16**	the youngest ever male Grand Slam singles champion at **17** .... months.
Pete Sampras	1971	American	**18**	He started hitting tennis balls at the age of 3
Andre Agassi	**19**	American	Eight	His first **20** .... was in La Quinta

Listening

SECTION 3   Questions 21 - 30

Questions 21 - 27

Complete the table below.

*Write **NO MORE THREE WORDS** for each answer.*

College Conference 2009	
Speakers	**Administration and Organisation**
Professor Harman - good at running 21	Invitations to all speakers have to be typed on the school's headed paper.
Mr Steve Bishop - **22** .... among many Universities in England.	The photographer will take pictures for the school **25** ....
Sandra Bolton will give some Drama 23	The caterers are called **26** ....
Mr Max Wallington will give a lecture about Shakespeare.	The conference will be in the main college hall and rooms 10, 11, 12 and 13.
Sean O'Brien has done a lot of work in the field of **24**	The date of the next meeting will be on **27** ....
Geoff O'Hara has a lot of knowledge about Albert Einstein.	

Questions 28 - 30

*Choose **THREE** letters, A - G.*

What **THREE** rules, given to them by the headmaster, do the students have to follow during the conference?

28 ....   29 ....   30 ....

A	Make sure they tidy up the hall and rooms after the conference.
B	Provide cleaners for the conference.
C	Provide lunch for the speakers.
D	Make a record of what each student at the conference wants to study at University.
E	Make a record of what each student at the conference is studying now.
F	Make a record of all students who attend the conference.
G	Help organise the travel arrangements for the speakers.

SECTION 4   *Questions 31 - 40*

Questions 31 - 40

Complete the notes below.

*Write **NO MORE THAN TWO WORDS** for each answer.*

To calculate your Body Mass Index you should first take **31** .... in kilograms and divide it by your height in metres.

Healthy Diets

- It is important to eat starchy foods with fruit and vegetables.

- There are people who **32** .... that starchy foods are 'fattening'.

- Eat a minimum of **33** .... of fruit and vegetables a day.

- People tend to eat too much **34** .... and you only need a certain amount to keep healthy.

- People say that **35** .... can help protect against heart disease.

Exercise is good for us because:

1) it strengthens the heart

2) it tones our **36** ....

3) it is good for the mind

- We do less exercise because we have domestic **37** ....
  to do things for us.

- Adults should do at least **38** .... moderate-intensity physical
  activity, five days a week.

A physical activity can be:

a) a lifestyle activity

b) a **39** .... activity

c) sports

Activities that produce **40** .... on the bones are necessary.

Reading

READING PASSAGE 1

*You should spend about 20 minutes on **Questions 1 - 14**, which are based on Reading Passage 1 below.*

A

The climate of the Earth is always changing. In the past it has altered as a result of natural causes. Nowadays, however, the term 'climate change' is generally used when referring to changes in our climate which have been identified since the early part of the twentieth century. The changes we've seen over recent years and those which are predicted to occur over the next 100 years are thought by many to be largely a result of human behaviour rather than due to natural changes in the atmosphere. And this is what is so significant about current climactic trends; never before has man played such a significant role in determining long-term weather patterns – we are entering the unknown and there is no precedent for what might happen next.

B

The greenhouse effect is very important when we talk about climate change as it relates to the gases which keep the Earth warm. Although the greenhouse effect is a naturally occurring phenomenon, it is believed that the effect could be intensified by human activity and the emission of gases into the atmosphere. It is the extra greenhouse gases which humans have released which are thought to pose the strongest threat. Certain researchers, such as Dr Michael Crawley, argue: 'even though this natural phenomenon does exist it is without a doubt human activity that has worsened its effect; this is evident when comparing data regarding the earth's temperature in the last one hundred years with the one hundred years prior to that.' Some scientists, however, dispute this as Dr Ray Ellis suggests: 'human activity may be contributing a small amount to climate change but this increase in temperature is an unavoidable fact based on the research data we have compiled.'

C

Scientists around the globe are looking at all the evidence surrounding
climate change and using advanced
technology have come up with predictions for our future environment
and weather. The next stage of that
work, which is just as important, is
looking at the knock-on effects of
potential changes. For example, are
we likely to see an increase in precipitation and sea levels? Does this

mean there will be an increase in flooding and what can we do to protect ourselves from
that? How will our health be affected by climate change, how will agricultural practices
change and how will wildlife cope? What will the effects on coral be? Professor Max
Leonard has suggested, 'while it may be controversial some would argue that climate
change could bring with it positive effects as well as negative ones'.

D

There are many institutions around the world whose sole priority is to take action against
these environmental problems. Green Peace is the organisation that is probably the most
well-known. It is an international organisation that campaigns in favour of researching
and promoting solutions to climate change, exposes the companies and governments
that are blocking action, lobbies to change national and international policy, and bears
witness to the impacts of unnecessary destruction and detrimental human activity.

E

The problem of climate change is without a doubt something that this generation and the
generations to come need to deal with. Fortunately, the use of renewable energy is
becoming increasingly popular, which means that less energy is consumed as renewable
energy is generated from natural resources—such as sunlight, wind, rain, tides, and geothermal heat—which can be naturally replenished. Another way to help the environment,
in terms of climate change, is by travelling light. Walking or riding a bike instead of driving a car uses fewer fossil fuels which release carbon dioxide into the atmosphere. In addition, using products that are made from recycled paper, glass, metal and plastic reduces
carbon emissions because they use less energy to manufacture than products made from
completely new materials. Recycling paper also saves trees and lets them continue to
limit climate change naturally as they remain in the forest, where they remove carbon
from the atmosphere. Professor Mark Halton, who has completed various studies in this
field, has stated: 'with all this information and the possible action that we can take, it
isn't too late to save our planet from over-heating and the even worse side-effects of our
own activity'.

Reading

Questions 1 - 5

Reading Passage 1 has 5 paragraphs, A - E. Which paragraph contains the following information?
Write the correct letter A - E in the boxes below.
NB *You may use any letter more than once.*

1   A natural phenomenon that could also affect climate change.

2   Steps we can take to help reverse the situation.

3   An explanation of what climate change is.

4   Organisations that want to help.

5   Possible effects of climate change.

Questions 6 - 9

Look at the following people (Questions 6 - 9) and the list of statements below.
Match each person with the correct statement, A - D.
Write the correct letter, A - D, in spaces 6 - 9.

6 Professor Max Leonard	☐
7 Dr Michael Crawley	☐
8 Professor Mark Halton	☐
9 Dr Ray Ellis	☐

A We have the ability to change the situation.

B Climate change is inevitable.

C Humans have made the situation much worse.

D Climate change might not be all bad.

E Human activity and natural weather phenomena have combined with equal influence to shape climate change

F While we may not be too late to save our planet, there are bound to be some extreme side-effects of past human activity, one way or the other.

Questions 10 - 13

Do the following statements agree with the information given in Reading Passage 1?

In spaces 10 - 13 below, write

YES	*if the statement agrees with the information*
NO	*if the statement contradicts the information*
NOT GIVEN	*if there is no information on this*

10 Man is not entirely responsible for global warming. ....

11 Scientists have come up with new evidence about the negative effects of carbon-free sources of energy such as nuclear power ....

12 One of the purposes of Green Peace is to find out which companies and governments are doing things which don't help the actions of environmentalists. ....

13 Most people aren't willing to start using renewable energy. ....

Reading

READING PASSAGE 2

You should spend about 20 minutes on Questions 14 - 26, which are based on Reading Passage 2 below.

PRIVATE SCHOOLS

Most countries' education systems have had what you might call educational disasters, but, sadly, in many areas of certain countries these 'disasters' are still evident today. The English education system is unique due to the fact that there are still dozens of schools which are known as private schools and they perpetuate privilege and social division. Most countries have some private schools for the children of the wealthy; England is able to more than triple the average number globally. England has around 3,000 private schools and just under half a million children are educated at them whilst some nine million children are educated at state schools. The overwhelming majority of students at private schools also come from middle-class families.

The result of this system is evident and it has much English history embedded within it. The facts seem to speak for themselves. In the private system almost half the students go on to University, whilst in the state system only about eight per cent make it to further education. However, statistics such as these can be deceptive due to the fact that middle class children do better at examinations than working class ones, and most of them stay on at school after 16. Private schools therefore have the advantage over state schools as they are entirely 'middle class', and this creates an environment of success where students work harder and apply themselves more diligently to their school work.

Private schools are extortionately expensive, being as much as £18,000 a year at somewhere such as Harrow or Eton, where Princes William and Harry attended, and at least £8,000 a year almost everywhere else. There are many parents who are not wealthy or even comfortably off but are willing to sacrifice a great deal in the cause of their children's schooling. It baffles many people as to why they need to spend such vast amounts when there are perfectly acceptable state schools that don't cost a penny. One father gave his reasoning for sending his son to a private school; 'If my son gets a five-percent-better chance of going to University then that may be the difference between success and failure." It would seem to the average person that a £50,000 minimum total cost of second level education is a lot to pay for a five-percent-better chance. Most children, given the choice, would take the money and spend it on more enjoyable things rather than shelling it out on a school that is too posh for its own good!

However, some say that the real reason that parents fork out the cash is prejudice: they don't want their little kids mixing with the "workers", or picking up an undesirable accent. In addition to this, it wouldn't do if at the next dinner party all the guests were boasting about sending their kids to the same place where the son of the third cousin of Prince Charles is going, and you say your kid is going to the state school down the road, even if you could pocket the money for yourself instead, and, as a result, be able to serve the best Champagne with the smoked salmon and duck.

It is a fact, however, that at many of the best private schools, your money buys you something. One school, with 500 pupils, has 11 science laboratories; another school with 800 pupils, has 30 music practice rooms; another has 16 squash courts, and yet another has its own beach.

Private schools spend £300 per pupil a year on investment in buildings and facilities; the state system spends less than £50. On books, the ratio is 3 to 1.

One of the things that your money buys which is difficult to quantify is the appearance of the school, the way it looks. Most private schools that you will find are set in beautiful, well-kept country houses, with extensive grounds and gardens. In comparison with the state schools, they tend to look like castles, with the worst of the state schools looking like public lavatories, perhaps even tiled or covered in graffiti. Many may even have an architectural design that is just about on the level of an industrial shed.

Questions 14 - 20

Choose the correct letter A, B, C or D.

14 The English educational system differs from other ones because
 A it tries to make state and private education equal.
 B more students are educated at private schools than state schools.
 C it contributes to creating a class system within society.
 D it is more expensive to run.

15 There are more private school children who go to university because
 A the lessons and teachers at the private schools are much better.
 B their parents are very rich and can help them.
 C they have more teaching hours.
 D the schools create a successful environment.

16 A lot of parents often send their children to private schools
 A because they are not well-informed.
 B to show how much money they have to their friends.
 C to increase their chances of succeeding in the university exams.
 D because of the better sports facilities.

17 It is suggested that some parents of children at private schools are
 A prejudiced and superficial.
 B more intelligent that those with children at state schools.
 C well-brought up and cultivated.
 D overly protective.

18 Private schools
 A always have their own beaches.
 B teach sports that state schools do not.
 C spend more money per student than state schools.
 D spend more money on hiring good teachers.

19 The writer thinks that private-school buildings
 A are very attractive and luxurious.
 B generally do not look very nice.
 C are too big for the amount of students who attend the school.
 D are not built to suit student's needs.

20 In general, what do you think the writer's opinion of private schools is?
 A It isn't fair that those without money can't attend them.
 B They divide social classes but they offer better facilities and a more creative environment.
 C There is little difference between private and state schools.
 D They have the best teachers.

Questions 21 - 26

Complete the sentences below.
*Choose **ONE WORD ONLY** from the passage for each answer.*

The fact that there are so many private schools in England, in comparison to other countries, makes the English educational system **21** ....

Most students in these schools are from **22** .... families. These students seem to do better at exams although statistics can be **23** ....

One of the advantages of private schools is that they seem to provide students with a better, more positive environment that encourages them to **24** .... themselves to their school work with more enthusiasm.

A lot of not very well-off parents make huge sacrifices for their children's **25** .... to help them go to respectable universities. Unfortunately, many state school buildings some times have the appearance of an industrial **26** ....

Practice Test 8

Reading

READING PASSAGE 3

*You should spend about 20 minutes on **Questions 27 - 40**, which are based on Reading Passage 3 below.*

Martin Luther King

A

Martin Luther King was born on January 15, 1929, in Atlanta, Georgia. He was the son of the Reverend Martin Luther King, Sr. and Alberta Williams King. He had an older sister, Willie Christine King, and a younger brother Alfred Daniel Williams King. Growing up in Atlanta, King attended Booker T. Washington High School. He skipped ninth and twelfth grade, and entered Morehouse College at age fifteen without formally graduating from high school. From the time that Martin was born, he knew that black people and white people had different rights in certain parts of America. If a black family wanted to eat at a restaurant, they had to sit in a separate section of the restaurant. They had to sit at the back of the cinema, and even use separate toilets. Worse, and perhaps even more humiliating still, in many southern states, if a black man was on a bus and all the seats were taken, he would have to endure the indignity of relinquishing his own seat to a white man. King could never understand the terrible injustice of this.

In 1948, he graduated with a Bachelor of Arts degree in sociology. Later, King began doctoral studies in systematic theology at Boston University and received his Doctor of Philosophy on June 5, 1955. King married Coretta Scott, on June 18, 1953 and they had four children.

B

Returning to the South to become pastor of a Baptist Church in Montgomery, Alabama, King first achieved national renown when he helped mobilise the black boycott of the Montgomery bus system in 1955. This was organised after Rosa Parks, a black woman, refused to give up her seat on the bus to a white man - in the segregated south, black people could only sit at the back of the bus. The 382-day boycott led the bus company to change its regulations, and the Supreme Court declared such segregation unconstitutional.

C

In 1957 King was active in the organisation of the Southern Leadership Christian Conference (SCLC), formed to co-ordinate protests against discrimination. He advocated non-violent direct action based on the methods of Gandhi, who led protests against British rule in India culminating in India's independence in 1947. In 1963, King led mass protests against discriminatory practices in Birmingham, Alabama, where the white population were violently resisting desegregation. The city was dubbed 'Bombingham' as attacks against civil rights protesters increased, and King was arrested and jailed for his part in the protests.

D

After his release, King participated in the enormous civil rights march, in Washington, in August 1963, and delivered his famous 'I have a dream' speech, predicting a day when the promise of freedom and equality for all would become a reality in America. In 1964 he was awarded the Nobel Peace Prize. In 1965, he led a campaign to register blacks to vote. The same year the US Congress passed the Voting Rights Act outlawing the discriminatory practices that had barred blacks from voting in the south.

E

As the civil rights movement became increasingly radicalised, King found that his message of peaceful protest was not shared by many in the younger generation. King began to protest against the Vietnam War and poverty levels in the US. On March 29, 1968, King went to Memphis, Tennessee, in support of the black sanitary public works employees who had been on strike since March 12 for higher wages and better treatment. In one incident, black street repairmen had received pay for two hours when they were sent home because of bad weather, but white employees had been paid for the full day. King could not bear to stand by and let such patent acts of racism go unnoticed. He moved to unite his people, and all the peoples of America on the receiving end of discriminatory practices, to protest for their rights, peacefully but steadfastly.

F

On his trip to Memphis, King was booked into room 306 at the Lorraine Motel, owned by Walter Bailey. King was shot at 6:01 p.m. April 4, 1968 while he was standing on the motel's second-floor balcony. King was rushed to St. Joseph's Hospital, where doctors opened his chest and performed manual heart massage. He was pronounced dead at 7:05 p.m. King's autopsy revealed that although he was only 39 years old, he had the heart of a 60 year old man.

Reading

Question 27-31
Choose the correct letter **A, B, C** *or* **D**.

27   From a young age Martin Luther King

    A wanted to protest for the rights of black people.

    B could not understand why black people were treated differently.

    C was not allowed to go to the cinema or to restaurants.

    D was aware that black people were being humiliated in many northern states.

28   What initially made Martin Luther King famous?

    A the black boycott of the Montgomery bus system

    B becoming a pastor at a Baptist Church

    C when Rosa Parks refused to give up her seat on a bus

    D when he persuaded Rosa Parks not to give up her bus seat to a white man

29   What influenced Martin Luther King regarding non-violence?

    A India's independence in 1947

    B Christianity

    C the Southern Leadership Christian Conference

    D the methods of Gandhi

30   What did Martin Luther King fight for in 1965?

    A the right of black people to vote

    B the actions of the US Congress

    C the right to win the Nobel Peace Prize

    D the right of black people to travel abroad

31   How did Martin Luther King feel about the civil rights movement?

    A It was helping the war in Vietnam.

    B It brought the younger generation together.

    C It had been exploited by politicians who wanted to get more votes.

    D The protesters sometimes behaved too violently.

Questions 32 - 34

Do the following statements agree with the information given in Reading Passage 3?

In spaces 32 - 34 below, write

YES	*if the statement agrees with the information*
NO	*if the statement contradicts the information*
NOT GIVEN	*if there is no information on this*

32   The black boycott of the Montgomery bus system was a success.   ....

33   In 1963 the white people in Alabama wanted desegregation.   ....

34   Martin Luther King achieved a lot in his protest against the Vietnam War.   ....

Questions 35 - 40

Reading Passage 2 has 6 paragraphs.
Choose the correct heading for each paragraph A - F, from the list of headings.
Write the correct number, **i - viii**, *in spaces* **35 - 40** *below.*

35	Paragraph **A**	....
36	Paragraph **B**	....
37	Paragraph **C**	....
38	Paragraph **D**	....
39	Paragraph **E**	....
40	Paragraph **F**	....

i   The memorable speech
ii   Unhappy about violence
iii   A tragic incident
iv   Protests and action
v   The background of an iconic man
vi   Making his mark internationally
vii   Difficult childhood
viii Black street repairmen

Writing

WRITING TASK 1

You should spend about 20 minutes on this task.

> *The graphs below provide information about the sales in England of three different kinds of music. The graphs together cover five decades and the sales are measured in pounds sterling. Summarise the information by selecting and reporting the main features, and make comparisons where relevant.*

Write at least 150 words.

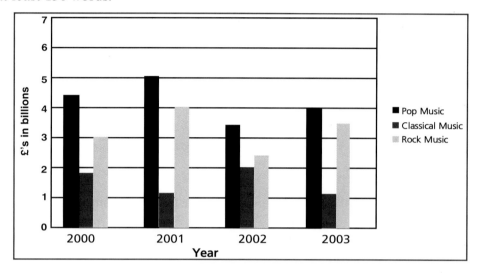

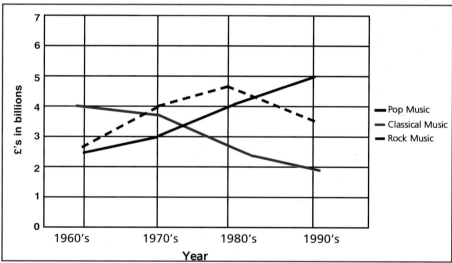

WRITING TASK 2

You should spend about 40 minutes on this task.
Write about the following topic:

> *It has become very common for people to borrow money. Most people have a credit card, a mortgage and often they will buy a car on credit as well. Is this a good idea or is it too risky? Discuss both views and give your own opinion.*

Give reasons for your answer and include any relevant examples from your own knowledge or experience.

Write at least 250 words.

Speaking

PART 1   (4-5 minutes)

The examiner asks the candidate about him/herself, his/her home, work or studies and other familiar topics.

Sports

- What sort of sports do you like to take part in?
- Why do you enjoy playing these sports?
- Do you think it's important for people to play sports? Why?/Why not?
- Do people of all ages in your culture enjoy sports? Why?/Why not?

PART 2   (2 minutes)

You will have to talk about the topic for one to two minutes. You have one minute to think about what you are going to say. You can make some notes to help you if you wish.

Describe some environmental voluntary work that you have done, or that you would like to.

You should say:
- What it was
- How difficult or tiring it was
- Whether it was effective or not

and explain why you decided to take part.

PART 3   (4-5 minutes)

Discussion topics:

Economic growth and environmental protection

- Businesses should be seen as partners in cleaning up the environment and not be treated as suspects by the government. What's your opinion about that?
- Can we afford to have both continued economic growth and environmental protection?
- Can we find the solution to our energy problems using renewable energy sources?

Technology and pollution

- Do you think that technology can play a key role in solving the pollution problem?
- We may lose some jobs as we move towards environmentally friendly technologies and lifestyles, but we'll create new ones in "green" industries. Do you agree with this statement?
- Do you agree with the opinion that preventing environmental damage can be more effective and less costly in the long run?

Test 9

Listening

SECTION 1   *Questions 1 - 10*

Questions 1 - 8

Complete the form below.
*Write **NO MORE THAN THREE** words for each answer.*

DENHAM'S SHIPPING AGENCY
customer quotation form

Example:
Country of destination: *Ireland*

Name: Tim **1** ....

Address to be collected from: **2** .... University

Town: Brighton

Postcode: **3** ....

Size of container:

Length:
2.5 m

Depth: **5** ....

Width: **4** ....

Contents: books

6 ....

7 ....

Total estimated value: **8** ....

Questions 9 - 10

Choose the correct letter, A, B, or C.

9 What is the minimum recommended cover by
   the agency?
   A   premium
   B   standard
   C   economy

10 Where does the customer want the goods
    delivered?
    A   port
    B   home
    C   business

SECTION 2   *Questions 11 - 20*

Questions 11 - 15

Label the plan below.
*Write **NO MORE THAN THREE WORDS** for each answer.*

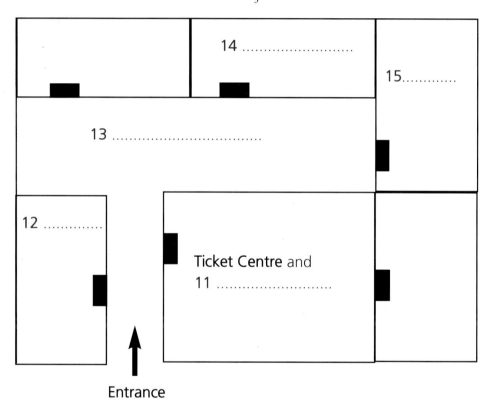

Questions 16 - 20

What does the tour guide tell her tour group about each of the following places on the day's itinerary?
Write the correct letter, A, B, or C next to questions 16 - 20 below.
NB *You may choose any letter more than once.*

16   The Aquarium   ☐
17   Solheim Country Club   ☐
18   Milltown Winery   ☐
19   The Zoological Gardens   ☐
20   The Stout Brewery   ☐

A They'll definitely go there.
B They might go there if time allows.
C They certainly won't go there.

Listening

SECTION 3   *Questions 21 - 30*

Questions 21 - 25

Complete the sentences below.

Write **NO MORE THAN TWO WORDS** *for each answer.*

Gyroscopes are used in laser devices and are found in many consumer **21** ....

The purpose of the project is to design a functional, **22** .... and beneficial consumer product.

The gyroscopic exercise ball can be set in motion by movements of the **23** .... and wrist together in synch.

The gyroscopic ball could help people in **24** .... who have lower-arm injuries.

The product could also be aimed at **25** .... for whom lower-arm strength is very important.

Questions 26 - 30

Complete the table below.
Write **NO MORE THAN THREE WORDS AND/OR A NUMBER** *for each answer.*

	PROTOTYPE DESIGN	TESTING
Estimated Cost:	£3,000	**26** ....
Numbers of Weeks:	**27**	**6**
	Numbers of test subjects:	**28** ....
	Breakdown of test subjects:	**5 professional athletes**
		29 ....
		5 **30** ....

Practice Test 9

SECTION 4   *Questions 31 - 40*

Questions 31 - 35

Choose the correct letter, A, B or C.

31   Speakers have to know
   A   their material.
   B   their audience.
   C   their limitations.

32   Experienced speakers
   A   always try to wing it.
   B   never arrive unprepared.
   C   give the best presentations.

33   You should always rehearse
   A   with friends who can advise you.
   B   with all the equipment you plan
        on using.
   C   more than once.

34   It is a good idea to
   A   be discreet with your audience.
   B   meet your fans.
   C   meet and welcome your audience.

35   Taking a few deep breaths before you begin
   A   will stop you having a panic attack.
   B   will guarantee that you feel more
        relaxed.
   C   will help turn your tension into
        enthusiasm.

Questions 36 - 40

Complete the sentences below.

*Write **NO MORE THAN TWO WORDS** for each answer.*

Useful Tips for a Successful Presentation

- Try to **36** .... yourself making a speech and imagine your voice loud and confident.
- Even if you make mistakes avoid making **37** ....
- Pay attention to your **38** .... - your words carry less meaning than your delivery.
- People usually remember less than **39** .... of what they hear.
- Be **40** .... about yourself; You don't become a perfect speaker overnight.

Reading

READING PASSAGE 1

*You should spend about 20 minutes on **Questions 1 - 13**, which are based on Reading Passage 1 below.*

Taking us back to the Paradise City

Formed in 1985 by Axl Rose and then lead guitarist, Tracii Guns, and taking its name from its two founding members, the hard rock band *Guns and Roses* reached heights of success that few could or would have ever predicted. Having sold more than 100 million albums worldwide, 46 million in the States alone, to date, the band that came to symbolise the hedonistic rebelliousness of the 1980s and 90s punk-rock period has, after much speculation, resurrected itself for one more assault on the music charts. GNR, as the band has come to be known, has just begun a new world tour. And as it embarks on another chapter of its journey, we take a look back at the colourful and often controversial history of the band.

1985 – 1986

The band line-up underwent many changes in the early days. Founding member Tracii Guns' failure to attend rehearsals led to him being replaced as lead guitarist by Slash. And once Rob Gardner, the band's original drummer quit for personal reasons, Slash brought his close friend Steven Adler into the fold. With the band members now settled and the line-up complete, Axl Rose (vocals), Izzy Stradlin (rhythm guitar), Duff McKagan (bass), Slash (lead guitar) and Steven Adler (drums) embarked on their first tour, nicknamed 'Hell Tour'. It was here on the road that the band established its chemistry and though it only managed to release one four-track EP, *Like a Suicide*, during this period, the seeds of success were being sown as the band quickly earned a reputation for its impressive live performances.

1987 – 1989

On July the 21st, 1987, the band released its first album, *Appetite for Destruction*. But success wasn't by any means instant; the album lingered low in the charts for almost a year before the band's agent managed to convince MTV executives to play *Welcome to the Jungle*, the first single off the album, during their afternoon rotations. Rock and punk fans soon took notice and began requesting the video en masse. *Sweet Child of Mine* was the album's second US single and, thanks largely to growing grassroots support, the song and its accompanying music video received regular airplay and shot to the top of the US charts. A world tour and invitations to appear at major international rock festivals followed. The band was now well on its way to achieving fame and fortune.

1990 – 1993

Band members lived life on the edge and, unfortunately, drummer Adler's lifestyle got the better of him. The extent of his dependence on drugs was so bad that he could no longer perform with the band and was fired in July, 1990, to be replaced by Matt Sorum. A sixth member of the group was also added as Dizzy Reed became the band's keyboardist. And, having gotten rid of its old management team as well, the band now launched its most ambitious project to date, releasing two albums, *Use Your Illusion 1* and *Use Your Illusion 2*, at the same time. The gamble paid off spectacularly with the albums shooting to numbers one and two in the charts respectively - GNR was the first band ever to achieve such a feat. But though they were riding the crest of a wave, controversy was never far from the band members, especially vocalist Rose who was, among other things, charged with assault and accused of inciting a riot that led to several fatalities. That said, the *Use Your Illusion* Tour ended on a high, registering record attendances and lasting an incredible 28 months.

1994 – 2008

But just when it seemed that the band could do no wrong, things slowly began to unravel. Rose and Slash had personal issues and the band went on a hiatus, not recording or touring together for the best part of two years, before Slash officially quit in 1996. Most of the other band members followed Slash out and, though Rose replaced them, it was a full nine years before a much-touted comeback gig was played in Las Vegas. The band's promised new album, *Chinese Democracy*, never materialised and tour schedules were interrupted and often cancelled altogether. It wasn't until 2008, with Rose now the only remaining member of the original band, that *Chinese Democracy* was finally released.

2009 – Present

A new world tour followed the release of *Chinese Democracy* and, although it received largely positive reviews, the band has continued to be plagued by controversy; Rose is notorious for arriving late for performances and his onstage behaviour has led to much criticism. But when all's said and done, there's no denying the enduring appeal of GNR. Loyal fans still line up in their thousands to get tickets for every new tour date, just as they did all those years ago at the height of the band's success. The only difference is that today they are more hoping for than expecting a great performance, but then that's rock and roll baby!

Reading

Questions 1 - 3

Questions 1 – 3 relate to the first paragraph only. Complete each sentence with the correct ending, A – G, from the box below. You may use each letter once only.

1	Guns and Roses
2	The band has enjoyed
3	The band became

A　takes its name from two former members.
B　was named after its founding members.
C　success in the States alone.
D　was never a predictable band musically.
E　considerable success in America.
F　a symbol of success in the 1980s.
G　representative of a certain attitude in music in the 80s and 90s.

Questions 4 - 7

Complete the sentences below.

Write **NO MORE THAN ONE WORD** *for each answer.*

Between 1985 and 1986 one of the original members wasn't capable of going to **4** .... which forced the band to replace him.

During their first tour they managed to have good **5** .... and play well together.

The album *Sweet Child of Mine* got regular **6** .... and reached the top of the charts.

Nobody can argue that they have not enjoyed long-lasting **7** ....

Questions 8 - 13

Look at the following statements (Questions 8 - 13) and the lists of periods of time below.

Match each statement to the correct period A - D.

Write the correct letter, A - D, in the spaces 8 - 13 below.

NB You may use any letter more than once.

A	from 1985 to 1986
B	from 1987 to 1989
C	from 1990 to 1993
D	from 1994 to 2008

8   The band took a long break, during which many members decided to leave.

9   There was an extremely long delay before the release of the band's next album.

10   The relationship between band members developed in a positive way while on tour.

11   A damaging addiction prevented one band member from performing well and led to him being sacked.

12   A new member joined the band playing an instrument that hadn't been played by previous band members.

13   The band registered its first number-one hit single.

Reading

READING PASSAGE 2

You should spend about 20 minutes on Questions 14 - 26, which are based on Reading Passage 2 below.

Surf's Up

There are two major subdivisions of surfing: longboarding and shortboarding. Their respective names represent differences in the type of surfboard used. Longboards are, as the name suggests, much longer and require a different riding style to shortboards.

Surfboards were originally made of solid wood, and were large and cumbersome, often weighing in excess of 100 pounds. Nowadays, they are more commonly constructed out of polyurethane foam making them much lighter, which means better manoeuvrability for the boarder. This is especially beneficial for longboarders, whose boards can measure up to 3 metres in length. Successful longboarders must learn to carry out difficult walking manoeuvres up and down the board so as to set themselves in the optimal position for catching and riding the wave. The lighter the board, the easier it becomes to execute such manoeuvres. Shortboarders, whose boards are usually between 1.8 and 2 metres long, also benefit from greater manoeuvrability though, and are able to turn and adjust more quickly thanks to the lighter boards.

It is claimed that surfing was first observed being enjoyed by native Tahitians in 1767 by European explorers. Later travellers also reported seeing naked locals, both men and women, amusing themselves in the surf off the coast of Hawaii. Perhaps this is one of the reasons why the sport is synonymous with the South Pacific and Hawaii in particular. Today, however, the popularity of surfing is such that surf clubs have popped up almost everywhere, from the windy West Coast of Ireland, to the ultra-chic Californian beaches. Indeed, it is in Northern California where perhaps the most famous and glamorous surfing takes place.

The prospective surfer would be well-advised to consider the dangers associated with the sport before he takes to the waves. Like all water sports, surfing carries with it the inherent danger of drowning. Although the board itself offers buoyancy, it can also be a hindrance, and a deadly one at that if its leash becomes entangled in a reef, holding the surfer underwater. Ideal water conditions for surfing can be extremely demanding on the body, too, and require the surfer to be an extremely competent swimmer.

Collisions with sandbanks, reefs, surf-boards and other surfers can also be extremely hazardous and can lead to concussion – a death sentence if the surfer is not rescued from the water quickly. Although rarer, attacks by marine animals are not uncommon, with sharks, rays, seals and jellyfish posing the greatest threats. You certainly need to be a courageous soul to brave the waves in this sport.

But for those who insist on giving it a go, the rewards can be very gratifying, and it isn't too expensive to get up and running either. Surf schools in popular destinations offer multi-day beginner and intermediate courses that focus on the basic fundamentals. Five-day courses start from as little as £100 and there are all-inclusive camps, too, which cover accommodation, meals, lessons and equipment. Longboards, given their superior paddling speed and stability, are usually preferred by coaches for use with beginners. Typically, the courses break

down the technique into separate skills: the first one being how to get into position to catch a wave, the second one being how to ride the wave and not fall off. Balance, of course, plays a crucial role, so a lot of time is dedicated to balance training exercises as well.

Difficult though it may be to master the art of surfing, it can also be extremely rewarding, and there are few feelings to compare with the exhilaration of riding out your first wave. So, for those of you daredevil adrenalin junkies who fancy having a go, details of a surf club near you can be found on the British Surfing Association's website, britsurf.co.uk.

And try to remember as your feet are dangling over the side of the board, *Jaws* was just a film; it ALMOST certainly won't happen to you!

Reading

Questions 14 - 19

Choose the correct letter **A, B, C** *or* **D**.

14 Longboards and shortboards

    A often weigh more than 100 pounds today.

    B are usually made out of solid wood.

    C require surfers to perform difficult walking manoeuvres.

    D are lighter and more manoeuvrable today.

15 The sport of surfing

    A was invented by a group of European explorers.

    B was first observed by native Tahitians.

    C is commonly performed naked by both men and women.

    D was first practised in the South Pacific.

16 Surfing has become very popular

    A in windy coastal areas.

    B on the fashionable west coast of Ireland.

    C in Tahiti in recent years.

    D all around the world.

17 Before a novice surfer takes to the water, he should

    A check the latest weather report.

    B avoid big waves.

    C have good buoyancy.

    D be aware of the risks involved.

18 Although a surfboard can help you stay buoyant, it can also

    A get in the way of your safety in some cases.

    B help you escape from dangerous sea life.

    C be a very dangerous weapon.

    D prevent concussion or death.

19 Unless you are pulled from the water quickly, a bad collision can prove

    A hard to escape.

    B life-saving.

    C fatal.

    D rare.

Questions 20 - 21

Choose **TWO** *letters, A - E.*

Which **TWO** of the following are hazards that surfers face?

    A being held underwater by reefs.

    B the potential for shark attacks.

    C frequent encounters with jellyfish.

    D demanding water conditions.

    E hazardous rescue attempts.

Question 22 - 23

*Choose **TWO** letters, A - E.*

Which **TWO** of the following are true about surfing?

A It can become a rewarding career.

B It can be very rewarding as you see yourself improve.

C It can be an adrenalin rush.

D It can be expensive to start.

E It can be dangerous for swimmers around you.

Questions 24 - 26

Complete the table below.

Write **NO MORE THAN TWO WORDS AND/OR A NUMBER** *for each answer.*

Subdivisions of surfing:	Longboarding	Shortboarding				
Surfing originated in:	The South Pacific					
Common dangers include:	24	if the board's leash becomes entangled in a reef, can be deadly	difficult water conditions	collision & concussion	attacks by local sealife	
Starting cost of five-day courses:	25					
26 .... **include:**	accommodation	meals		lessons	equipment	

Reading　　READING PASSAGE 3

You should spend about 20 minutes on Questions 27 - 40, which are based on Reading Passage 3 below.

Making a sound Investment Decision

As investors tire of stock market instability, the idea of owning a piece of real estate is gaining in popularity. Now, not everyone has what it takes to become a landlord, but if you can make a go of it, it certainly has the potential to become a good money-earner. Here are some tips from successful real estate mogul, Janet Anderson, on how to start building up your property portfolio.

According to Janet, one of the best ways to identify a bargain is to hunt for foreclosures. Foreclosures are properties banks have repossessed because their owners were unable to meet the mortgage repayments. Banks want a quick sell on these places, Janet says. They want to cut their losses and get their money back as quickly as possible. Developing a network – making connections with city clerks and bank employees who know which properties are about to be sold – can be an excellent way to identify such bargains. And bargains they certainly can prove to be; in a recent firesale auction ('firesale auction' is the phrase that has been coined to describe auction-room events dedicated entirely to the disposal of repossessed assets) a house with a market value nearing $1,000,000, but with a low reserve price designed to encourage bidders and secure a quick sale, went for $450,000; that's a whopping 55% discount.

It's also important to be realistic though and not stretch yourself too far financially. Janet says the biggest mistake you can make is to borrow too much or over-borrow. For first-time investors, lenders usually demand bigger down payments because you haven't got a proven track record. That's more of your money on the table and, therefore, should anything go wrong, you're in for a big financial hit.

Her business partner, James Nylles, is in complete agreement on this point. He also highlights the fact that the mortgage payments and deposits are only part of the long-term cost of buying a rental property. There is also the cost of repairs, administration and maintenance, rental manager's fees, insurance and so on, all of which require you to hold a significant amount of money in reserve. Failure to factor this in when calculating how

much you can afford to part with in mortgage repayments can lead to disaster.

One of the biggest traps for first time investors, according to Nylles, is the temptation to pay over the odds to get the property you desire. Buyers often get carried away, especially in the auction-room setting, which can get quite competitive and even descend into a racket of one-upmanship. They end up paying top-dollar and landing themselves in a financial situation they can ill afford to be in. Remember, you are in the property game to make money, so the more money you have to pay upfront for a property, the less likely you are to recoup your investment in the long run. The good news, however, is that the housing market is not very hot at the moment, which means the danger of overpaying is not so great. Always set emotions to one side and think from a purely business perspective. The question of your liking or disliking the property is irrelevant. As Nylles points out: "you will not be living there." Business decisions are made in the cold hard light of day; your objective is to minimise your outlay and maximise your return. Whether you secure a huge home in pristine condition or a tiny flat with barely room to stretch in is irrelevant – if the tiny flat gets you a better return on your investment then the choice is a no-brainer.

And last of all, do your homework. You've got to get to know the location in which you are going to invest. Look out for areas which are earmarked for government investment. Urban renewal areas are often very attractive since house and rental prices in such places are low right now but can be expected to rise in the not too distant future. The range of local amenities, safety and the state of the local economy are all important factors to consider, too. As the old saying goes; 'location, location, location'. Invest in a good location and you will maximise your rental income.

Questions 27 – 33

*Answer the questions below using **NO MORE THAN THREE WORDS** for each answer.*

27   What are investors getting fed up with?

_____

28   Janet Anderson is involved in the sale of property. What is another phrase used in paragraph 1 to describe this type of business? _____

29   What is one of the best ways to identify a bargain in the property market?

_____

30   Failure to meet your what, can cause your home to be repossessed?

_____

31   What do banks want to get back quickly on foreclosed properties?

_____

32   Developing networks is an excellent way to find what?

_____

33   What is the biggest error of judgement first-time investors can make, according to Anderson?

_____

Questions 34 - 40

Do the following statements agree with the information given in Reading Passage 3?
In spaces 34 - 40 below, write

YES	*if the statement agrees with the information*
NO	*if the statement contradicts the information*
NOT GIVEN	*if there is no information on this*

34	Banks demand larger deposits from first-time property investors.	_____
35	By making a larger deposit, investors can limit their personal financial risk.	_____
36	There are a lot of long-term costs to take into consideration before purchasing a rental property.	_____
37	Banks require you to hold a lot of money in reserve to meet your long-term property maintenance costs.	_____
38	Many investors are tempted to pay more than they should for their investment properties.	_____
39	At the moment, house prices are extremely high in general.	_____
40	There are a lot of urban renewal projects that have been earmarked by the government.	_____

Writing

WRITING TASK 1

You should spend about 20 minutes on this task.

> *The chart below shows the percentage of Irish language speakers by province (Leinster, Munster, Connacht and Ulster) in the Republic of Ireland (State) in five different years.*
>
> *Summarise the information by selecting and reporting the main features, and make comparisons where relevant.*

Write at least 150 words.

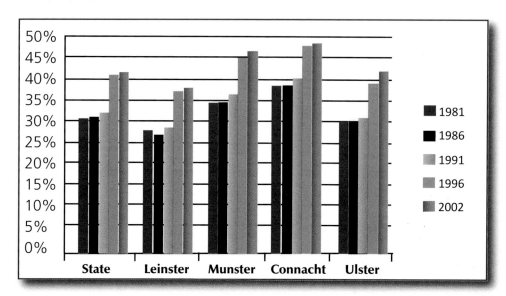

WRITING TASK 2

You should spend about 40 minutes on this task.

Write about the following topic:

> *Nuclear power is a necessary evil. Despite the potential human and environmental consequences of radioactive fallout, nuclear energy is a genuine alternative to non-renewable energy sources like oil and coal, which are quickly running out. In short, the benefits of nuclear power far outweigh the risks of using it.*
>
> *To what extent do you agree or disagree?*

Give reasons for your answer and include any relevant examples from your own knowledge or experience.

Write at least 250 words.

Speaking

PART 1   (4-5 minutes)

The examiner asks the candidate about him/herself, his/her home, work or studies and other familiar topics.

Music
- Do you like listening to music?
- Is music an important part of your life? Why?/Why not?
- For what occasions is music important in your culture?
- Do you think people will always enjoy listening to music? Why?/Why not?

PART 2   (2 minutes)

You will have to talk about the topic for one to two minutes. You have one minute to think about what you are going to say. You can make some notes to help you if you wish.

> **Describe a habit that is good for your health.**
> **You should say:**
> - why you do it
> - whether it is difficult or easy to do
> - whether it requires self-discipline or not
>   and finally explain why this habit is
>   good for your health.

PART 3   (4-5 minutes)

Discussion topics:

Eating healthily
- What do you think of fast-food restaurants?
- "Ninety per cent of the diseases known to man are caused by cheap foodstuffs. You are what you eat." Do you agree with this statement?
- Do you eat a lot of red meat or do you prefer healthy alternative foods such as fish, vegetables etc.?
- A lot of young people are presently suffering from eating disorders, such as anorexia, because they want to look thin and beautiful. What are the reasons for this obsession with weight?

Health issues
- Why do you think some people turn to drugs?
- What do you think of the health service in your country?
- How would you try to persuade a friend of yours not to smoke cigarettes?
- Do you believe the day will come when we will be able to cure all diseases?

IELTS Scoring

IELTS is scored on a **9-band scale**. Candidates will be given a score for overall language ability as well as another score for each of the four skills (Listening, Reading, Writing and Speaking).

IELTS 9-band scale

9 Expert User	Has full command of the language.
8 Very Good User	Has full command of the language with occasional inaccuracies.
7 Good User	Has operational command of the language, although occasional inaccuracies do occur.
6 Competent User	Has generally effective command of the language despite some inaccuracies.
5 Modest User	Has partial command of the language and understands the overall meaning in most situations. Can handle basic communication in own field.
4 Limited User	Basic competence in familiar situations. Frequent problems in understanding; no use of complex language.
3 Extremely Limited User	Only understands general meaning in familiar situations. Has many problems communicating in English.
2 Intermittent User	No real communication is possible except for the most basic information. Has difficulty understanding spoken and written English.
1 Non User	Has no real ability to use the language beyond a few words.
0 Did not attempt the test	His performance cannot be assessed.